from

Billy Fury to YouTube

~

MICHAEL PARKINSON (THE OTHER ONE)

Published by Michael Parkinson

Publishing partner: Paragon Publishing, Rothersthorpe
First published 2018

© Michael Parkinson, 2018

ISBN 978-1-78222-588-1

Book design, layout and production management by Into Print
www.intoprint.net
+44 (0)1604 832149

Contents

FOREWORD 5

1   Billy Fury Dance - Nottingham Arts Theatre 7

2   Billy Fury Dance - Lytham, Blackpool 23

3   Billy Fury Dance - Mansfield. 28

4   Billy Fury Dance - Floral Pavilion, New Brighton 33

5   Billy Fury Dance - Shaw Theatre, London. 41

6   American GI and English Girl. 47

7   Billy Fury Biography. 53

8   Billy Fury Graveside Tribute 60

9   YouTube, How I started. 63

10 Saara Aalto X Factor 65

11 Jessica May George, Jessie's Fund 68

12 Thames Path Walk, Barrier to Windsor. 74

13 Thames Path Walk, Windsor to Oxford 83

14 Thames Path Walk, Oxford to Source. 91

15 Blackpool Tower Ballroom - Phil Kelsall 98

16 Joanna Forest, Feel your Boobs. 100

17 Cricket - Notts and England. 104

18 The Seekers - Judith Durham. 110

19 Scarborough Spa Music. 112

20 Disneyland, Paris 119

21 Eric Coates - Viola to Composer 122

22 Thursford Christmas Spectacular 131

23 Nottingham Organ Society. 139

24 Royal Academy of Music 146

25 Phab, Fanfare for Christmas 150

26 London Concerts 154

27 Scottish Army Invade Trafalgar Square............ 159

28 Victorian Ballads to Limericks..................... 161

29 Southwark Cathedral to Bonington Theatre 180

30 Promotions, Concerts and Shows.................. 183

31 Coeliac Disease - Gluten Free Diet................ 187

32 Childhood Memories.............................. 190

33 National Service 197

34 Back Home 205

35 Gardener and the Alzheimers Lady................ 208

36 Tuneless Choir 212

37 Chamber Choir, Drake University, Iowa........... 215

38 YouTube Subscriptions 220

39 Danilo Mascetti, piano 222

APPENDIX... 223

ACKNOWLEDGEMENTS 231

Foreword

by Michael's grandson, Dr Craig Woods BSc PhD ARCS

MY GRANDFATHER TOLD ME HE was writing a book. This shouldn't be as surprising as it was. He's always told stories, he's always up to something. Michael started writing about his experiences producing Billy Fury shows and producing his YouTube channel. Included are some of the more interesting episodes in his life. He pours acclaim on what he has found inspiring or joyful, some of which are charmingly niche.

I don't think my Grandpa is aware of the gift he possesses which is to get on and do what you want to do. Producing shows or uploading videos did not seem on the cards. So many people don't know where to start, but for him it seems to always start with a person. In conversation both frank and honest and to the point. I suspect this is why he gets things done. Reading this book was, for me, a lesson in how to take pride and enjoyment in what you do. Take yourself seriously with fun. My grandfather combines fearlessness with reverence and respect while meeting people. I expect that's why they seem to open up to him and to be happy to work with him. He was amazed at the patience Sara Aalto had for him when happening across her in Leicester Square.

For me the most enjoyable parts of this book were the biographical chapters. Memories of Nottinghamshire life followed by national service in London and then the transition to civilian work. I suspect that this is my preference because of my relation to him. For other people perhaps they will prefer the chapters which are very different in style, they describe various cultural events or persons of interest.

You may now look forward to reading this book and imagine the places described along the way. Better than that though, you can read this while accessing YouTube and search for the titles Michael recommends as you go through. This allows you to see for yourself what he is talking about. I found this to be a valuable addition and it's something I haven't encountered before in a book.

6

Billy Fury Dance
Nottingham Arts Theatre

ONE SUNDAY AFTERNOON IN MARCH 2009 my wife Joan and I were driving near Nottingham, when Paul Robey on BBC Radio Nottingham announced a Billy Fury song. Joan jumped about with enjoyment as it was being broadcast because she is an ardent Billy Fury fan. Paul Robey is Joan's favourite presenter who has a Sunday afternoon slot which he refers to as 'nostalgia and nonsense'. I had arranged for Phil Kelsall, principal organist of the Blackpool Tower Ballroom, to perform an afternoon concert at Nottingham Arts Theatre in July of the following year. For an additional eighty pounds I knew that I could put an evening show on as well. I had long believed that the songs of Billy Fury were suited to routines by dancers so I thought about putting a Billy Fury Dance Show together. I mulled over the idea and had two obstacles. One was that some of Billy Fury's backing group, the Tornados, were currently performing a show called Halfway to Paradise - The Billy Fury Story, I did not want to risk them complaining so contacted Chris Raynor (one of the Tornados who lives near Nottingham). I explained my idea asking if he had any objection. He assured me that he thought it was a great idea and said that he and his wife would want to come to the show. I then asked him about my other worry which was 'would I get permission from the owners of Billy's recordings to use them in my show?' Chris's reply was not what I wanted to hear. He said, 'if you ask the people in London they may say no so it is better not to ask and just do it'. I thanked Chris for his input but made a mental note that I would not consider doing the show without getting permission to use the recordings.

After much investigation I discovered that most of the tracks were owned by Universal Music and some Parlophone recordings by Lisa Voice who had been Billy's partner for a number of years. I contacted Paul Veitch who is Head of Creative Licensing at Universal Music London. He gave me permission to use the tracks owned by them provided that the Theatre had a Performing Rights Society license. After more work I got permission from Lisa Voice to use the tracks that she owned. That was the easy bit accomplished, my next objective was to write a script (something I had never done before). It was easy to obtain information about Billy Fury and I had soon downloaded loads from the internet. Putting it together in a show format and deciding which songs to use was a huge challenge. Joan had many Billy Fury recordings but by no means all. I started to put something together but lacked inspiration so decided to go to the grave of Billy Fury in the hope that it would trigger creativity. Looking back, it was a strange idea that paid great dividends.

On 26 August 2009 I went to Westminster Paddington Cemetery at Mill Hill in North London and asked a groundsman where the grave of Billy Fury was. He replied 'I am asked that question nearly every day and it is the most visited and best maintained grave in the whole cemetery'. It transpired that he was the Head Groundsman and was going that way so escorted me to the grave. On arrival, there was a man sitting on a wooden bench and a lady kneeling down tending to the grave. I explained the reason for my visit to the man who said, 'you should speak to her, she is Billy's number one fan'. The lady looked at me and said, 'just one of many'. The lady was Marina Weedon and the man on the bench was Paul her ex husband who is a taxi driver. They were divorced but once a month he took her from her home in Chiswick to look after the grave. Marina told me that there were two Billy Fury fan clubs. She was in one called The Sound of Fury, and she suggested that I speak to a man called Chris Eley at that club. Paul was in the newer one called 'Billy Fury In Thoughts of You' and my contact there would be Mags Cummings. *(I understand that this club has now closed down)* The fact that one of them was in each club meant that they shared information from both clubs.

Marina told me a story; When she was 16 her Father bought her an expensive watch for her birthday present. Her elder sister took her to a Billy Fury Show at the Southall Dominion Theatre in April 1962 as her treat. Marina was captivated by Billy's performance. She joined the other girls screaming with delight and throwing her arms in the air. At the end of the show she realised that the watch was missing, perhaps it had shot off her wrist. She and her sister searched for a long time but could not find it. Not only were they late home but Marina had to tell her Father that the watch was lost. He was annoyed and vowed never to buy her another one. After Marina and Paul had gone I made a note of the words inscribed on the headstone which were:-

IN LOVING MEMORY OF

RONALD WYCHERLEY
(BILLY FURY)

PASSED AWAY 28TH JANUARY 1983
AGE 42

SADLY MOURNED BY LISA, PARENTS,
RELATIVES AND FRIENDS

HIS MUSIC GAVE PLEASURE TO MILLIONS

REST IN PEACE DARLING BILLY

I decided to use the words 'His music **still** gives pleasure to Millions' in my script because there I was, twenty six years later, and people were still enjoying his music.

(My later investigation revealed that the Sound of Fury Fan Club arranges for regular professional annual cleaning and any necessary repairs to the grave, on behalf of the Billy Fury Estate, Ms Lisa Voice and that Marina does a regular general tidy up also on behalf of the Sound of Fury).

The following evening I contacted Chris Eley and told him of my plan. He was enthusiastic and promised to send CDs of all the Billy Fury recordings. True to his word over the next few days various CDs, information and pictures dropped through my letter box. Joan and I found the task of deciding which songs to use in the show time consuming but enjoyable. After much deliberation we decided on the songs. I decided on a format of some narration telling the Billy Fury Story interspersed with songs and choreographed dance of varied tempo. I broke this down into scenes of around twelve minutes per scene.

This is a list of songs which finally made it into the script:-

Give me your word
Do you really love me too
Please love me
Margo don't go
Maybe tomorrow
Don't knock upon my door
It's only make believe
We were meant for each other
I'd never find another you
I love how you love me
Once upon a dream
Gonna type a letter
Running around
I'll show you
Last night was made for love
In my room
Collette
Wondrous place
Like I've never been gone
Jealousy
Because of love
Lady
King for tonight
Stand by me
How many nights, how many days
Run to my loving arms
In thoughts of you
I'll never fall in love again
In summer
Turn my back on you
Letter full of tears
Forget him
I will
I'm lost without you
Devil or Angel
I'll never quite get over you
Somebody else's girl
A thousand stars
Halfway to paradise

In addition to the songs I included a special scene where the cast sang the 23rd psalm, Billy reading a poem that he had written himself and 'Sweet Jessica' a reference to my chosen charity Jessie's Fund.

I continued to work on script writing and at the same time exercised my mind on how I would get dancers and narrators to perform in the show. I was not getting on well with this until November 2009 when dame fortune smiled on me. I went to a small dance show in a studio at the Nottingham Arts Theatre. I thought it would be a good opportunity to meet dancers. Maggie Andrew appeared to be in charge and I spoke to her about my plans. I had met Maggie four years previously when I had collaborated with the London Studio Centre in putting on three performances of 'Oh What a Lovely War' at the Nottingham Arts Theatre. Maggie had done 'front of house' and told me how much she had enjoyed the shows every time I had seen her since. Maggie offered to direct my Billy Fury Dance Show for me and I accepted her offer, she wrote these words in a confirmation email to me a couple of days later:-

'Could we meet for coffee this week and I will tell you all about me and what I think I could bring to the show in terms of help etc. I am anxious that you will see that it is my love of theatre etc that motivates me. I think it is important that we get it out there as soon as possible to dancers, they get really busy! Maggie'.

I accepted Maggie's suggestion and we agreed a deal. Maggie had directed a few youth group productions at the Arts Theatre and had contact with many young performers in the Nottingham area. We organised an application form and circulated it to various dance schools, drama and theatre groups. We set up and I negotiated payments to the Arts Theatre for rehearsals. There is a lot of boring, expensive, but necessary stuff to do in promoting a show like theatre hire contracts and insurance for instance. Maggie had a close relationship with the Nottingham Post and BBC Radio Nottingham and they helped by giving publicity involving details of the show and the dancers that we wanted. It was decided that there would be one performance on Sunday evening 11 July 2010, the day that Phil Kelsall played his concert in the afternoon. It was then that Maggie pointed out to me that I had caused her a huge problem. She wanted all of the theatre for the whole day of the show but was not able to have it because Phil was arriving at around 12 noon and had to get theTechnics organ on stage and set up for his performance at 2pm. It was rather a strange situation because if I had not been putting the Phil Kelsall concert on the Billy Fury Show would not have happened.

Many dancers applied to take part in the show but the first audition had to be cancelled on the day because of heavy snowfall. Another audition was arranged (more expense) and we finished with 32 performers, mostly dancers but some would do narration as well and some of the dancers would assist Maggie by choreographing routines. I had to book and pay for many rehearsals. Maggie had banned me from attending rehearsals but, to my surprise, invited Joan and I to go into the theatre studio for a preview that she had arranged for us. I was impressed that the combination of Billy's songs, narration and dance worked beautifully. After the preview Maggie told me her reason for putting it on. She wanted me to pay for the theatre for another performance the day after the original Sunday night show. I thought, 'more expense' but agreed so a further performance was booked making a two night show. I had invited Jean Wycherley (Billy's Mother) to the show but had not received a reply. Maggie and the girls composed a letter to her which they all signed. This is exactly what the letter said:-

Dear Mrs Wycherley

We are writing to invite you to an event we are putting on honouring Billy Fury's memory. Although Michael Parkinson has already contacted you regarding our performances on the 11th and 12th of July 2010. We thought it would be beneficial to hear from us exactly why we are involved with this project.

The Billy Fury Show is being performed at the Nottingham Arts Theatre with all proceeds going to a charity called Jessie's Fund. Originally it was a one night charity event but tickets went so fast we felt we needed to add another night to be able to spread Billy's music further. All the dances are being choreographed to his music and we loved it so much we felt the need to inspire others with it as well. We have thirty two girls dancing throughout the show. Some of us being responsible for the choreography also. The age range of the girls is between ten and twenty five although the majority are between thirteen and sixteen.

We hope you can attend, however even if you can't we wanted to let you know how much we've enjoyed being allowed to use both Billy Fury's music and clips from his films to be able to tell his life story through dance and narration.

Yours faithfully

Maggie Andrew (and signatures of all the girls)

Maggie was proud to tell me a few day's later that Jean wanted to come and that John and Mags Cummings (of the 'In Thoughts of You' fan club were going to bring her). Maggie found additional inexpensive rehearsal space about four miles from Nottingham at the Patricia James dance studio in Carlton so many of the girls travelled out there. I was welcomed to one of them. One of the difficulties that Maggie and I endured was the constant demand for rehearsals causing my costs to escalate well above what I had anticipated. Maggie never had all the girls together at a rehearsal until the day of the performance. Although they were only young performers they all had huge demands on their time.

I included these tributes to Billy Fury in the programme and printed them exactly as they were sent to me with no editing:-

From Mags Cummings of the Billy Fury In Thoughts of You Fan Club

I first met Billy at Manchester Hippodrome when I was fifteen and was hooked. I was fortunate in getting to meet him many times and eventually became a friend. One of my first encounters at the age of sixteen was when I slid under a locked gate at Buxton Pavilion Gardens where Billy was waiting in his car whilst his manager had gone to find someone to allow them out. I'd given Billy a birthday cake during the show and when I approached the car he mentioned it and then motioned for me to come closer and gave me my first 'proper' kiss. He was a lovely gentle man. A complete contrast to his electric persona on stage. It was a very sad day indeed when he was prematurely taken from us.

From Vince Eager - My Pal Bill

It's not until you have the opportunity to reflect on life that the significance of certain events take on their full meaning. My first meeting with Ronald Wycherley was outside the Birkenhead Essoldo stage door in October 1958. That chance meeting, I was going for a Wimpy burger with drummer Brian Bennett when Ronnie approached me, proved to be a stellar moment. What if Ronnie had not been a determined guy, what if I had not been going for a Wimpy, what if I had ignored his approach, what if Larry Parnes had not been in the theatre. Would Ronnie have ever become Britain's greatest Rock 'n' roller? I think he would. Someone with his undoubted talented eventually shows up on the show business radar.

Ronnie soon became Billy and he set off for the royal suburb of Knightsbridge in London. During the year Billy and I were flatmates we never looked upon each other as something more than flatmates. We both experienced difficult and great times together. Our bond was being away from our parents and in an alien environment. From not having two halfpennies to rub together to being lorded in high circles was all part of our experience.

A more caring, gentle or kinder person than Billy you couldn't find. Of all the stage names Larry Parnes gave his protégés, I think 'Billy Fury' was genius. Larry's choosing of boy next-door first names, such as Tommy, Marty, Billy and then second names, Steele, Wilde and Fury certainly gave the artistes something of a split personality. The off stage 'Billy' and the on stage 'Fury' were just that. You would not believe that 'Billy' could become 'Fury' but he did with consummate ease.

Billy was two different people, and one person who recognised Billy's potential was the 'Oh Boy' TV show Producer Jack Good. He presented Billy to the nation and got it spot on. There is no doubt that had it not been someone who hadn't the skill and enthusiasm for his artistes that Jack had, then things could have turned out very differently. I was asked a few years ago if I had any suggestions as to who might be suitable to unveil Billy's statue in Liverpool. At the time I had just rekindled my friendship with Jack and he was an obvious choice. The only problem was that Jack had become a recluse and was happy to get on with his painting whilst the world 'rocked' by. After a few glasses of Lager and Merlot, Jack agreed to take on the task. Jack's acceptance was punctuated by him insisting that he would not do it for anyone other than Billy. It was Jack who first presented Billy to the nation, and it was Jack who was to present his statue to the world. Jack's actions in unveiling Billy's statue were the final seal of approval that Billy Fury was without doubt Britain's greatest rock 'n' roller.

(I recorded Vince speaking about Billy and have loaded a video to YouTube: *Billy Fury by Vince Eager, Billy Fury Dance Show*)

From Alvin Stardust

I first met Billy Fury when I was a teenager. It was the first tour I'd ever done with my band The Fentones.

As soon as Bill came on stage at the soundcheck it was obvious he was 'A STAR'. Only a couple of times in my life in the music business have I had that feeling. Elvis, The Beatles, Buddy Holly and maybe a couple more. Not bad company eh?

Often we shared dressing rooms and we became good friends. He was a great bloke and a fantastic natural performer. A great loss to us all when we lost him. But his memory lives on alongside his fabulous recordings.

Very sincerely Alvin Stardust

From Chris Eley - The Sound of Fury-Official Billy Fury Fan Club

When I was first approached by Michael Parkinson and informed of his intention to stage a tribute in song, story and dance to the late great Billy Fury, my first impression was 'How original and refreshing'. That perception has not changed, because indeed this is the first time such a show has been produced without the use of singers. Tribute acts do a sterling job in promoting Billy's legacy but this really does promise something different. Since having the privilege of becoming involved in the project I have become aware of just how sincere Michael is in this venture-both in his love of Billy's music and in his dedication to Jessie's Fund, which is about helping children with special needs and which he has been supporting for about eight years now. Choosing songs for the performances from among the wonderful three hundred or so numbers recorded across several labels from 1958-83 has not been an easy task, and whilst the show is based primarily on most of his hit singles, a few of the other less well known but equally valid, some might say better tracks, found on B sides, albums, EPs and even from the inexplicably chart-barren Parlophone, or wilderness years, have been included. Were the show able to be longer the diversity of Billy's wonderful output would have been further displayed. Because of the charity aspect of the show Universal/Decca and Ms Lisa Voice of the Billy Fury Estate have kindly consented for the wonderful selection of tracks you will hear, to be played as indeed have the owners of various clips and photos you will experience during the show. Best of all, in addition to promoting surely some of the finest popular music ever to be recorded, your participation by attending this event will be helping a very good cause, named Jessie's Fund.

We lost what many feel was Britain's finest performer of his era and genre all too soon on 28 January 1983, when Billy finally lost his battle against the heart valve problem that had dogged him since his childhood. Since then his fans have maintained and enhanced his grave at Mill Hill in London, placed a lectern in Liverpool Anglican Cathedral, held tribute weekends nearly every year, placed a bronze statue at the Liverpool pier head, and worked with music companies on various vinyl and CD releases. Various tribute acts and bands have appeared, with many of the best remaining on the circuit today, and three Billy acts have appeared on 'Stars in their Eyes' over the years. In

1998 an excellent Omnibus TV documentary was screened, bringing back many fans to the fold. In 2008 Billy, who has two fan clubs in the UK and an excellent independent website, enjoyed the incredible feat for a 'Retro' artist in achieving a top 10 DVD (re-entry from 2007) and a Top 10 CD. Together with Dusty Springfield, Billy is the most requested (and played) solo artist on Brian Matthews long running Sounds of the 60's BBC 2 radio show. 'Forget Him' - not likely! This tribute in song and dance has been produced with a high level of integrity and genuine resolve and provides a rare opportunity to hear the original 'Sound of Billy Fury' on a theatre stage. So sit back and enjoy the musical legendary Billy Fury, presented in a unique, tasteful and enjoyable way.

Chris Eley

A few days before the concerts were to take place I was driving near to where Maggie lives and saw her walking along the pavement so stopped and got out of the car to speak to her. To my dismay she was distraught and threw her arms around me and between tears told me that it was not going to happen as there were so many problems. She calmed down after we had spoken for a few minutes and I was able to reassure her about a few things. The incident may have helped Maggie but left me worried about what would happen on the first night.

When the big day dawned Maggie, technical staff and others were in the theatre at 7am and got to work on the technical and dress rehearsal. When Phil Kelsall arrived, at around 12 noon for his 2pm concert the stage had to be allocated to him. The technical crew helped him get the organ on stage and speakers set up. He had got up early that morning to collect the trailer that he hires to transport the organ and travelled to Nottingham from Blackpool. He was not allocated a dressing room because they were all occupied by dancers so just before the audience were allowed into the theatre Phil (who had just been awarded the MBE) and myself had to get changed at the back of the stage. Phil was not happy and I can distinctly remember his words 'I have performed in Church Halls that are better organised than this place'. I felt guilty because it was my fault in arranging two shows in one day and not the fault of the Arts Theatre. His performance went well as usual and the audience departed leaving Maggie with sole control of the theatre for the remainder of the day.

There was just one parking space near the front of the theatre and I wanted to make sure that this was saved for Mags and John Cummings when they arrived with Jean Wycherley. I borrowed four white painted wrought iron chairs and table from the coffee bar and situated them on the road in the parking space which Joan, myself Linda Shawley and Chris Eley sat on until Mags and John Cummings arrived with our special guest. This caused much laughter amongst early arrivals and passers by so we all started to enjoy ourselves. Many bus and car drivers gave us a hoot and a wave, it was great fun. When Jean arrived we took the chairs back into the theatre and I went on to my role of selling programmes inside. Someone came to me and suggested that I should go outside and give a programme to Jean which I did. Unknown to me, my friend, whose YouTube name is catman2007, had set it up and was videoing. It is still on his YouTube Channel with the simple heading *Mrs Jean Wycherley*. She can be seen standing and chatting with Billy Fury fans who had come to the show before I gave her a programme. The performance was brilliant but poor Maggie did have her problems because amongst other things one of the girls was sick at the back of the stage whilst one of the numbers was being performed. It was a full house and everyone enjoyed the show. At the end Chris Eley presented pictures of Billy to Jean Wycherley, Joan and myself. The picture that we received featured Billy Fury and these words:-

This endearing picture of Billy Fury from the mid sixties is presented to Michael and Joan Parkinson in recognition of their promotion of the musical legacy of Billy. In coupling a varied selection of recordings from Billy's entire career output, with dance, they have created a unique show in laudable support of Jessie's Fund. With grateful thanks Chris, Linda and the team of The Sound of Fury (Official Billy Fury Fan Club)

Nottingham - 11th July 2010

A surprising thing happened after the show whilst the presentations were being made and all the dancers were on stage with the curtain closed. My wife, Joan who is very shy and had never made a speech before in her life suddenly said that she wanted to speak to the performers, she said, 'That was the most fabulous thing I have ever seen, you all did really well and I really enjoyed it'. The feedback that I received through this and subsequent Billy Fury Shows is that the young people involved like the Billy Fury songs and enjoy dancing to them and I hear the same comment over and over again. The audience loved listening to the Billy Fury recordings coupled with the dance routines. The show was performed again the following night, everyone was more relaxed this time and even director Maggie Andrew could enjoy it.

A few days after the shows Chris Eley sent me his review, it is rather long but I include it here because it gives a good explanation of the show:-

During the afternoon we were treated to a performance, for Jessie's Fund, by Phil Kelsall MBE, the lead organist from the Blackpool Tower Ballroom. The venue was well attended and the performance magnificent, as might be expected, and very well received by Phil's fans. During the early evening Billy's Mum arrived (Michael had been sitting on a theatre chair in the road saving her a parking space - told you he had humour!). She was actually brought along by a very nice couple, John and Mags Cummings, the latter of course from Billy Fury in Thoughts of You Fan Club team. It was great to see Jean again and as always her presence was to add greatly to the event. Mags and I were allowed in for a little while to take photos of the girls who would be performing for us shortly afterwards. This was because taking photos during the performance may have been off-putting for the girls, although no doubt some proud parents did snap away. What was outstanding whilst talking to the girls, aged from about nine to early twenties was that they now loved the music of Billy Fury; an artist even most of the parents didn't know about. That said they were going round singing his songs. This was so heartening and the photo shows them yelling out Billy Fury and punching the air when I asked them to say his name for the photo. Their enthusiasm and infectious sense of fun boded well for the performance and we were not to be disappointed. During act one we were treated to a mixture of narrations of Billy's life, mostly well delivered indeed and never less than competent throughout the show, and nineteen songs in the first act, beginning with *Give me Your Word* and ending with *Like Iv'e Never Been Gone*. The narrations were rendered even more effective by the well known Halfway to Paradise picture of Billy kneeling with his guitar which Michael had had extended, illuminated and positioned at the side of the stage. Every number was different in approach and each was highly enjoyable, with many novel twists throughout the whole evening. The girls, of whatever age, danced their hearts out for us and it was such a wonderfully innocent show, quite the opposite to what I envisaged until I met the girls in rehearsal. Prior to attending I had thought of sexily dressed over sixteen year olds, pouting and go-go dancing raunchily 60's style (wishful thinking I guess!). I had been looking forward to Billy's sensuality being somehow transferred to dancing girls-a sort of reversed erotic effect yet demonstrating his highly sexualised image. However, this unexpected combination of ages and dance styles, (which was down to the show director) coupled with the innocence and cheeriness actually worked on a very different level was, perhaps as it should be for such a fund, highly wholesome; although this is not to say that there were not attractive girls on stage. To hear recordings of such numbers as *Please Love Me* and others not normally performed by tribute acts, played in public for the first time was terrific. Difficult to pick out individual routines but *Gonna Type a Letter* was perhaps the major show highlight. With its office setting, a sub plot and a lot of movement including tap dancing, it really was great fun. *I'll Show You* was the total opposite, nicely done and the gold ponchos were a lovely touch; *In My Room* was highly poignant and the idea of having 'French' striped tops for *Collette* was clever. The dancing combined summersaults, tap dancing, twist, jive and various other styles and it was a credit to the girls and their marvellous stage manager, Maggie Andrew, and there was not an obvious falter or mis-step in either act-they had worked, and been worked that hard. For an amateur production, with some girls who had never been on stage before it was incredible. It would be unfair to single out any individual but one must be, albeit for a different reason. Lauren Pringle, a young cast member had been working so hard for weeks but was taken ill during the final rehearsal and so missed the show. We really felt for her, and her family and friends and hope she is now fine. The show also featured projected images of Billy on a big screen and being the anorak that I am had to tell Michael that some of the images were reversed and will need changing for any future shows. Also Billy did not cut the *One and only* in 1980 but in 1982, wonder how I missed that, but these are only very minor constructive criticisms for what was a great show.

Act 2 followed the pattern of narration and dance and opened with a great tango scene for *Jealousy,* the girls stunning in all Red and Black dresses, setting the tone for the rest of the act. *Because of love* featured a hula style dance, quite neat and I am sure *Lady* impressed Billy's Mum. *King for Tonight* had a great ending as did several others, how the girls could get into some of the tableaux positions they did beats me, and the delight and exuberance was there especially during *How Many Nights, How Many Days.* I made a note, gymnastics amazing but I cannot recall exactly which numbers featured it, great stuff anyway. *In Summer* was, as it should be, very bright and happy-these girls never stopped smiling, *Turn My Back On You* really rocked away with two older girls jiving, and the postman's hat was a nice touch during *Letter Full of Tears.* Quite how the girls managed such rapid costume changes I don't know and whoever provided the costumes needs a major thank you. Having very young girls in the show allows for cute-and this was typified by a brilliant *Devil or*

Angel where the 'imps' appeared behind a barrier with devils ears on and were joined by Angels for a mock encounter-clever stuff, and so well performed. Great ideas from Maggie, such a talented and professional director, as well as a lovely warm person. Her genuine love for 'her girls' and a fierce protectiveness bear testament to this. *Halfway to Paradise* inevitably closed the Billy part of the show, and there had been really poignant moments, especially during scene eleven which combined Psalm 23, poetry by Billy (from *Paper Aeroplanes)* and *Forget Him* but the performance of *Sweet Jessica* which closed the show was both highly poignant and truly beautiful. The girls sung the tribute to Jessica with a lovely acoustic guitar backing and some solo verses. Unfortunately the girl who played the guitar injured her hand and could not play on stage, which would have added even more pathos to the number. I did say there was such a lot of talent involved in this production and that is an understatement, from the writer, through producer and assistant, the cast, technicians and the theatre staff, a very professional and wonderfully enjoyable production. What I know about dancing you could write on a matchbox-but I know what I saw and it was splendid. In addition to supporting the excellent fund it gave Billy's musical legacy a great uplift and crossed generations, which is what we need to do. A total of forty of Billy's songs were used, mostly hits but mixed with other Decca, Parlophone and Polydor tracks in an excellent mix. One more act would have meant even more varied songs, but two acts was about right. The detailed programme contained personal tributes from Vince Eager, Alvin Stardust and notes from both fan clubs, plus full credits.

To round off the evening Billy's Mum received a presentation photograph of Billy from the cast all involved in the production, and a signed photo list of the cast. Then Michael and Joan received a presentation, with gratitude for promoting Billy so positively. from the Sound of Fury and on behalf of Billy's fans everywhere. Linda and I would like to thank Michael and his wife Joan, a massive Billy fan, for their courtesy and friendship. Michael thanked the fans who attended and we in both fan clubs would echo that without such support all this talent and work would have been wasted. Without the original idea and script of course nothing would have happened, so thanks Michael and Joan, from us all and Billy, who would I am sure be as usual, bemused at the fuss, but chuffed to bits.

Chris Eley *(Sound of Fury Fan Club)*

Whilst I was pleased with the audience reaction and this review I was aware that some of the narration was not clearly audible to the whole of the audience and knew that I would improve it for subsequent shows. Chris was too modest to point out that it was he who donated the framed pictures. Director, Maggie Andrew lived that show and though she demanded high standards from the performers they liked and respected her. The Father of one of the performers videoed the show, I have used it to load many of the dance routines to YouTube and list just three of them here:-

Billy Fury Dance, Lady, Nottingham Arts Theatre
Billy Fury Dance, How Many Nights, Nottingham Arts Theatre
Billy Fury Dance, Gonna Type a Letter, Nottingham Arts Theatre

The performers had made a collection and presented a bottle of champagne to Joan and I with a note thanking us for giving them an opportunity to perform in a wonderful show.

As a result of the shows I donated £1246 to Children's Music Therapy Charity Jessie's Fund. The figure included members of the cast donating travelling expenses and costume makers donating fees that I had offered, another example of the lovely attitude of people in amateur theatre. See Chapter Jessica May George.

The Performers were:-

Lauren Banks
Helen Belcher
Alice Bentham
Holly Cuffley
Vikki Dixon
Frankie Farish
Skye Fletcher
Zoe Garton
Helen Greatorex
Jasmine Hardy
Hania Hickling
Megan Hill
Imogen Jesson
Erin Keogh
Emily Kirk
Charlotte Lawley
Fabiane Leame

Amy Pickance
Lauren Pringle
Chloe Richardson
Sarah Robinson
Alice Sikora-Bradley
Amanda Tate
Paige Taylor
Lily Taylor-Ward
Faith Tucker
Cora Vanaman
Pippa Waite
Isabella Walker
Kirsty Walton
Lizzy Whynes
Laura Wilbraham

2 Billy Fury Dance Lytham, Blackpool

AFTER THE SUCCESS OF MY Billy Fury Dance Show at Nottingham I wanted to put the show on at other venues and had learned a few lessons. I decided to change the way that dancers were selected and rehearsed. My plan was to engage four dance schools and allocate some of the songs to each of them. Every school would select their own performers, choreograph their own routines and rehearse in their own space. The schools would be paid for their contribution including rehearsals and would be responsible for their own chaperones and child protection policy (where applicable). I wanted two narrators situated at a lectern so they could consult the script if necessary, with a good microphone system, and each would understudy the other. I decided not to have projected images during the performance because many people had told me that it distracted them from what was happening on stage at the Nottingham shows.

Whilst I was preparing to put the show on at Lytham I was interviewed by a reporter from the Blackpool Gazette and they published a request for anyone with stories about Billy Fury to contact me. I received a letter from Robert McDougall who lived at Marton near Blackpool. This is the gist of what he wrote:-

I worked on the Liverpool Langton Dock in 1957. I remember Ron as a tall lanky lad with sleeves rolled up handling an assortment of ropes in a most athletic manner. We became friends and Ron would sometimes sprint from his berthed tugboat to the timber unloading quayside to tell me a joke. We often sat together on the River Wall during lunch breaks and Ron would show me batches of songs he had written. Later, in March1960, I saw a picture in a newspaper and recognised it as the friendly scouser I had met on the docks. The article stated Billy was in a stage show at Liverpool Empire with Joe Brown and two American big stars, Gene Vincent and Eddie Cochran. I went to the Liverpool Empire stage door and asked for Billy who came down from the dressing rooms, recognised me immediately on sight and invited me up two floors to the stars dressing rooms which faced the rear of the Old Lime St Station. Billy introduced me to the other stars and said that I was his old dockside pal.

I thanked Robert for the information and just before the date of the show offered him a complimentary ticket but sadly he told me that he had terminal cancer and would not be able to attend, he died a couple of weeks later but his words live on in my script.

I booked the Lowther Pavilion Theatre at Lytham St Annes near Blackpool for Sunday 2nd October 2011 with a 'get in' time of 1pm, for a combined technical and dress rehearsal at 2pm with the performance starting at 7pm. Prior to that date I had supplied the theatre with all the necessary sound CDs, running order and given some guidance to sound requirements with fine details to be arranged at the technical rehearsal.

I had arranged four dance groups as planned but suffered a major problem at the end of August when one had to pull out because of illness of the principal. Nicky Figgins, from Blackpool, whose group were already doing their share of the show agreed to take on the role of the missing school. This meant that they had to choreograph, rehearse and find performers for eleven additional songs and they only had four weeks. In the true tradition of show business they pulled out all the stops and achieved it.

Joan and I travelled to a hotel in Lytham four days before the show and on arrival went into the theatre to makes sure everything was going to plan and were assured it was.

However, we were disappointed that there were no flyers of our 'Billy Fury Dance Show' displayed in and around the theatre, on investigation, these were discovered in an unopened box that we ourselves had delivered to the theatre some weeks before.

A more serious problem occurred on performance day, we arrived at the theatre at 12-30 for the 1pm 'get in' and were kept waiting in the foyer for well over half an hour until I demanded to know what was happening.

We were allowed in to be greeted with an apology and the news that, due to a mistake, the 'multi faceted' venue had been let out for a craft fair the previous day and not converted back to theatre use overnight or in the morning. There were tables and chairs all over the place and one man was slowly moving them away. Our offer of help was refused on grounds of 'elf and safety' so we just had to wait helplessly as plans for our rehearsals were shattered. The dance groups arrived and did bits of rehearsal in whatever space they could find and I found some space and rehearsed the narrators who were excellent. The leaders of the dance groups and the dancers repeatedly asked if they could help prepare the theatre but all offers of help were refused. After 4pm it became apparent that the front stage extension had not been set up. This is essential for a dance show and was delayed even more because the area had been used for storage and had to be cleared. The staff then experienced difficulty fitting the extension.

One group leader threatened to leave and take all her dancers with her if the stage was not available at 6pm. I managed to placate her and we finally got use of the stage at ten minute past six. The dance groups 'blocked' many scenes (this is a term they use for just doing bits of the dance and not the whole piece) but only the first half could be rehearsed. At that point a decision was taken not to rehearse the second half at all. I asked the lighting and sound technicians to 'just use their discretion' because the proper technical rehearsal was impossible.

The show started on time, it was brilliant and the audience loved it. The individual dance groups knew what they had to do. The narrators confidently conveyed the story which was clearly audible throughout the auditorium and no one suspected that the technical staff were 'flying on the seat of their pants'. The only people who knew what had happened were relatives of the performers, they had rehearsed in their own schools during the morning and it had been planned that they would have a break after the dress rehearsal in the afternoon and come back for the performance. They had personal stories of exhausted dancers, missed meals and cancelled hair appointments.

I was pleased that my system of using dance schools who rehearsed in their own space with their own choreography and costumes worked well. I shudder to think what would have happened, because of the theatre rehearsal fiasco, if that had not been done.

These were the groups who defied all the odds to put on a magnificent show:

Nicky Figgins Centre Stage Academy, Bispham, Blackpool

Athina Aristidou
April Shillingford
Bethany Potts
Britney Quirk
Brittany Armer
Courtney Burgess
Elle Daley
Ellie-jay Heatley
Emma Wood
Gavin Field
Hannah Peel
Isabelle Foote
Katy Simms

Kelly Jump
Kelly Smith
Lauren Simkin
Lucy Shuttleworth
Marcus Glen
Meagan Todd
Melissa Banks
Melissa Mills
Miss Nicky Figgins (Principal)
Rachel Sadler
Rosie Grindley
Sammy Jump
Stephanie Nickson
Wei Wei Wu
Yazzmin Knapman-Fletcher

Claire Knight Dance School, Wirral

Abi Preston
Cerys McNee
Claire Pearce
Elizabeth Davidson
Ellena White
Hannah Bennet
Hannah Smith-Richards
Harriet Cavanagh
Katy Poyser
Kirsten Oelofse
Lauren Thirsk
Leah Furlong
Lucy Johnson
Lucy Mulcrone
Lucy Smith-Richards
Luke Bennet
Lucy Bramhall
Olivia Grace
Tim Beckett
Vicky Cowell
Vivien Rees
Wendy Garnett

Whittaker Dance and Drama Centre - Blackpool

Chloe Hinds
Danielle Woodhouse
Grace Holliday
Johanna Rutherford
Laura Eastwood
Lauren Bryne-Fraser
Leonie Bradley
Natalie Coleman
Nikita Coulon
Samantha Enright
Tara Crawforth

Narrators Kimberly Edge and Sarah McFadyen had both trained at the Whittaker Drama Centre. The principals and staff of all the groups and the sixty-three performers worked well together ensuring that the continuity and performance was excellent.

The Lowther Pavilion now has now been refitted with a state-of-the-art seating system giving greater flexibility in how the space is used and allowing a quick transition from a flat floor event to a theatre set up. This is good though I believe it has to be managed effectively.

My next show was only six days away at the Palace Theatre, Mansfield and although this was in a conventional theatre and not a 'multi faceted venue' I contacted them and was assured that they were properly prepared.

3 Billy Fury Dance Mansfield

I STARTED PLANNING FOR MY Billy Fury Dance Show at the Palace Theatre at Mansfield, Nottinghamshire in September 2010 for a performance on Saturday 8 October 2011.

Two dancers who had performed in the first show at Nottingham Arts Theatre were members of dance schools at Mansfield Woodhouse and Kirkby in Ashfield respectively. The proprietors of those two schools situated within ten miles of Mansfield immediately agreed to take part in the show. The Rollo Academy of Performing Arts situated in Nottingham also agreed to take part. This left me seeking one further group, I approached another dance academy, Joan and I had attended their shows and were impressed with them. We met the principal one Saturday morning and I agreed a deal for her school to take part. This was the fourth dance group sorted so I was very pleased. Imagine my disappointment on the following Monday when I received an email message from the principal. She had noticed the name of one of the other groups that she did not like. She gave me an ultimatum to get rid of the other group or her group would not take part in the show. I decided to keep the other group and this is an illustration of the rivalry between dance groups and the difficulty which I experienced, some get on really well together and others hate each other.

I agreed to pay additional travelling expenses to the fourth group that I selected. They were situated thirty miles away at Loughborough and had to use a coach to get their dancers and back room staff to Mansfield. I allocated twelve songs to each group, supplied CDs and the script and each group got on with choreographing their routines and rehearsing in their own space.

Vince Eager who had regularly performed with Billy Fury was booked to speak a tribute to Billy Fury at the show but found that he had to cancel through no fault of his own so I filmed him speaking the tribute instead. Vince was present at that famous interview where Larry Parnes put Billy straight on stage following an unofficial interview. The YouTube name is *Billy Fury by Vince Eager, Audition at Birkenhead Essoldo*

The 'get in' time was 1pm at the Mansfield Palace Theatre on performance day, Saturday 10 October 2011. Joan and I arrived in good time and the dance groups arrived as planned. An unusual thing happened to Joan as we were preparing for the rehearsal. She was setting up raffle prizes at a table in the auditorium and moving them from the backstage area where we had gone in. Whilst she was in the auditorium the fire curtain was lowered for testing and Joan was stranded in the darkened theatre and not able to get back because of the fire curtain. She shouted for help and fortunately a young lady who was setting up the bar heard her and let her out through the bar area. We often have a laugh about it when we are in a theatre and the safety curtain comes down.

Mansfield Palace Theatre host many dance shows and they are good at it. The back stage facilities are excellent, everyone was gathered together and were given instruction on procedures, health, safety and backstage etiquette. The dress and technical rehearsal went well and the performers had some time off before the show which started at 7pm. The show was a great success, it was enjoyed by performers and audience alike and received enthusiastic applause. Of course there were many family and friends of the performers as well as Billy Fury fans in the audience. I was very proud of everyone involved and include names of the groups and performers who took part:-

Narrators

    Georgia Munnion
    Helen Greatorex

Excelsior School of Dance and Gymnastics - Mansfield Woodhouse

    Alana Mullis
    Amelia Pidduck
    Angela Stirland
    Chloe Carlin
    Chloe Smalley
    Demi Hodgkinson
    Ellie Pheasant
    Emily Sykes
    Emily Wiseman
    Greer Taylor
    Hollie Matthews
    Jazmine Vessey
    Kaye Beastall
    Kimberley Smith
    Lauren Banks
    Lauren Pidduck
    Leah Carlin

Lucy Taylor
Natalie Smith
Natasha Vessey
Olivia Weaver
Rachael Spencer
Rebecca Wiseman
Rebecca Spencer
Samuel Holden
Shannan Clay
Sian McIntyre
Tammy Wilcockson
Tia Clay

Christine March School of Dance - Kirkby in Ashfield

Amber Otten-Miller
Amy Marshall
Cora Vanaman
Jessica Johnson
Katie Beecroft
Niamh Beardsley

Charnwood School of Dance, Loughborough

Amie Cunningham
Amy Walker
Angela Mawman
Cathy Barnes
Charlotte Davis
Chloe French
Danielle-Grace Gudger
Ellie Tack
Emily Ralph
Emily Rice
Emma Doherty
Evie Marshall
Evie Martin
Hannah Lanes
Hannah Purvis
Heather Rignall
Helen Pilkington
Holly Oliver
Holly Prangley
Jodie Green

Joella Senior
Georgia James
Katherine Smith
Maisie Wade
Megan Price
Molly Ogle
Molly Sutton
Rebekkah North
Sophie Barraclough
Stacey McGrath
Stacey Pitchford

Rollo Academy of Performing Arts - Nottingham

Abbey Marvin
Amy Meadows
Amber Hudson
Ashleigh Morris
Beth Ursell
Charlotte Burrows
Chloe Hopcroft
Destinee Needham
Erin Keogh
Ffion King
Gabbie Tempest
Ella Roebuck-Swain
Fabiane Leame
Georgia Buda
Lillie Wildman
Lydia Thacker
Melissa Dudley
Millie Dearie
Mollie McGugan
Shanade Williams
Shayna McPherson

The 2 narrators and 87 dancers made a total of 89 cast members and during the finale I made a heartfelt speech which was videoed by a friend and loaded to YouTube with the name *Michael Parkinson's Billy Fury Show, Mansfield Palace* so I have been able to use it to print the actual words that I used 'ladies and gentlemen, if this were a television program eighty six of these dancers would have been thrown out like so much dross and we would just be left with one who would be considered the champion. To me, we have eighty seven champion dancers tonight and I am grateful to every one of them'. The video finished with the dancers acknowledging applause from the audience.

A couple spoke to me after the show who told me that they live in Manchester and had attended the Billy Fury Dance Show at Lytham St Annes on the previous Sunday. They enjoyed it so much that they travelled to Mansfield six days later to attend this show which of course had a different cast. I wanted to know which show they had enjoyed the most but they insisted that they derived equal amounts of enjoyment from each and were interested in the varied approach to the same songs.

The only slight reservation that I had about this show was that sometimes there were little breaks between some of the numbers so the continuity was not quite as slick as it had been at Lytham St Annes or Nottingham. I made myself a note to do better at my next show at the Floral Pavilion, New Brighton which overlooks the Mersey where young Ronald Wycherley had worked on a tug boat before achieving fame as Billy Fury.

I made a donation of £521 to Jessie's Fund from the shows at Lytham and Mansfield bringing the total to over £5700 (see chapter Jessica May George).

4 Billy Fury Dance
Floral Pavilion, New Brighton

IN MARCH 2011 I BOOKED The Floral Pavilion Theatre at New Brighton, Wirral for a performance of my Billy Fury Dance Show on 1 April 2012. It is an attractive venue overlooking the Mersey Estuary with Liverpool Docks on the other side of the water. Booking this attractive 800 plus fixed seated auditorium with plush surroundings and state of the art lighting, sound and acoustics is the most ambitious project I have ever undertaken.

I had already used the Claire Knight Dance School, in my show at Lytham St Annes in October 2011 so they were first on my list. They were soon joined by Wallasey School of Ballet and Anamal Dance Company of Hoylake so all three companies were from the Wirral and happy to work together. I formed an agreement with another dance school who originally wanted to be included but pulled out. I decided to ask Nicky Figgins, although her academy is based near Blackpool and would incur additional travel expense to me. I was full of admiration for them because they had pulled all the stops out to replace the group who had pulled out of the Lytham show only four weeks before the performance date.

This is part of my message to them:

'Hi Nicky, I would like you to take part in my Billy Fury Show at the Floral Pavilion, New Brighton on Sunday 1 April 2012. This opportunity has arisen because a group have pulled out stating the reason that they have just received their competition schedule for 2012 which clashes with my show. I don't understand how a dance group can state categorically that they will take part in a show and then pull out. By a huge coincidence the three scenes are those that you did at Lytham, 4, 9 and 13' Best wishes Michael.

This is the reply I received:-

Thank you Michael. When I opened my school 6 years ago after many years of successfully performing I promised myself I would train my pupils but also give them the opportunity to perform in fantastic shows along the way. As far as I am concerned I am not only a teacher to teach but I can give these children memories that will last forever. I believe that live entertainment has been dying for years and am proud to be in a show that brings that back. I will also never let anyone down, if you say yes then mean yes. We are really looking forward to it again although when I told my pupils that we were doing the original 11 they said but what about Glad all over and Hippy Hippy Shake!!!!!!!! they're very funny NickyXX

That was a lovely response to my request and the reference to the two songs has been echoed by many dance groups, they are both fast and dancers love performing to them.

So my revised line up was fixed:-

Claire Knight Dance School *Wirral,* Wallasey School of Ballet *Wallesey Wirral;*

Nicky Figgins Stage School *Blackpool and* Anamal Dance Company *Hoylake Wirral.*

The next objective was to find two narrators. After much work I selected Zoe Vaux and Lois Moon, both from Liverpool. After I had agreed terms with Zoe and Lois I received a further application from Jenny Hammond, an experienced TV presenter so decided to include all three with Zoe playing the role of leader and the other two joint narrators. It transpired that Zoe and Jenny had previously worked together and were looking forward to being involved again. They arranged rehearsals in their own homes and I met them for a final rehearsal at the Queen's Royal Hotel (where Joan and I were staying) on 27 of March. I invited Jean Wycherley (Billy Fury's Mother) to the show but was told that she would be away in Germany so would not be able to attend.

The first scene of my show includes a song called 'Sweet Jessica' it was written by Susan Raasay who was Associate Director of London Studio Centre's 'Oh What a Lovely War'. I had collaborated with them in putting on three performances of that show at the Nottingham Arts Theatre in 2005. Susan learned about Jessie's story during preparation for the shows and was inspired to write the song. It had been performed by the Claire Knight group at Lytham St Annes with singer Hannah Bennet. I wanted to video this for loading to YouTube in a studio setting because videoing in a live performance is difficult with varying lighting conditions and other factors. Joan and I went to Claire Knights Dance Studio which is now known as Irby Dance Studio four days before the performance day where Claire had arranged for some of the dancers to stay after the normal lessons and some to come in specially. The first attempt looked terrible because they were performing in the middle of a huge studio with no backdrop but Claire said 'no problem I can draw a partition across' so they tried again but this time the sound was weak because it was coming from the other side of the partition. Claire said 'we have a speaker this side, I just need to alter the connection to the amplifier' so we tried again but this time I noticed that some of the dancers were masked by the ones in front, I said to the group 'if you can't see the camera, the camera can't see you' Claire changed things taking sight lines into consideration and we tried again. Eventually I was satisfied and thanked the dancers, one of them said they were pleased to do it for Jessie's Fund. Claire, Hannah and the dancers put a lot of effort and stayed late to do this video for me, I felt a bit guilty because I had put them to so much trouble but the next day received a message from Claire thanking me for my efforts and stating 'they had learned a lot from me' that made me feel twelve feet tall, the YouTube title is *Sweet Jessica, Hannah Bennet, Billy Fury Dance Show.* Hannah is now her first year at college in London (February 2018).

Joan and I had travelled to New Brighton on 27 March and I had a meeting with the Floral Pavilion management and technical team. I was able to convey my wishes about sound, lighting and continuity to them. It was also arranged that I would be allocated a technical area to myself because I planned to film the show on my Super VHS camera which housed a full size three hour super VHS tape.

On performance day everything went to plan. The performers arrived in good time, Joan busied herself preparing the raffle and prizes for Jessie's Fund. The dress/tech rehearsal was under way and I was situated on my own in the technical area at the rear of the theatre.

I was approached by a member of staff who told me that Billy Fury's mother was in a car outside the theatre and wanted to know if she could come to the show. I went down to see her and arranged to introduce her to the audience at the end of the show. I had been planning to make a speech but asked Jean to do so instead. I suggested to Jean that she announce an encore of 'Half Way to Paradise'. I went back to my position, the rehearsal finished and everyone had a couple of hours off before showtime.

We returned to the Floral Pavilion in good time to see the audience arriving and just before the show started I returned to my position in the technical area with the Super VHS camera. I needed to continually adjust the camera focus according to lighting conditions and was all prepared to do so. The show started and I was totally unprepared for something that happened to me. Everything was superb, the lighting, sound, costumes, colour, dancing, speech all brilliant. I suddenly dissolved into tears, not just moist eyes but uncontrollable shaking and tears of emotion. Everything that I had been working for since I first had the idea of the show worked. I was a total wreck and all idea of operating the camera vanished. I was not able to compose myself until just before the interval and it was such a relief to meet people and hear how they were enjoying the show.

The second half started and I was not much better and towards the end of the show I made my way to the front row of the auditorium leaving the camera running but unattended. When the finale finished I introduced Billy's Mother to the audience and shared a few words to the audience with 91 year old Jean. When this was finished Jean suggested an encore of 'Halfway to Paradise' but she did not sit down next to me as planned. Instead she grabbed the microphone from me and proceeded to accompany her son singing. The audience loved it and gave her a standing ovation. This can be seen on YouTube with terrible picture quality but the sound indicates what she did, the title is *Jean Wycherley, Mother of Billy Fury, Speaks and sings, Tribute*.

There were 118 dancers and 3 narrators in the show:-

Leader, Zoe Vaux, Narrators, Jenny Hammond & Lois Moon

Anamal Dance Company, Hoylake

Georgina Barlow
Harry Barnes
Jodie Beauchamp
Evie Cheung
Frankie Clarke
Rosie Connor
Annie Corke
Errin Coull
Oliver Courtney
Amy Cowley
Beth Cumming
Sophia Dollery
Alex Doran
Jessica Doran
Sophie Evans
Libby Farrar
Megan Fletcher
George Fletcher
Mya Flowerdew
Rebecca Gerety
Courtney Goddard
Lucy Harrison

Kelly Hayden
Charlie Holmes
Aimee Jackson
Hollie Amy Jarvis
Ella Johansen
Jodie Kelly
Erin Kidd
Adam Ledgerton
Ellie Malone
Belen Manley
Kelsey McCarthy
Margarita McGrath
Leah McNay
Chris McNeilis
Stacie McNeilis
Rebecca Morgans
Katie Moruzzi
Danuelle Murray
Anna Riley
Brogan Roy
Margaret Saunders
Olivia Smith
Grace Speed
Izzi Steele
Jen Suaby
Laura Suckley
Hannah Waywell
Pippa Welch

Claire Knight Dance School, Wirral

Tim Beckett
Hannah Bennet
Luke Bennet
Harriet Cavanagh
Gemma Crutchley
Lizzie Davidson
Leah Furlong
Wendy Garnett
Olivia Grace
Emma Hopwood
Elise Johnson

Lucy Johnson
Cerys McNee
Millie Metz
Lucy Mulcrone
Kirsten Oelofse
Claire Pearce
Katy Poyser
Abi Preston
Viv Rees
Lauran Thirsk
Ellena White

Nicky Figgins Centre Stage Academy, Blackpool

Athina Aristidou
Brittany Armer
Melissa Banks
Mr Gavin Field
Miss Nicky Figgins
Miss Rosie Grindley
Miss Kelly Jump
Samantha Jump
Karis Lomax
Melissa Mills
Stephanie Nickson
Hannah Peel
Britney Quirk
Lauren Simkin
Katy Simms
Miss April Shillingford
Lucy Shuttleworth
Miss Wei Wei Wu
Emma Wood

Wallasey School of Ballet, Liscard

Nicola Barr
Lisa Beattie
Chloe Bryan
Molly Chrishan
Laura Collison
Katie Dodd
Faye Edwards

Natalie Edwards
Melissa Fearnley
Erin Haig
Zoe King
Katie Lewis
Katie Lindon
Sophie Lyons
Sophie McGregor
Sophie Nelson
Sarah Perkins
Rachel Pickford
Melissa Pugh
Bethany Richards
Hannah Ridge
Jessica Roberts
Kimberley Roberts
Rachel Sefton
Katie Sheridan
Kirsty Walsh
Nicole Yee

One of the songs in the show was 'In My Room' Larry Parnes, Billy's manager had wrongly claimed that it was written by Billy Fury but in fact it had been written by fellow Liverpudlian Jimmy Campbell who died on 12 February 2007. He is commemorated by a seat and plaque situated on the sea front about a mile from the Floral Pavilion. Jimmy's family were regular visitors to the Hotel where Joan and I were staying so I gave them tickets and they attended the show as my guests. Katie Sheridan from the Wallasey School of Ballet performed a solo routine to this lovely song, the YouTube title is *Billy Fury In My Room, Wallasey School of Ballet*

Other videos from the show are on my YouTube channel Michael nottha-tone Parkinson

I have selected one of each group as suggested viewing:-

Billy Fury That's All Right Floral Pavilion New Brighton
Billy Fury Running Around, Floral Pavilion New Brighton
Billy Fury Maybe Tomorrow, Floral Pavilion New Brighton
Billy Fury Died 1983 Speaks & sings Forget Him

It had been a memorable and emotional experience for me. To see things that I had planned come to fruition, words I had written spoken so well, the combination of Billy Fury singing and the dancing routines culminating in the standing ovation for Jean was brilliant.

As a result of the show I donated £530 to Jessie's Fund *See Chapter 11, Jessica May George*

5 Billy Fury Dance Shaw Theatre, London

IN 2015 I DECIDED TO put my show on in London using professional performers and asked Cora Vanaman if she would be interested in directing it for me. Cora had an impressive CV of song, dance, choreography, teaching and narration and she had performed in my first Billy Fury Dance Show at Nottingham Arts Theatre. Though she was only fourteen at the time she had danced, narrated and choreographed routines for the other dancers. In addition, in October 2011 she took part in my Billy Fury Dance Show at the Palace Theatre Mansfield, as a member of the Christine March Dance School where she had been a member from the age of three. In that show the script required a group of dancers to sing the 23rd psalm (as part of the scene depicting the death and funeral of Billy Fury). Two days before the show most of the girls dropped out of the singing leaving just two who were to sing as a duet. On the day before the show the other girl dropped out and I asked Cora to sing solo which she did beautifully. She had then gone on to the Mountview Academy of Theatre Arts in London where she had done a Foundation Course in Musical Theatre. When I contacted Cora to ask if she was interested in directing my London show she had just finished at Mountview so the timing was ideal.

We held a meeting where we discussed various things and arranged a second meeting for a week later. At that second meeting Cora introduced Craig Canning who she wanted as assistant director to work with her over rehearsals and the shows and we discussed many aspects of the show, content, cast required, rehearsals and much more.

In the meantime I investigated various theatres in and around London before deciding to hire the Shaw Theatre situated near St Pancras Station and the British Library on Euston Road. The plush 446 seater theatre is only a mile and a half from the West End and appeared ideal. It is part of the Pullman Hotel, owned by the Accor Group. There would be fourteen performances between 14th and 23rd April 2016 with some matinees. The difficult part of promoting a show is that you have to book a theatre long before the event so this was done in June 2015.

The next obstacle was rehearsal space, again necessary long before the show and not easy to find in London but we found what appeared to be ideal premises, Pulse Studios, situated on Liverpool Road Islington and booked the studio for 13 days starting on 29 March with final date on 12th April 2016 before our dress rehearsal at the theatre the day before the first performance. At that point Cora and Craig had not seen the studios. I had gone in, looked around, done the booking and paid a deposit of £768.

Our next objective was to audition performers and I formed an agreement with SCA Management at Italia Conti and an audition took place in their premises near the Barbican on 20 October. I loaded video clips to YouTube under the title *Billy Fury Dance audition, Michael Parkinson,* Many dancers and a narrator took part in the audition and the hard working but relaxed environment can be seen on the video. When the audition finished Cora, Craig and myself were on a high. It was the first really enjoyable episode in the planning for the show. We had a couple of hours to spare before our train back to Nottingham and I suggested that we go to the rehearsal studios so that Cora and Craig could see the facilities. I telephoned Pulse Studio to tell them that we were calling in but no one answered even though they should have been open. We decided to go anyway and on arrival found the studio dark and locked with a notice on the door - 'Studio closed until further notice. All lessons and bookings cancelled' Our feelings of elation were dashed and though rehearsals were not due to start for five months, I was worried about the outcome, what was going to happen and what about the deposit I had paid?

On the train back to Nottingham Cora busied herself with her copious notes about the audition and selection ideas. We had already decided on a second audition to look at performers who had applied to us individually and were planning to hold that at Pulse Studios.

I telephoned my contact at the studio the next morning and learned that there was a huge dispute between the owner of the dance studio Jonathon Laidlaw and the owner of the building. This had resulted in the studio being closed. I was given the telephone number of the studio owner and had to leave a message so I feared he would not contact me. To my surprise Johnathon phoned me a couple of hours later and explained the situation to me. It was not good and there was little chance of it being resolved. He advised me that it would be better to cancel the rehearsal bookings and he would reimburse the £768 deposit that I had paid. He promised that the money would be paid back by bank transfer and to my delight he telephoned me within twenty minutes to say it was done. Imagine my relief when I checked my bank statement to see the money had been repaid. I spoke to Johnathon whilst preparing this book and he told me that the dispute with the owner of the building had led to the closure of his dance studio business.

My next task was to find another rehearsal space and discovered Husky Studios at Amelia Street which is situated underneath the railway arches at Elephant and Castle. It was closer to central London so more expensive than Pulse but I booked various dates for our rehearsals and 10 November for our second audition. Cora, Craig and I attended this audition.

Cora believes that dancers should warm up before dancing because it helps to avoid stress and strains. She put the dancers through a vigorous warm up and it can be seen on YouTube title *Dance Warm Up, Leader Cora Vanaman, Husky*. If you think that dancing is easy, take a look at this. An audition video can also be seen on YouTube title *Billy Fury Dance audition 2 Husky*. Cora made her final selection of dancers and we agreed on the narrator so these were the performers selected to take part in the 14 Billy Fury Dance Shows at the Shaw Theatre:-

		From:
Ronald Wycherley	Ryan Mockridge	Hastings, Sussex
Billy Fury	Charles Ames	London Borough of Wanstead
Narrator (Mickey)	Scott Westwood	West Bromwich, W. Midlands
Dancers	Becky Basset	Liverpool, Merseyside
	Paige Blackwell	Borehamwood, Herts.
	Ellen Bleasdale	Warrington, Cheshire
	Eleanor Byrne	Dublin, Southern Ireland
	Abigail Cleary	Dundee, Scotland
	Hollie Dorman	Underwoo, Nottinghamshire
	Lara Greenhow	Coventry, Warwickshire
	Alice Gribben	Scunthorpe, Lincolnshire
	Zoe Price	Hullbridge, Essex

I got contracts agreed by all the performers and loaded informative videos to YouTube of Cora and Craig speaking about their involvement in the show. The video titles are:-

Billy Fury Dance Show, Cora Vanaman, Director

Billy Fury Dance Show, Craig Canning hit by David Essex

In the second video Craig talks to Cora about being hit in the face whilst performing as a stuntman with David Essex.

Cora located accommodation for herself and Craig which I viewed and booked for the duration of rehearsals and shows, she took measurements of the performers and arranged for a dressmaker to make some of the special costumes and others were bought on Ebay.

On 7 February 2016 Cora sent me this message:

'Hi Michael, Hope you are OK. I have just spent the entire day with my Dad and we have completely reworked the script for the narrator. Whilst the content of your script was very factual and informative, I hope you understand that to work in this type of show would have been extremely difficult, therefore the script needed to be more audience friendly and entertaining.The revised script, albeit a first draft at this stage, has been tailored to suit Scott and will allow him to use his skills to interact with both the cast and the audience and I have every confidence that it will work well. I appreciate that it only summarises key points out of your original script but for a dance show I felt it important to keep the focus on entertainment. Please find it enclosed for your perusal'. Thanks Cora

This was a bombshell because I liked my original script and there had never been any problems with it in previous shows. However, I took the view that it would be pointless to pay a young person to direct my show, because I wanted a young feel to it and then stifle her initiative. Apart from that I liked some of the ideas that Cora and her father had introduced. Whilst researching this book I discovered that Cora's grandfather was in fact an American GI who had been sent to England in 1944 prior to the D-Day Normandy landings. He had met and eventually married a young lady from Mansfield, Nottingham. They lived in America for a few years before moving to England. That story will be Chapter 6 in this book. The result of this was that Cora'a Father needed no introduction to American music and his knowledge was invaluable when he assisted his daughter Cora in revising my script. A few years later young Ronald Wycherley was influenced by records brought in by American workers that he met whilst working on a tug boat in Liverpool docks. It is strange how the Billy Fury story and my London show had such a strong American influence.

I am grateful to Universal Music, London and Lisa Voice who gave permission for the Billy Fury tracks to be used in all my Billy Fury shows. The dress and technical rehearsals went on with the normal amount of hassle and the first performance on Thursday 14 April was well received by the audience. I sat on the front row with my camera mounted on a tripod and videoed some performances so that I could edit and load videos to my YouTube channel name Michael notthatone Parkinson.

The first scene starts with Heartbeat playing, Ronald Wycherley enters stage, dances a little, goes to sit downstage right, starts writing. Mickey enters, music fades but remains on quietly, Mickey speaks *'The dockside, Liverpool.*

What a place. It's grey, it's dark, but d'you know what, I love it, Oh, I'm Mickey by the way, yer' alright, I work on the tugs with me mate over there (indicates 'Ron') *'whatcha whack'* (Ron screws up paper and throws it away, Mickey picks it up and reads paper. *That's my mate Ron. Ronny. And this* (waves paper) *is gonna make him famous one day, you mark my words, cus' my bessie Ronny, he writes dead good songs. Now do you see that, over there,* (points) *that's the Mauretania it's just docked. up. That has come from from the big apple, NYC, the Empire state. It's New York, New York, what a wonderful town. Now something very special is happening in the states at the moment, it's called Rock and Roll. It's gonna' blow your socks off Daddy-o* (in corny American accent, with Elvis move)

(Girl runs through auditorium with record in hand). Girl *Ronny, Ronny, look what I have got for you straight off the boat can you believe it, look here for you.* (Runs on stage) *this record, Girls, check it out. come on, come on, check it out* Eight girls run on stage, one with a record player (Mickey) *You see because this boat's full of Yanks and these guys bring records, now I'm not talking about How Much is That Doggie in the Window, no, no no, I'm talking about You Ain't Nothing but a Hound Dog, crying all the time, Well you aint' gonna Rabbit, you aint' no friend of mine. (*Girls slap thighs and laugh-Once upon a dream plays, Mickey and four girls exit with record player. Remaining girls dance, joined by Ronnie who is attracted by one of the dancers and the scene ends with the two of them together.

I have included the dialogue from scene one because it illustrates how Ronald Wycherley was influenced by records brought in by American boat workers.

The YouTube video titles in order of performance are:-

Billy Fury Dance 1 Heartbeat, Narration, Once upon a Dream
Billy Fury Dance 2 You're having the last dance with me
Billy Fury Dance 3 Give me your word, Narration
Billy Fury Dance 4 It's only make believe
Billy Fury Dance 5 Margo
Billy Fury Dance 6 Running around
Billy Fury Dance 7 I'll never fall in love again
Billy Fury Dance 8 Gonna type a letter
Billy Fury Dance 9 When will you say I love you
Billy Fury Dance 10 Wondrous place
Billy Fury Dance 11 Maybe tomorrow
Billy Fury Dance 12 In thoughts of you

Billy Fury Dance 13 Don't knock upon my door (subject to video blocking)
Billy Fury Dance 14 Nothin' shakin' like the leaves on the trees
Billy Fury Dance 15 I'd never find another you
Billy Fury Dance 16 Like I've never been gone
Billy Fury Dance 17 Run to my loving arms, Dialogue
Billy Fury Dance 18 Colette
Billy Fury Dance 19 That's alright (last one before the interval so have a cup of tea)
Billy Fury Dance 20 Glad all over
Billy Fury Dance 21 Jealousy
Billy Fury Dance 22 My Christmas Prayer, Narration
Billy Fury Dance 23 Devil or Angel
Billy Fury Dance 24 Somebody else's girl
Billy Fury Dance 25 Hippy Hippy Shake
Billy Fury Dance 26 Because of love
Billy Fury Dance 27 Lady
Billy Fury Dance 28 Last night was made for love
Billy Fury Dance 29 In my room, Narration
Billy Fury Dance 30 In Summer
Billy Fury Dance 31 Psalm 23 Crimond, Sung by dancers
Billy Fury Dance 32 Billy speaks self written words, Forget him
Billy Fury I will, Michael Parkinson Show
Billy Fury Dance 34 I'll never quite get over you, I'm lost without you
Billy Fury Dance 35 A thousand stars, Narration
Billy Fury Dance 36 Halfway to Paradise (Finale)

I have incorporated these song titles as YouTube names but any of them can be blocked either Worldwide or in Certain Countries and that can happen at any time so please understand if you are not able to see certain scenes. Also the type of device you are using can influence what can be seen. At the time of writing (Feb 2018) Billy Fury Dance 13 is subject to blocking by copyright holders.

The artistic and performance side of the show was brilliant and we received many glowing comments from people in the audience, I watched every one of the shows and thoroughly enjoyed them. Readers can form their opinion by looking at some of the YouTube links but the message that shines through to me is that the Billy Fury recordings were as popular with dancers and audiences either amateur or professional as the music of today.

6 American GI & English Girl

WHEN I ASKED CORA VANAMAN to direct the London version of my Billy Fury Dance Show she enlisted the help of her father in an ambitious project of revising the narrator part to make it more audience friendly and entertaining. The first scene illustrates how young Ronald Wycherley was influenced by music brought in by American workers and I was intrigued as to how John, her father, appeared to know so much about the American influence. I asked him and discovered the amazing story of his father (Cora's grandfather). Here is the story as told by John Vanaman:-

Robert Elgie Vanaman was born on 7 May 1921 in Winamac, Indiana, a small mid western town in the heart of America's farming belt. The youngest of 5 he had three brothers and one sister. He was born and lived with his family on a working farm which had been in the family for at least three generations.

The two story wooden building had several rooms and a full sized barn, cow shed, pig sheds and chicken runs plus various out buildings. Fruit orchards of apple, peach and plumb and several hundred acres of arable land which was used for crops such as corn, beans, peas, wheat plus whatever was decided would be good to grow and sell. A gravel pit which was fed from a small stream gave a constant supply of fresh fish such as catfish, sunfish and the occasional snapping turtle.

Life was hard and started at 4am with 60 head of dairy cattle which needed to be milked by hand, originally the land was farmed using a team of horses and a hand plough but when funds allowed, a small tractor became invaluable. The morning jobs were usually finished by 11am and after lunch there was always something else to attend to. All produce grown was either sold, stored or bottled for later consumption. This was a self sufficient family who were living through the great depression. At least a couple hours a day Robert would disappear with either a rifle, shotgun or fishing rod to 'bag' something for the table and larder. Rabbit, squirrel and pigeon being the most common. He soon became a crack shot, something he would later be rewarded for during his time in the army.

Robert was always messing with engines and soon could repair not only the family vehicles but neighbours too and he was able to earn some spare cash as the local repairman. He could drive his daddy's car at 14 and often would drive into town to buy provisions from the Mercantile store. He passed his driving test at 16 by driving the town judge around in a breakdown truck! Shortly after this while driving his daddy's 1932 Chevrolet Coupe he had a serious road accident and almost killed himself.

In his mid teens Robert became unsettled at home and tensions between him and his elder brothers resulted in an altercation which upset Robert so much, in desperation, at the age of 18, he drove to the nearest main town and joined the regular Army, (The Army of the United States).

Basic training was held at Fort Wayne, Indiana and subsequently he was assigned to the National Guard where his first duty of action was to riot control in Chicago where a racial demonstration had gotten out of hand and looting was taking place. Generally an Army presence whenever needed was the order of the day.

Obviously at the time, the Americans were aware of the tensions that were building in Europe and the rumours about an American involvement. It had been suggested that the extreme northern coast of Canada may be an invasion point so Robert's company was about to spend the next 6 months in Upper Michigan doing snow warfare. This involved using skis, snow shoes, extreme survival techniques and sniper training all in temperatures of minus 30 degrees. When a series of German U Boats had been sited in and around the Caribbean Islands, it was decided that Robert and the rest of his company would be better placed guarding the coast of Trinidad than the frozen waste of nowhere so they were all shipped out.

I guess you can imagine that life was somewhat different now and Robert was enjoying the peace and tranquillity of a Caribbean island. After a few daily exercises and patrols, life was pretty sweet. No one was really expecting the order to ship out, especially as the destination was New York. Once new orders were issued that said England everyone knew what to expect.

Getting troops over to England for the invasion was no easy task and many large ships were commandeered to act as troop carriers including the Cunard liners Queen Elizabeth and Queen Mary. Stripped of their luxury cabins and state rooms they now housed cots and bunks making homes for well over 10,000 troops each. Robert travelled over to England on the Queen Mary docking at Liverpool sometime in 1944. Stationed at several places he ended up at Mansfield, Nottinghamshire. Now the rank of PFC, private first class, being a seasoned soldier he offered support to the young draftees, (United States Army), many who were both scared and homesick. One Friday evening, while out on leave in the town, Robert and his friend spotted a couple of local girls walking together. Noticing the girls stopping to look in a shop window, Robert, grasped the opportunity and said 'You girls lonesome?' Spending the rest of the evening together, Robert and Joan agreed to meet again and from then on would meet as often as they could. I am not sure how much the lure of American chocolate, coffee and nylons helped but many British girls fell helplessly in love with the GI's with their clean cut uniforms, smooth accents and boy could they cut a rug on the dance floor. The poor British guys really didn't stand a chance.

Joan introduced Robert to her parents and received the approval she was hoping for and after a short time Robert asked Joan to marry him. Without any real plans she agreed and all the arrangements were made. The wedding was to be at St Barnabas church Pleasley, Derbyshire sometime in May 1944. You cannot really imagine Joan's heartache at being left at the altar when Robert didn't turn up. It was common knowledge that many Americans had already left brides to be waiting usually because they were already married back in the States. However, Joan was convinced that Robert would not do this and after giving her apologies set out with her mother for his last known camp address. On arrival she was told that he, along with his entire company had been shipped out under tight security to a holding area on the south coast. Not knowing anything else they proceeded to travel to Nottingham where they boarded a train and headed to London. From there they headed to what they believed to be the holding area and on arriving at a gate patrolled by an armed MP were told literally nothing. Heartbroken they spent the night at a very dirty B&B and returned home the next day. Joan continued an anguished existence not knowing what had happened to Robert, she hoped that the invasion was the real reason that he had not turned up at the alter but had he survived?

In the holding area, secrecy was paramount. No letters or messages were allowed even leaving your bride at the alter was not reason enough to put the invasion at risk. Poor weather conditions hampered the invasion attempt but finally the day came and Robert, along with an old friend from training days who he just had happened to meet with by chance found themselves on a landing craft heading for Utah beach. Strong currents caused them to drift several hundred yards off course and therefore they had not arrived at the designated landing point however after meeting some resistance they finally met up with the 101st airborne and Robert had survived the beachhead landing, unfortunately, his friend had not been so lucky. His company quickly moved forward taking Cherbourg and then became part of Operation Cobra, a sweeping offensive to drive the Germans back across France now a foothold had been maintained after the invasion. Robert's campaign in the European theatre was suspended at this point when a shell from a German 88mm exploded close to where he was dug in. This was just outside St Lo in France. Shrapnel damage was enough to render him unconscious and he was evacuated to a safe point for hospitalisation where he was returned to the UK and coincidentally to Kings Mill hospital, in Mansfield, for convalescence in July 1944.

Whilst making his recovery Robert was able to ask a nurse to get a message to Joan's place of work. They were reunited for a very short time before Robert was soon returned to his company who were now deep into Europe and he continued his front line duties.

On his return to combat, Robert encountered the fierce battle known as the Battle of the Bulge as his unit was pinned in for 12 days without food or water, eventually, the weather cleared enough for air support to help clear the way for ground troops to relieve them and they were able to press on into Germany. Pockets of resistance along with the concentration camps were daily occurrences the units were dealing with. A skirmish in a small town resulted in Robert sustaining a head injury and this time the seriousness of his injury resulted in him being transported to hospital in Paris where he spent two weeks recovering before being returned to the UK for light duties along side the 9th Air Force.

Robert was not able to see Joan on his return to the UK, it is possible that he was stationed somewhere in Suffolk and was only able to send letters updating her of his situation. (John still has one of the letters and has transcribed it for inclusion in this story, it was dated 14 September 1944 and arrived postmarked 20 September 1944):-

Dearest Joan

I have waited a few days to write to you so I would be able to send you my address so I could get some mail from you. I haven't received any mail from you yet. I sure hope you have received my mail. Honey, I sure wish I could be with you for I sure miss you since I left you. We could still take those short walks like we did when were there before. I am some place in Belgium so you can see that my mail never catches up to me. Honey will you play that one record you have just for me and my heart will be right with you. I haven't heard it since that last night I was with you. I will be listening for it. It maybe a long way away but my heart will hear it. Do you remember what I wrote in your autograph book?

Since I came over here I have a better one. As I lay sleeping in my Fox hole and getting up black as coal, waking up in the morning dew and thinking of you.

Lots of love, Bob

Officially Robert was assigned into Company E 11th Infantry 4th Infantry Division, (The Ivy Leaguers) and because of his ability with a rifle and sidearm he was tasked as a BAR man, (Browning Automatic Rifle). This light hand carry machine gun was used to support units of men and carriers were usually well protected. Two or three ammo carriers would also support the BAR man. Drawbacks were that they were always upfront trying to clear a path and weighing almost twice as much as a standard M1 rifle it was heavy to carry around. He received the Air Medal for his outstanding contribution to the war effort with his work with the Air Force. Apart from his assigned duties he often volunteered to repair the jeeps and other vehicles needing attention as the Air Force mechanics were working full time keeping aircraft flying.

Robert was officially demobbed in May 1945 and he finally married Joan in July 1945 at St Barnabas Church Pleasley as originally planned. After the wedding Robert had to return to the States for his official release from the Army. Joan joined him in January 1946 docking in New York on the Queen Elizabeth where she and Robert made a new life together in Winamac living on the family farm. Life was good, and Joan enjoyed being there and was readily accepted into the family. After about a year it was decided that Joan's parents would come out to the States and join them so they could all be together. Joan and her mother worked on the farm whilst Robert and father in law Reg found work locally as Robert did not want to work on the farm again.

This worked well and everyone enjoyed their new life in the States until, sometime around 1954, Reg fell ill with cancer and wanted to return home to Mansfield. Joan felt the need to return to Mansfield with her parents and Robert decided to go with them so it was decided that Joan, Robert and her parents would return to the UK.

On arrival in Mansfield Robert applied for a job as a mechanic at a General Motors garage. It so happened that the garage had an old American MACK truck waiting for an engine overhaul and none of the mechanics were familiar with the engine so Robert's timing was perfect and he was given a job immediately, being tasked with getting the MACK back on the road. Robert stayed in this job for a few years before he secured a job with the National Coal Board and worked there for the rest of his working life. Robert and Joan had one child, John, who was born in 1956, I am very grateful to John for supplying this very interesting story. This of course is Cora's father who was such a big help on revising the script for the Billy Fury Dance Show at the Shaw Theatre.

On their return to England, Robert bought a little bit of America with him including clothes, ornaments, photographs and vinyl records. Robert particularly loved music and immediately started to build on his collection by buying singles and EP's by artists such as Cliff Richard, Billy Fury and Marty Wilde all of which would be played on a beautiful polished wood stereophonic radiogram while, as a family, card games such as Canasta or Pinochle were played on a Sunday evening. They remained married until his passing in 1991. The Vanaman farmhouse in Winamac, Indiana still exists but does not belong to the Vanaman family. Some members of Robert and Joan's family still live in the United States and some in the United Kingdom.

7 Billy Fury: Biography

WHILST WRITING THE SCRIPT AND producing my Billy Fury Dance Shows I have put together biographical details and stories about Billy some of which were spoken by cast members or narrators. This forms the base for my short biography of Billy Fury and is not intended to be a full and complete biography.

Billy Fury was a stage name. He was born on 17 April 1940 his real name was Ronald Wycherley. His mother was Sarah Jane Wycherley but for some reason became known as Jean which was the name that she was referred to in my knowledge of her from the year 2009. His father, Albert was in the Army during the 1940s and on returning to civilian life worked as a cobbler. His mother sang a lot and during my conversations with her convinced me that is where young Ron developed his interest in singing and song writing. The family lived in the Dingle area of Liverpool. A young brother, Albert, the same as his father was born on 26 June 1943. Ron attended St Silas Infants School and then went on to Wellington road secondary school. He lost much time at school because of ill health. At six years of age he suffered rheumatic fever and was in Alder Hey Children's Hospital for two months. At the age of 12 he was in hospital again, reportedly this time in Wales. He was not a good patient and after two weeks he got out of the second floor window and climbed down a drainpipe to what he thought was going to be freedom. He was caught in nearby fields and put back in the room with the window securely locked this time.

Ron was given piano lessons from the age of 11 and his parents bought him a guitar for his 14th birthday. He became a good strummer but never progressed beyond three chords. He left school at the age of 15 and worked in an engineering factory for a year. He then worked on a tugboat called 'Formby' in Liverpool docks. Country and western records brought in from America inspired Ron. He formed the Formby Sniffle Gloup (he must have had a sense of humour) and performed in pubs and clubs. Ron liked the lyrics of Hank Williams but decided he wanted to write songs in his own style. This was the deep broken hearted mood evident in much of his work. Ron changed boats but later went to work in a department store. Here he was influenced by a fellow employee, Margo King. He became very fond of her but to Margo Ronnie was just a good friend. He wrote Margo (Don't Go) for her. She got married and emigrated to Australia and did not hear the song for many years.

Ron started to perform gigs and the small audiences were impressed with his singing and song writing abilities. In April 1958 he recorded six demo tracks on a 78 rpm acetate record at Percy Phillips recording studio at 38 Kensington, Liverpool (this premises now has a Blue Plaque). Some reports say that his mother sent this to Larry Parnes but others say that Ron sent a picture of himself and a tape of his songs to impresario Larry Parnes but did not get a reply. He entered a local talent show 'Carroll Levis Discoveries' at the Liverpool Empire but failed to win the heat. His mother wrote again to Larry Parnes who this time replied. Larry invited Ron to see him at the Birkenhead Essoldo on the 1 October 1958. One of his shows, 'The Larry Parnes Extravaganza' was being staged that night. A member of the tour company, who spotted Ron at the Essoldo was Brian Bennett, the backing drummer in Marty Wilde's band. He said later 'Ron had a guitar in a pillow case and wore a pair of brothel creepers, sort of big suede shoes. He had this wonderful swept back blonde hair'. Ron took his guitar out of the bag and sang some of his own songs to Marty Wilde and Larry Parnes. He hoped that Marty would like what he heard and record some of them.

Instead, in an episode that has become music legend, Parnes took Ron on stage during the interval. When the curtains opened a frightened 18 year old made his public debut as a singer. He sang Margo, Maybe Tomorrow and Don't knock upon my door. Ron said later that his knees were literally knocking together but the fans thought it was part of the act. The audience loved his performance and the girls loved his appearance.

At the end of the show Larry Parnes asked Ron to join his Extravaganza tour. He wanted him to appear the very next night when the show moved to the Stretford Essoldo. His parents could not believe it when he got home and told them what had happened. Next morning Ron was packing his suitcase to go to Manchester. His mother got really worried about him going off on his own. Ron convinced her that it was the best chance he would ever have.

Larry Parnes had decided that Ronald Wycherley was no name for a rock star. He told Ron that his first name would be Billy after Billy Cotton the popular bandleader. The second name would be Fury to compensate for his shyness. Ron argued, he wanted to be called Stean Wade, Parnes insisted and the name Billy Fury was born. Billy continued to perform in the Extravaganza shows of Larry Parnes. It was not only his singing voice that impressed the fans. The girls went wild with delight. They screamed louder and louder as he gyrated in a sensual manner. His good looks, singing voice and brilliant stage presentation made him a hit where ever he performed. Billy's influence at this time was Elvis Presley. He copied and accentuated Elvis's sensual moves on stage. In fact he was banned in Dublin because his act was considered to risqué. The show toured extensively and ended in London. Before the end of the tour Billy had more than proved his worth. He got a new, and better, contract, with Larry Parnes. In November 1958 he recorded his first single. This went straight into the top twenty chart in February 59. It was Maybe Tomorrow, written by Billy himself. It was the first song he sang at the Larry Parnes audition. Decca records gave him a seven year recording contract. More singles were released.

A long playing 33rpm record, The Sound of Fury was released in 1960. This reached the top 20 long player chart and has been re-issued in various forms on four occasions. Experts regard it as Britain's finest example of rock n roll, rockabilly, music. Billy had written all ten songs himself, something unheard of until the Beatles came along. Some were credited to Wilbur Wilberforce, a name Billy used to avoid Larry Parnes taking commission on his writing.

In 1960 Billy had three more hits including Collette. She was, according to Billy, an actress in a subtitled French Film that Billy went to see. He wrote the song on a cigarette packet found on the floor of the cinema. I read his explanation of his song writing method. I find it absolutely amazing. He said 'I get an idea, usually when I'm depressed over some girl. I scribble a lyric and sing the thing straight into a tape recorder. It never gets on to paper until someone at the music publisher puts it there. Then they send me back an arrangement, which I can't read. So, I just record it the way I thought of it'.

His mum, Jean, used to find bits of song on scraps of paper all over the house. This included her bills and important papers.

In the 1960s Billy had more top twenty UK hits than anyone except, The Beatles, Cliff Richard and Elvis Presley. He and his fans were disappointed that he never reached number one. In May 1961 Billy recorded a cover version of Tony Orlando's Halfway to Paradise. This was an immediate hit and got to number three in the charts followed by Jealousy in September 1961, this got to number 2 giving him his highest ever UK singles chart placing.

Billy's heart problem continued to plague him. On some tour dates he had to cut his act short. Sometimes he had to be replaced altogether. The fans were told that he was suffering from exhaustion or the flu.

In 1962 Billy and Larry Parnes flew to Los Angeles to present Elvis Presley with Gold and Silver discs for Decca UK sales. They spent the day on the film set of 'Girls, Girls, Girls'. Billy recalled 20 years later 'We didn't really say much at all, I was on the set watching him, all we got to say to each other was **Hi.** He was one of the nicest people I have ever met, he called everyone Sir'. As a result of this visit Billy's last release of 1962 was 'Because of Love' a song used in the Presley film. Elvis said in a later interview, 'I could not understand Billy Fury, he came all the way from England to see me and all he said was **Hi'**. This was an example of Billy's shyness offstage. Billy's good looks made him a natural for television. His first appearance was in Ted Willis's drama 'Strictly for Sparrows'. He appeared on television in Jack Good's 'Oh Boy' in February 1959. He and Marty Wilde were two favourite performers in another Jack Good television show. This was called 'Boy Meets Girl' and ran for seven months from September 1959. In 1962 he made his film debut in Michael Winner's 'Play it Cool'. He played his own character as Billy Fury in 'I've Gotta Horse', (this is my favourite Billy Fury film). He loved animals and persuaded the studio to include some of his own in 'I've Gotta Horse'. He made a cameo appearance in 'That'll be the Day' and this reached number one in the album charts.

Mansfield resident Christine Newton told me a personal story, she said; 'I was nearly 15 years of age and the family were staying in a caravan at Caister on Sea in Norfolk. I had pestered my parents to take me horse riding. On 24 September 1964 we went to a stables near Yarmouth and had a great surprise. There was no riding that day because the stables had been hired out to a film company. They were filming 'I've Gotta Horse'. Billy Fury, The Batchelors and Leslie Dwyer were there. We were allowed to stay and watch the filming because they did not want us going off and telling other people. Later, we went into Yarmouth to see the Billy Fury show and saw fire engines roaring up to the theatre. They were filming there as well'. Christine has photographs of herself taken with Billy Fury but had never seen the film. I presented her with a copy, as a reward for her story, when she attended my Billy Fury show at the Mansfield Palace Theatre in 2011. In 1964 he bought a racehorse called 'Anselmo' my wife, Joan, wanted to back the horse in the 1964 Epsom Derby but was too young to place the bet. She persuaded her Mother to do it for her and Anselmo came third at 100 to 1.

I experienced difficulty relating dates and events in Billy's career and found the reason. Larry Parnes knocked a year off Billy's age to make him more attractive to girl fans. On his 22nd birthday he had to pretend to be 21 and so on. This probably made little difference to the fans but it made my research difficult. Frequent health problems started to depress Billy. He struggled through many variety shows and pantomime. 'In Thoughts of You' was his last top ten hit in 1965. Then he began taking time to indulge his love of wildlife. He was always a passionate animal lover, rather surprising, because at the age of two he was badly bitten by a dog. He was permanently scarred on the right cheek and this shows in some of his pictures. Billy signed with the Parlophone label in December 1966. Over the next four years he released eleven singles. He continued to write songs and make TV and radio appearances but his worsening heart condition prevented much promotional work. He played cabaret when health allowed and found peace, whenever possible, at his home in Ockley, Surrey, where he had a mock Tudor mansion with ten acres of land.

I found an interesting story that may have happened around that time, Mark Kozlowski wrote:

> *My friend Mike Manges, who lives in Akron, Ohio USA is a Billy Fury fan despite being American, he loves 1950s Rock n Roll and he met numerous brits who share similar interests. They introduced him to Billy Fury's work and he loves it so in 2005 there is someone in Ohio playing and loving Billy's recordings. Apparently a friend of his knew someone who, as a child lived in Surrey near where Billy Fury lived at the time. One day, this lad and his friends were sailing their toy boats on a pond, when along came Billy Fury, he stopped and chatted with the boys, asking them what they were doing. He looked at their boats, and said 'I've got a boat'. He went back to his house, and returned with a model yacht, he put it in the pond and sailed it with the boys as if he did that sort of thing very day. Then he looked at his watch and said he had to go. 'What about your boat?' said one of the lads. 'Don't worry' said Billy 'you keep it'. The lad who kept it was a friend of my workmate. My workmate said 'the friend became a real Billy Fury nut after that episode, because Billy was such a nice, down-to-earth guy.*

He assembled a large menagerie and played host to the greats of the show business world. Billy eventually needed open heart surgery in December 1971. He could not afford private treatment and was admitted to a National Health Service ward. He started performing again in March 1972 and enjoyed renewed health for a while. By the early 1970s Billy was living in Wales, on a hundred acre farm, with his long term Partner Lisa Rosen. He experienced happiness, breeding horses and sheep. He spent a lot of time bird watching, a boyhood hobby he never gave up. Once he accidentally killed a bird whilst driving, it upset him so much that he brooded for hours. This was the gentle side of Billy, he detested blood sports and attempted to save injured birds. He was involved in work to preserve the Red Kite. He appeared at the 1972 Wembley Rock 'n' Roll Festival. In 73 he appeared in the film 'That'll be the Day'. He did a major tour in 74 and the Russell Harty Show in 76. He needed a second heart operation in 1976 and retired the next year. In 1978 he was declared bankrupt, he owed the Inland Revenue sixteen thousand seven hundred and eighty pounds. Billy always blamed his manager for the problem. In the early days, Larry Parnes paid him a wage but did not take care of the tax. As part of the arrangement with creditors, he re-recorded some hits for K-Tel. He was discharged from bankruptcy the following year and went back into retirement.

In 1982 Billy decided to make a comeback. He went into the studio to record tracks for another album. This was eventually called 'The One and Only' but was not released until after his death. In 1982 he recorded 'Devil or Angel' on the Polydor label.

On the 7th of March 1982 Billy collapsed at the farm in Wales. He suffered partial paralysis and temporary blindness. Lisa drove him to hospital in London and he made a good recovery. Billy performed at a number of venues from June to December 1982. He did many radio interviews. He made three TV appearances; two had to be shown posthumously.

On the 28th of January 1983 Billy, or to be precise, Ronald Wycherley was found unconscious. He was taken from his London apartment and pronounced dead on arrival at St Mary's Hospital, Paddington. The heart weakness that had dogged him all his life had finally claimed him. He was 42 years old. The funeral service was at St John's Wood Church, London on 4 February 1983.

Ironically both Billy Fury and Elvis Presley died at the same age of 42.

He left a legacy of over 340 recordings. He was in the singles charts for 281 weeks and the album charts for 51 weeks. He had a career total of 29 hit singles and 11 top ten hits. His recordings are regularly played on Radio and his films are being sold and watched today.

A DVD video 'His Wondrous Story' was released in 2007 by Odeon Entertainment Ltd, it has achieved excellent sales and is still available for purchase today.

A DVD video 'The Sound of Fury' was released in April 2015 and has reached number one in the UK Music DVD charts, it is available for home viewing and has been shown in many cinemas and extensively on BBC television.

The final episode in the story of Ronald Wycherley was the death of his Mother, Jean on the 17 May 2017 aged 96. Joan and I travelled to Liverpool for the funeral which went from her house in Aigburth called 'Wondrous

Place.' The service was at St Anne's Church, Aigburth where Colin Paul spoke a tribute to Jean and then sang 'In Thoughts of You' in a voice trembling with emotion. I have put video clips together from that day and happier times backed by Billy Fury singing 'In Thoughts of You' in my tribute to her and loaded this to YouTube, at the time of writing (Feb 2018) this has attracted nearly four thousand views and lovely comments, I believe this is a token of the admiration and respect that people had for Jean and her influence on the career of her son. The YouTube name is

Billy Fury Mother died age 96 Tribute, In Thoughts of You

Numerous videos of Billy Fury including interviews and songs are available on YouTube enabling people of today and future generations, in many countries, to discover the songs and backing tracks that dedicated followers have been enjoying for many years. In my opinion the words of the songs are as relevant today as when he first recorded them.

8 Billy Fury: Graveside Tribute

TUESDAY 28 JANUARY 2014 WAS the 31st anniversary of the death of Billy Fury, I usually go to London each Wednesday so had decided to go to the grave at Mill Hill Cemetery in North London on that day to video the floral tributes that had been placed the previous day. I woke at around 3am on the Wednesday with an idea that I should speak a tribute to Billy at the grave. I tried to dispel the thought from my mind and get back to sleep but could not, the idea would not go away. I decided that a certain scene of my show script would be ideal so, went down stairs, switched the computer on and printed off the appropriate page. I placed the A4 page into a thin plastic folder and placed it by the front door with my small tripod to take with me. I went back to bed and on wakening a few hours later I was disappointed to see that it was raining heavily. Joan told me that she had heard the forecast and it was going to rain for most of the day in London but I said 'I will still go to the grave, perhaps it will have stopped by the time I get there'.

When the train reached St Pancras it was 'chucking it down' but I decided to go anyway. I travelled on the underground Northern line but on arrival at Edgware it was still raining. I went on a 221 bus and it was still raining as I got off at Salcombe Gardens. As I walked up Milespit Hill I questioned my sanity. It was cold, raining heavily and blowing a gale but I thought 'it may get a little better when I get to the grave'. It didn't and as I walked along I realised that I was the only living person in the cemetery (apart from the ground staff who were sheltering in their shed). I tried videoing whilst standing with the iPhone under my chin out of the rain but speaking, holding the phone and script was impossible. I gave up on that method and placed my camera on my portable tripod halfway along the grave and knelt on the stone surround at the foot of the grave. I leaned forward so that I could hold the script and plastic cover over the phone to keep it dry and had to lean forward to read it. My first two attempts of reciting the words were terrible, I tried again but was still not satisfied. I was trembling with cold and saturated so had to stop. I went down to the Chapel, squeezed water from my trouser legs and played my video. It was not good, the rain on the plastic cover and the wind sounded terrible and I had stuttered a bit on the third take as well. I decided that it was not good enough for YouTube but looked again at home the next day and loaded it with 'apologies for the background noise caused by rain on the camera cover'. Within three hours the video had received many views and a comment from 'soundsmagic' saying 'that was fantastic - the rain makes it sound like the crackles on an old record, the words you spoke were great and thank you' that comment meant a lot to me and illustrates the beauty of YouTube that a complete stranger wrote such words of encouragement. The video can be seen on YouTube under the title *Billy Fury Graveside Tribute by Michael Parkinson* at the time of writing (Feb 2018) it has had over forty four thousand views, 268 likes only 3 dislikes and 60 comments, it is receiving about 40 views every day. I believe it shows how many people are still interested in Billy Fury.

These are the words that I recited on the video:-

'29th of January 2014, yesterday was the 31st anniversary of the death of Ronald Wycherley, Billy Fury. Billy left a legacy of over 340 recordings. He was in the singles charts for 281 weeks and the album charts for 51 weeks. He had a career total of 29 hit singles and 11 top ten hits. His recordings are regularly played on Radio and his films are being watched and sold today. He is buried here at Paddington Cemetery, Mill Hill, North London. The grave is frequently visited and maintained by fans. The headstone bears the inscription, *His Music Gave Pleasure to Millions*. His music still gives pleasure to millions. Here we are 31 years later, listening to his unique voice and those lovely songs, many written by Billy himself. A bronze statue stands on the riverside at Liverpool. It features Billy looking out over the Mersey where he used to work on a tugboat. It took The Sound of Fury Fan Club six years four months to raise over forty thousand pounds for the statue. The inscription on the plaque reads:-

BILLY FURY (RONALD WYCHERLEY)

17TH APRIL 1940 TO 28 JANUARY 1983

LEGENDARY BRITISH ROCK 'N' ROLL STAR

MAJOR UK CHART ARTIST

OUTSTANDING AND CHARISMATIC LIVE PERFORMER, SONGWRITER, ANIMAL LOVER AND GENTLE MAN

THIS STATUE HAS BEEN ACHIEVED THROUGH THE DEDICATION OF BILLY FURY FANS WORLDWIDE

SCULPTED BY FELLOW LIVERPUDLIAN TOM MURPHY

These words are a lasting memorial to Billy Fury. People often ask why Billy Fury was buried in London and not his native Liverpool. Of course he had been away from Liverpool for over twenty years. I was told by a fan who lives nearby that Billy had lived close to Mill Hill for a while so he chose Mill Hill as his final resting place. His grave is situated at one of the highest points of the cemetery, next to the roadway where a bench seat memorial to Billy is situated.

The Sound of Fury Fan Club is heavily involved with the management and maintenance of the grave and the bench seat. Regrettably the original dove on the top was damaged, perhaps deliberately, but possibly accidentally by a grass strimmer but an attempt to remove one of the photos was deliberate and resulted in damage. Both of the original photos, one loosened and both faded, were therefore replaced in consultation and with the help of Frank Bull a dedicated fan and friend of Mrs Jean Wycherley and Billy's manager, Hal Carter. Frank Bull, then hailing from Enfield where he was an undertaker with obvious connections in the trade arranged for the original photos that were made in Italy and paid for by fans, to be produced and fitted. Frank, together with Hal Carter, Billy's mum Jean and several fans attending Mill Hill, some of whom later became the SOF team, had previously had a surround put in place in addition to the oval photos. All of this was graciously permitted by Billy's long-term companion Ms Lisa Voice, who owns the grave. The fan club also pays to have the grave cleaned professionally once a year and has the non-formal but very generous assistance of a dedicated reasonably local fan, Marina Weedon, for general tidying and checking up on the sites condition. I met Marina on my first visit to the grave and subsequently at my Shaw Theatre Show, her story is included in chapter one.

Many fans put floral and written tributes on the grave throughout the year and the way it looks is a testimony to his continued popularity.

9 YouTube: How I Started

A FRIEND OF MINE REPEATEDLY told me that I should set up a YouTube channel and load some videos, my answer was always 'I can't be bothered with anything like that, too difficult for me'. This started back in 2010 and my friend always countered 'with your interest in music and your dance shows you have the perfect opportunity to load some interesting videos'. His YouTube name is catman2007 and his most watched video was simply called *Blackpool Tower catman2007* with a short description stating 'A trip on the lift ascending Blackpool Tower'. He had loaded it on 1 November 2006 and it had received over fifty thousand hits. (Now over sixty seven thousand). Something happened on 9 November 2011 that persuaded me to have a go.

I attended a piano recital at Steinway Hall, The Piano Showroom on Marylebone Lane, London. The pianist was a pretty young lady from Italy, Vanessa Benelli Mosell who was studying at the Royal College of Music which is situated near the Albert Hall in London. Vanessa played music composed by Domenico Scarlatti, Richard Dubugnon and Franz Liszt. As I enjoyed the performance I noticed that the lady sitting next to me was apparently making a sound recording but just before the end she sighed and pulled the connections out of her recording device. The pianist finished playing and as she was acknowledging applause I said to the lady who had been recording 'has your battery gone flat'. She replied 'Yes, I'm her Mother and I've come all the way from Italy to record her and my battery has run out'. At that point Vanessa went off stage but returned and proceeded to play an encore which was a fast piece that excited me. On impulse I took my iPhone from my pocket and recorded the remainder of the piece. At the end, as Vanessa was being applauded her Mother asked me if I could put it on YouTube. To my shame I said no because I did not know how to do it and I was worried that I should not have recorded it anyway.

We all went downstairs to wine and nibbles provided by Steinway. During the reception her Mother introduced me to Vanessa who herself asked if I would put the encore on YouTube and and I heard myself saying 'Yes'. It was easy to ignore Mother's request but how could I ignore Vanessa? She told me that the piece was called 'Grand Galop Chromatique' by Franz Liszt, I asked and obtained permission from Steinway to load the piece to YouTube and pondered how I would do so on my train journey back to Nottingham. Over the next couple of days I investigated how to set up a YouTube channel. An obstacle was my name because I have the same name as the well known TV personality Sir Michael Parkinson. I decided to call my channel Michael notthatone Parkinson and loaded the video with the name *Liszt Grand Galop Chromatique, Vanessa Benelli Mosell, Piano.*

The video got many views and comments so I was hooked. At the time of writing it has had 5,600 views, (February 2018). Vanessa has gone on to achieve fame with many videos on YouTube, you can see them by searching for *Vanessa Benelli Mosell.*

From that unusual beginning, I have loaded over a thousand videos to my YouTube Channel with total views of well over 645,000 (six hundred thousand) and I plan to tell the background stories about some of them later in this book. I make sure that I have permission from the performer before loading but I sometimes have a problem where a performer wants me to load a video but I am not keen on it. An example of this occurred in July 2017, I had been invited to video the whole performance of a show called 'Theatricality' an amateur group called 'Bear Left Theatre Company' at the Bonington Theatre at Arnold in Nottinghamshire. They trusted me to load what I considered suitable to YouTube and I just loaded a few scenes. My favourite was a comedy routine which I called *All That Jazz, Comedy version, Bear Left Theatre Company.* After I had loaded these few scenes I received a message from a young Lady who had performed a scene from Hamlet which I had not loaded but Lauren pleaded with me to at least let her see what she had done. I relented and loaded other scenes from the show thinking why should I censor what they had done. I therefore loaded it with the title *Hamlet, Ophelia's Flower Speech, Lauren Nicole, Bear Left Theatre.* At the time of writing this had only attracted 13 views but I can salve my conscience by knowing that I have given viewers the chance to decide.

That story epitomises my opinion about YouTube in that viewers can watch what they want to watch and not just things that have been cleared by an editor or put on a television programme.

10 Saara Aalto: X-Factor

A FUNNY THING HAPPENED TO me on the way to the Theatre (to use an old music hall line) on Wednesday 7 December 2016. I had travelled by train to London from my home in Keyworth, Nottingham as I usually do on Wednesday and made my way to the box office of the Noel Coward Theatre on St Martin's Lane. I hoped to obtain a cheap late booking ticket to see the show 'Half a Sixpence', and to my delight there was just one seat near the end of the front row available for £20. I could not believe my luck and snapped the offer up with a 'flash bang wallop'. I had seen an amateur production of the show by the Carlton Operatic Society which was performed at the Nottingham Playhouse in March 1999 but had not seen the famous professional version in which Tommy Steele played Arthur Kipps. I then had a decision about timing to make because I had planned to attend the lunchtime concert at St James Church Piccadilly and curtain up for Half a Sixpence was due at 2-30pm. It was 12-30 when I came out of the box office with my prized ticket in hand and the lunch concert was due to start at 1-10pm and finish at 2pm so I decided to time my walk to St James so that I could be sure to be back at the theatre in good time for the 2-30 start. With this in mind I set off with some purpose towards St James and made good time as I crossed Charing Cross Road and walked along Irving Street towards Leicester Square.

On arrival at the lower part of Leicester Square I witnessed something that made me forget all about my timing mission because an unusual scene unfolded in front of me, there was a camera crew and a lady dressed in a white flowing cape being interviewed by a well dressed man. I sidled up to the camera crew and asked if I could video as well. To my surprise one of the men said 'yes but just wait until I give you the go-ahead'. After a couple of minutes the camera man invited me to go up to the lady and ask a few questions, I did this but found it very difficult because I did not know who she was or anything about her. I stumbled through and found out that she was Saara Aalto, one of three finalists in the X Factor and the winner would be decided the following weekend. She told me that she was from Finland I asked her about what type of songs she sang and she told me that she loves to sing all kind of songs including ballads and sometimes she dances and sings and that she is very versatile. At this point one of the film crew said 'just one more question' but I could not immediately think of anything so the crew directed Saara to walk into the entrance to the Global Radio studio and to walk out towards them for their next sequence. As Saara walked out again I thought of another question and said to her 'Saara can I be really cheeky and ask you to sing a few notes? Saara paused for a moment and sang. 'Somewhere over the Rainbow, way up high. There's a land that I heard of, once in a lullaby'. It was a beautiful experience because she was right next to me and her singing voice sounded lovely. I was impressed that Saara was so polite and patient with me because I was an old man who admitted that I knew nothing about her or about the current X Factor shows. I watched the finals programme on the following Saturday evening and Saara finished second. She has been selected to represent Finland in the 2018 Eurovision Song Competition to be held in Lisbon, Portugal. I loaded a video to YouTube the following day with this title *Saara Aalto X Factor Sings in Leicester Square for Michael Parkinson*. The scene is exactly as I have described it with no pre planning other than me having my iPhone constantly ready for action. This video is my second most watched with over 28,400 views (February 2018).

I proceeded to walk to St James Church for the lunchtime concert which featured three harp players from Trinity Laban Conservatoire of Music and Dance. They 'used a lot of pluck' to perform a lovely programme so the day was getting better and better. At the end of the concert I hurried back to the Noel Coward Theatre but called in to Global Radio in Leicester Square to take some post production video and to check that it was all right to load what I had done to YouTube.

I arrived at the Noel Coward Theatre ten minutes before the performance of Half a Sixpence and I loved it. I don't usually wax eloquent about a male performer but Charlie Stemp was brilliant as Arthur Kipps. During the interval I went outside and videoed some of the posters and then into the foyer where there was a large screen showing some video of the show. I asked the staff if I was allowed to video the screen but had to wait whilst they consulted a senior manager. The answer was rather strange 'you haven't asked' so I did it and loaded my review to YouTube the next day with the title *Half a Sixpence, Review by Michael Parkinson*. I enjoyed the second half of the performance and went outside to a cold, dark December London evening.

I went across to St Martin in the Fields Church overlooking Trafalgar Square and attended the Transport for London Festival of Carols concert. There was a poignant section in which they spoke about the terrible tram crash near Croydon in November where seven people had lost their lives and over fifty were injured. Joan and I had travelled on the same tram line the previous

April and we were both scared because of the speed of the tram downhill and round a steep bend over that section.

When the concert finished I walked to a bus stop on the Strand and got on a number 91 bus which took me to St Pancras Station in time for the 10pm train to Nottingham. I arrived home at just after midnight, tired but happy after a wonderful day. It reminded me of the famous quote from Samuel Johnson 'when a man is tired of London, he is tired of life; for there is in London all that life can afford.'

As this book is going to press (April 2018) it has been announced that:-
Saara Aalto will represent Finland at the 2018 Eurovision Song Contest in Lisbon with the song Monsters. In the Finnish national selection UMK, Monsters was chosen over the other candidate songs Domino and Queens.

Jessica May George: Jessie's Fund

THIS IS A STORY WHICH has influenced me to donate over Seven Thousand Pounds to the fund over the past sixteen years.

Jessica May George was born on 22 October 1984; her parents were both professional musicians. Mother, Lesley Schatzberger, plays clarinet, Father, Alan George plays viola in the Fitzwilliam String Quartet. They had retained their original surnames to further their musical careers. Jessie was lively, bright and musical but when she was nine years old she became ill and was diagnosed with a rare and inoperable brain tumour. She was admitted to Leeds General Infirmary for a course of radiotherapy treatment. Jessie had written poetry from the age of five and continued during her time in hospital, here are the first two she wrote.

For Ada

I like the nurse called Ada
And her daughter is sweet too
When I first got very ill
I thought it was just the flu

Ada showed me to my bedroom
On my very first day
I really liked her ever so much
I didn't want her to go away.

She's pretty in an oriental way
Her little Francesca, too
If you were ever poorly
Perhaps she would look after you.

To the Nurses on Fleming Ward

Here is a verse
About a nurse
In fact about a few
I wanted to thank you
But I didn't know how to
So I wrote this poem for you

Jessie wrote a little rhyme which she suggested should be sung to the 'Ode to Joy' tune from Beethoven's Ninth Symphony:

Day by day I fight my tumour
I'll kill every rotten cell
One by one I kill them off
And I will soon be fit and well

Jessie had to wear special glasses because of double vision, caused by the tumour, and used the name Billy because it rhymed with silly.

Glasses

"Glasses are silly"
Said little Billy
"Every day passes
And I still need glasses
Why should it be
That it has to be me?"

Jessie had a mischievous sense of humour

Janet and Bill

Janet and Bill
Don't live on a hill
They live in a second floor flat
It's very small
And our house is tall…
And they don't think much of that

Radiotherapy and steroid treatment caused Jessie to be constantly hungry and she was given reasonably healthy snacks between meals in an attempt to keep it under control

Hungry

I am starving
Are you starving, too?
I would like to eat
And eat it with you.

I would like to eat
And eat and eat
I would like to eat
Potatoes and meat.

I am hungry
Hungry as can be
So won't you just give me
A crumb or a pea?

This is Jessie in defiant mood, she referred to her tumour as a 'bloomin blob'

Bloomin' Blob

I will fight my bloomin' blob
I'll fight it away and away
I will fight it till it's gone
I'll fight it till the great day

Jessie's parents hoped that revolutionary treatment in America may help their daughter and money was raised to do this, Jessie herself thought of the title. So Jessie's Fund was established to meet the cost of treatment planned for her in the USA and Jessie put a collection of her poems in a little book which she sold for fifty pence a copy.

Jessie finished the course of radiotherapy and was able to go home for a while and was even able to attend school for a few half days. This is a poem that she wrote at school on 13 April 1994:

The Evening Sun

I was walking along the beach
I saw the evening sunlight
It was really so very bright
The sun was orange and yellow
Whilst I heard the wind's big bellow
The sun was twinkling on the sea
How nice and beautiful could it be
It twinkles on the water bright
When I go home in the night

Jessie's condition suddenly worsened and she was admitted to Martin House, a Children's Hospice at Wetherby where she died after only six day's on 6 May 1994 aged nine and a half years.

Whilst Jessie received excellent care in Martin House there was no form of music therapy so her parents decided that the money already raised would be used to encourage music therapy in children's hospices and in April 1995 it was established as a registered charity.

Jesssie's Fund helps children in children's hospices to express themselves by using music as a language. They establish posts for music therapists, provide appropriate instruments, and offer training in simple musical techniques to staff. In schools for children and young people with special needs they give pupils the opportunity to participate actively in making music. They create their own music, and then perform or record it, in a programme called Soundtracks. They place just as much emphasis on training staff in special schools to use music as a tool for communication and learning: in this way they leave a legacy after every one of their projects. They also offer support to other organisations aiming to help children with disabilities through music, as well as to individuals who struggle to access music therapy.

The first Patron of the fund was Victoria Wood, a well known writer, actor, singer, songwriter, musician and comic. Victoria died on 20 April 2016 after 17 years as Patron.

A serious but humorous YouTube video is, *Victoria Wood talking about Jessie's Fund*.

As a mark of respect to Victoria the fund managers decided to wait for well over a year before appointing Maxine Peake as the new Patron. Maxine is an actor in theatre, television and film. As a writer she focused on social issues and stories of women who have achieved greatness in the face of adversity. On accepting the role she said: *'I am very honoured to have been approached by Jessie's Fund to become their new Patron. No one could ever replace the extraordinary Victoria Wood: to be able to continue her work with an organisation that she held so dear to her heart is an absolute privilege.*

'Music has always played a very special part in my life, as a healer and an inspiration. To be able to reach out to young people with complex needs and to allow them to communicate through the power of music is a must. What a wonderful and essential charity'.

More information about the fund can be seen on their website: **www.jessiesfund.org.uk**

In conclusion, here is a personal story:-

A few years ago Joan and I were on holiday in a little island called Formentera. It has no airport so can only be reached by boat from Ibiza. We have enjoyed two weeks there for over twenty years. The Cala Saona Hotel, where we stay, overlooks a small sandy bay with rocks and fisherman's boats on either side. It is ideal for swimming and paddling in the sea. One day I saw a man throwing and catching a Frisbee by himself and before long I had joined in and we were enjoying ourselves in the water, just like two small boys. Our respective wives were not as energetic, or as stupid, as us and were content to sit on the beach. After a few days I asked my new friend if he and his wife would like to have a drink with us after dinner one evening. So, we went to small open air bar which overlooked the moonlit bay, a million miles from reality. During the conversation the Frisbee thrower's wife mentioned that she worked at a children's hospice and I asked 'have you heard of Jessie's Fund' to my surprise she said 'yes, they trained me to make music with the children'. It was the first time I had met someone using music therapeutically and it was the first time that she had met someone who had donated to the fund. We chatted for some time and I asked if I could ask a personal question. It was this 'do you feel depressed by working with children whose life expectancy is very limited' she replied 'on the contrary, I feel privileged that I am able to help them at a time when they desperately need it'.

One strange quote came from a Mother, 'my daughter loved it when the music therapist came to see her because she was the only one who did not pull her about and stick needles in her'.

Thank you to Jessie's parents for giving me permission to use those lovely poems which illustrate what a perceptive child she was. Jessies Fund has been running since 1995 and in addition to their work with the fund Father Alan George is still a member of the Fitzwilliam String Quartet and Mother Lesley Schatzberger still plays clarinet and teaches at the University of York and Royal Northern College of Music. It is a great tribute to them that they have turned a personal tragedy into an organisation that helps many children through music therapy.

My YouTube tribute to Jessie features a young lady speaking her story and reading some of her poems, it can be seen by typing in the title *Jessie's Fund, Jessica May George by Charlotte Griffin.*

12 Thames Path Walk, Barrier to Windsor

IN SPRING 2014 I HAD a zany idea of walking along the Thames Path from Blackfriars Bridge in the Centre of London as far as I could in a westerly direction. I usually went to London on Wednesdays and had often walked between Putney and Barnes so I decided to set myself a challenge. I only walked when the weather was good because it had to be enjoyable and not a chore.

My first effort was from Blackfriars Bridge to Chelsea and the next week I walked from Chelsea Bridge to Putney. The next section from Putney to Chiswick was interesting because it followed the course of the Oxford/Cambridge University Boat Race which starts near Putney Bridge and finishes at Mortlake very close to Chiswick Bridge. I continued the walks through Kew, Richmond, Hampton, Elmbridge, Shepperton, Staines, Runnymede and by the end of the summer had reached Windsor.

The following spring I decided to continue my walks and entertained grandiose ideas about walking all the way to the source. My first walk in 2015 was from Windsor to Maidenhead and other efforts took me through Bourne End, Henley, Reading, Goring, Wallingford reaching Shillingford Bridge on 6 September 2015.

Shillingford to Culham Bridge was the first section walked in May 2016 and I continued on various dates through Oxford, Bablockhythe, Tadpole Bridge, Lechlade, Cricklade, Ashton Keynes, Ewen and on 17 August 2016 I achieved my objective by walking to the pile of stones in the field which indicates the source near Ewen Bridge in Gloucestershire.

My friend, catman2007 had been following my progress with interest but was quick to deflate me by stating that I could not claim to have walked the Thames Path because I had not walked from the Thames Barrier to Blackfriars Bridge. He was right of course so on 25 August 2016 I walked from the Barrier through Greenwich to Canary Wharf and on 31st August achieved my objective by walking the final section from Canary Wharf to Blackfriars Bridge. The distance from the Barrier to the source is about 180 miles. I had travelled by train from my home near Nottingham to St Pancras Station for all of my individual walks and then used buses, trains, underground or taxis for the start and finish of my walks. I am proud of my achievement as I am an old man in my late seventies.

I loaded video of all the sections in geographical sequence to my YouTube channel Michael notthatone Parkinson and list them with a few stories about my experiences along the way. When I first started the walks I did not take any video until I walked the section from Hampton Bridge to Elmbridg but when I had completed the whole 180 miles I walked the sections from Blackfriars to Hampton Bridge again and videoed so that the whole walk is on YouTube in geographical but not chronological order.

YouTube title
Thames Barrier to Greenwich Thames Path Michael Parkinson

I started this walk from Charlton Station and on reaching the side of the River I had to turn right, away from my intended destination reach the strange looking flood barrier but then had to retrace my steps to walk towards Greenwich. There is a garden centre on stilts, and reed beds created so that they are flooded at high tide whilst overhead the Emirates Airline cable cabins glide across the river on their way from Greenwich to the Royal Docks. Much of the walk is dominated by views of the huge O2 Arena and there is a golf driving range which looks small by comparison. An interesting exhibit at the side of the river is a one eighth segment of a sand dredger ship called 'A slice of reality'. Parts of this walk were interesting with views across of the River from the Thames Path but other parts were horrible taking me away from the River alongside busy roads and constant difficulty deciding which way to go.

I hope this situation is temporary. Something should be done to make a better walkway and cycle path for the many thousands of people who will live in the accommodation already built or under construction between the barrier and the centre of Greenwich. I was relieved to arrive at Greenwich where the old Royal Navel College is occupied by Trinity Laban Conservatoire of Music and Dance. It was a hot summer day and there were hordes of visitors around the *Cutty Sark*.

YouTube title
Greenwich to Canary Wharf, Thames Path Michael Parkinson

Although this is a separate video it is a continuation of my walk from the Barrier to Canary Wharf that I did on the same day. It starts with a walk through the Greenwich Foot Tunnel because I had decided that it was better to walk along the North side of the River, known as the Isle of Dogs between Greenwich and Canary Wharf. There are signs and relics describing the infamous Brunel Iron Ship *SS Great Eastern* and fatalities during an unsuccessful sideways launch operation in 1857.

There are many places where I had to walk away from the river along various streets and alley ways before regaining close proximity to the river with views towards central London or across to the south bank. I learned that the name Millwall is derived from a row of Windmills that stood along the River wall and videoed a sign in memory of forty people killed when a bomb hit an air raid shelter on 19 March 1941 at Bullivant's Wharf. My research revealed this explanation *On the night of March 19, 1941, a public shelter on Bullivant's Wharf, off Westferry Road, was hit by a landmine. Over 40 people were killed, and dozens were injured. Some families lost all but one member. This was the Isle of Dogs' biggest wartime disaster.* (See wordpress.com for the full story). I continued past Limehouse dock, West Ferry and West India pier before reaching the busy area around the swanky Gaucho Restaurant and Canary Wharf.

YouTube title
Canary Wharf-Blackfriars Thames Path Michael Parkinson

It was a lovely late Summer day when I walked from Canary Wharf to Blackfriars Bridge on 31 August 2016. There were many places where I had to deviate from the riverside before regaining the river views from the Thames Path. One of the famous public houses is called 'The Grapes' and an unusual view from the window is a statue of a nude man who appears to be standing on the water. A plaque on the wall indicates that the Statue was created by Antony Gormley in memory of a neighbour 'Paul Cottingham' a former East Enders Actor who died in 2014. The walk continued past many relics of London Docks which had been converted to expensive looking houses and on past Limehouse, Shadwell, Wapping, Tower Bridge, Southwark Bridge and finally to my destination Blackfriars Bridge.

Although this was the final stage of my Thames Path Walk it may be confusing because I had started at Blackfriars Bridge and walked west to the source and then done the section from the Thames Barrier to Blackfriars to complete my mission.

YouTube title
Blackfriars to Chelsea, Thames Path Walk Michael Parkinson

I started this walk along the Thames Path travelling on the North side of the river in a Westerly direction towards my intended destination at Chelsea and mention just a few of the things that you can see on the video. Cleopatra's needle looks very impressive situated at the side of the river and next is the monument to W.S.Gilbert who wrote the words for the famous Gilbert and Sullivan operettas, the inscription reads 'HIS FOE WAS FOLLY & HIS WEAPON WIT'. The Charing Cross walking bridge looked very slender in contrast to the extremely wide railway bridge. There were views of the London Eye and the Battle of Britain Monument which has the famous words spoken by Winston Churchill 'NEVER IN THE FIELD OF HUMAN CONFLICT WAS SO MUCH OWED BY SO MANY TO SO FEW'. I then climbed the steps onto Westminster Bridge and walked across to the South side of the river where I was able to capture video of the Houses of Parliament and of course Big Ben.

I continued past Lambeth and Vauxhall Bridges before having to make some detours away from the side of the river because of extensive building work. I hope that when all the work is complete the Thames Path will be reinstated and the general public will be able to enjoy it. The worst diversion was around the large Battersea Power Station site. Again I am sure it will be fantastic when it is finished and many people will enjoy living there but the deviation from the side of the river spoiled my enjoyment of the walk. I walked through the impressive Battersea Park and admired the Peace Pagoda with its large gilded bronze sculptures. They have to be seen to be believed. I walked past Chelsea Bridge and reached the Albert suspension bridge where there is a sign stating 'ALL TROOPS MUST BREAK STEP WHEN MARCHING OVER THIS BRIDGE'. This is because of a suspension bridge collapse at Broughton, Manchester in 1831, due to the vibration created by rhythmically marching soldiers. The army issued orders that, in future, columns of troops should not march in step when traversing a suspension bridge. It was suspected that the bridge at Broughton had not been constructed properly and collapsed after only three years service. I crossed over the impressive looking Albert Bridge arriving at my destination as Cadogan Pier on the North side of the river came into view.

YouTube title
Chelsea to Putney Thames Path Walk Michael Parkinson

I walked from the Albert suspension bridge on the South side of the river on 14 September 2016, a lovely summer day and soon reached Battersea Bridge. A little path took me past St Mary's Church Wandsworth as I approached Lambeth Railway bridge. It was noisy when a helicopter took off as I passed the Oyster Pier Helipad and there was another detour away from the river because of more construction work but it appeared that the builders are making plans to restore the Thames path on completion of the work.

I continued past Plantation Pier and Battersea Reach before crossing the footbridge where the river Wandle runs into the Thames, Wandsworth Park merges with the path making a very pleasant walk before reaching Putney railway bridge and eventually the graceful looking Putney Road bridge and St Mary's Church.

YouTube title
Putney to Mortlake Thames Path Walk Michael Parkinson

Four days after the 2015 boat race I walked along the North bank of the Thames from Putney Bridge through Bishops Park and around the Fulham Football Ground before regaining the side of the river. Views across the river of Harrods furniture depository which has now been converted to apartments preceded more construction work at Putney Reach before I walked under the end of Hammersmith bridge. There are many restaurants and public houses on the next stretch whilst people were enjoying the sunshine at Furnival Gardens, a little island called Chiswick Eyot is another familiar name on the boat race commentary.

There is a little road which floods at high tide with houses on one side of the road and separate gardens across the road that border the edge of the river. The setting became more rural as I walked along Dukes Meadows, reaching Barnes railway bridge, I had to use a small walkway constructed at the side of the railway to cross the river before continuing my walk along to the south side of the river and videoed a train going across the bridge very close to me. Having crossed the bridge I continued to Mortlake where an unimpressive post marks the finishing point of the boat race. The winning post is situated just before Chiswick Bridge which the Oxford and Cambridge crews go under before continuing their celebrations and throwing the cox of the winning crew into the river.

(I was in the area in 2017 and noticed that two very impressive finishing posts have been erected, one on each side of the river.)

YouTube title

Mortlake to Richmond Thames Path Walk Michael Parkinson

This walk from Mortlake to Richmond was the most enjoyable of the sections that I had experienced since starting at the barrier and travelling through central London hampered by the many places where I had to leave the side of the river. The most pleasant feature was the rural surroundings and the absence of construction work. On leaving Mortlake I walked under the end of Chiswick Bridge enjoying peace and tranquillity before reaching Kew railway bridge and then Kew road bridge. Soon, I was walking along with Kew gardens to my left and the river to the right. There is a huge island on the other side of the river called Brentford Ait, a bird sanctuary and Heronry. Eventually, I saw a sign indicating Richmond Deer Park to my left before passing the impressive Richmond Lock bridge then Twickenham road and rail bridges. I eventually walked past Richmond rail bridge before reaching my destination at Richmond which resembles a seaside place when the Sun is shining.

YouTube title

Richmond to Hampton Court Thames Path, Michael Parkinson

On 21 September 2016 I enjoyed walking along the South side of the river from Richmond and the first thing of interest was the Puppet Theatre Barge but I resisted the temptation to watch 'Brer Rabbit Visits Africa' (their spelling, not mine). I passed Petersham Lodge Woods, Hammertons Ferry, Eel Pie Island and the entrance to Ham Lands South nature reserve before reaching Teddington lock, this is the most important lock on the river because the Thames ceases to be tidal here. The water is controlled by a series of locks and sluices so it is affected by sea water and the tide on the Richmond side with fresh water on the Kingston side.

There are many boat clubs and boat yards on the approach to Kingston where I went under Kingston railway bridge before going up the steps and crossing the road bridge and going down the steps on the other side to Barge Walk where I continued my journey on the North side of the river. On the Surbiton side of the river Ravens Ait is a two acre island with high class wedding and reception facilities and there is an immaculate looking golf course on my right as I approach Hampton Court. A sign stating DEER CULL IN PROGRESS warned me not to go into the park and further along I saw a huge set of closed and locked ornate gates. I guess they would be used to allow certain people access to the river. Further along, Hampton Court Palace, dominated by many ornate looking chimneys, came into view.

I reached Hampton Bridge and am convinced that this section from Richmond is one of the most interesting and enjoyable sections of the Thames Path.

YouTube title

Hampton Bridge to Elmbridge Thames Path Michael Parkinson

Picturesque East Molesey cricket ground was the first attraction as I started this walk on the South side of the Thames on 21 August 2014 whilst on the river there is a weir and expensive looking houseboats, many of them are triple decked. Further along there was a boundary wall for Molesey reservoirs on my left hand side with lovely views over the river to my right. Words from Wind in the Willows written by Kenneth Grahame are etched on a plaque at Molesely 'Believe me my young friend, there is nothing, absolutely nothing, half so worth doing as simply messing about in boats'. I walked past Hurst Park, Port Hampton, and Walton Bridge before arriving at Elmbridge.

YouTube title

Elmbridge to Shepperton Ferry, Thames Path, Michael Parkinson

After leaving Elmbridge I walked through West Molesey enjoying peaceful and rural tranquility only interrupted occasionally by few boats chugging along. There were some very expensive looking houses boasting manicured lawns sweeping down to the river on the opposite bank. A few more islands appeared before I walked past Sunbury Lock and eventually arriving at Weybridge where I had to use the ferry to cross to the North side of the river.

YouTube title

Thames Ferry Weybridge/Shepperton, Nauticalia

There is a bell fixed to a post on the Weybridge side of the river which I had to ring to summon the ferry and sure enough a man appeared on the other side and soon arrived in a small boat fitted with an outboard motor. Bob was operating the Nauticalia ferry service and soon took me across to the Shepperton side of the river. (On another occasion he took me round the nearby Doyle Carte Island which was interesting as I am Gilbert and Sullivan devotee, the title of that video is *Doyle Carte Island and House, River Thames)*

YouTube title

Pike caught in Thames at Shepperton, Michael Parkinson

An angler was in the process of landing a fish as I approached him on the bank of the Thames at Shepperton on 27 August 2014 his rod was bending as he played in a large pike. The Angler, whose name was Neil posed proudly with his catch and then placed it back in the water. Neil assured me that the Pike would be fine as it swam away. Videoed at around 5pm on 27 August 2014 as I walked along the Thames Path between Shepperton and Staines. He was pleased that I had videoed the magic moment and was happy for me to load it to YouTube where it has achieved over 560 views (February 2018).

YouTube title

Shepperton to Staines, Thames Path, Michael Parkinson

I used the ferry boat to get from Weybridge on the South side to Shepperton on the North side of the river before walking past the lock and Shepperton Island and arriving at Chertsey Bridge near the Kingfisher public house. The next point of interest was Chertsey lock and a huge weir which goes around an island before walking under the M3 motorway and passing Laleham Leisure Park. I walked past Penton Hook Lock before thankfully reaching the outskirts of Staines and eventually the comforting seat on a train at Staines Station for my journey back to London and Nottingham.

YouTube title

Staines to Windsor, Thames Path, Michael Parkinson

The start of this walk was in the built up area from Staines Bridge, I walked under two bridges that make up the M25 motorway and past Bell Weir Lock before eventually reaching quite, rural, countryside towards Runnymede. I spotted the Air Force War Memorial at the top of a hill to my left and read that the Campus of Brunel University was close by. Soon I could see Magna Carta Island where, in 1215, King John signed the famous document. I understand this has great significance to Americans because it forms the basis of their Declaration of Independence. A large sign informed me that I was walking past Old Windsor and I saw many large pleasure boats as I approached Old Windsor lock and weir. The path took me over the Albert Bridge and there was a detour around the edge of Windsor Great Park and through a village called Datchet. When I walked into the centre of Windsor I walked past the Castle on my way to Windsor & Eaton Central Station for my journey to London and home.

13 Thames Path Walk, Windsor to Oxford

THE SECOND SECTION OF THE Thames Path walk was full of interest and enjoyment though from a practical point of view it was more difficult for me to get to the starting points and back home from the finishing points which were progressively further from St Pancras. I live at Keyworth in South Nottinghamshire and use my senior railcard to book my journeys to London. Frequent stops to take video cause the walks to take longer than if I just concentrated on walking. The advantage of the video is that you, the reader, can have a look at the views and comments that I made whilst recording them. You just have to type in the names at the head of each section.

YouTube title
Windsor to Maidenhead Thames Path, Michael Parkinson

Walking past Windsor Castle at the start of my walk I crossed Windsor bridge and walked along 'The Brocas' on the Eton side of the river where there was a detailed sign:-

THE BROCAS

THIS IS PRIVATE LAND OWNED BY
EATON COLLEGE
PUBLIC ACCESS IS ALLOWED
SUBJECT TO THE FOLLOWING:
PLEASE
TAKE ALL RUBBISH AWAY WITH YOU
CLEAR UP AFTER YOUR DOG
DO NOT LIGHT FIRES OR BARBECUES
DO NOT FISH
RESPECT THE PRIVACY OF LOCAL RESIDENTS

THANK YOU

It was a lovely sunny day and there was a happy atmosphere of many people enjoying themselves on the boats and banks. I walked past the Windsor railway and road bridges and round a steep curve in the river where there is another detailed and interesting sign about nude boys in the river:-

BATHING REGULATIONS AT ATHENS
Fifth Form Nants in First Hundred and Upper and Middle Divisions may bathe at Athens. No bathing at Athens on Sundays after 8-30 a.m.
At Athens boys who are undressed must either get at once into the water or get behind the screens when boats containing ladies come into sight. Boys when bathing are not allowed to land on the Windsor Bank or to swim out to launches and barges or to hang onto, or interfere with boats of any kind. Any boy breaking this rule will be severely punished From School Rules of the River 1921.

I wonder if that sign is there for historical reasons or if boys are still allowed to bathe nude at that point. I continued past Boveney lock where I witnessed an interesting display of piloting skill as the captain eased 'The Georgian' into the lock with just a few inches clearance. Next up was St Mary Magdalene Church, Boveney, which is owned by 'The Friends of Friendless Churches'. This organisation was founded in 1957 by Ivor Bulmer Thomas who saw beautiful ancient Churches doomed to disuse and decay and vowed to do something about it. In 2018 the Friends own nearly 50 Churches and do what they can to allow people to visit. I walked under the M4 motorway and Bray bridges before arriving at Bray which is famous for the connection with the famous song 'The Vicar of Bray' A film was made at Riverside Studios, Hammersmith with Stanly Holloway as the vicar, an excerpt can be seen on YouTube *The Vicar of Bray-Stanley Holloway-1937*. I can remember singing the song at school and being taught the philosophy behind it.

I was impressed with the slender arches of the Brunel railway bridge, known as the sounding bridge and I had to cross over the next bridge to continue my walk on the opposite side of the river. As I walked into Maidenhead I was approached by a lady who was too shy to appear on video and would not give her name but wanted to tell me a story about the Brunel bridge and the Gaiety Girls, see YouTube *Gaiety Girls, Gaiety Row, Brunel Bridge, Maidenhead*.

This concludes my account of the walk from Windsor to Maidenhead and I recommend it to anyone because it is packed with interest and enjoyment.

YouTube title
Maidenhead to Bourne End Thames Path, Michael Parkinson

The first place of interest on leaving Maidenhead was Boulters lock followed by Ray Mill Island with colourful birds in the Aviary and a Commemorative statue called 'The Companions'. It has a boy a dog and a football dedicated to:-

Michael Taylor aged 13 years

Daniel Howton aged14 years

Andrew Watts aged 14 years

Lee Powell aged 15 years

Who died on 4th April 1988 in Salzburg.

They were on a a a skiing trip from Altwood School in Maidenhead and the memorial was made by local artist Eunice Goodman.

The power and noise of the water impressed me at Boulters weir before continuing my journey to Cookham where the Thames path took me through the Churchyard and the next signs stated Bell Rope and Cockmarsh Meadow. On arrival at Bourne End I walked across a combined rail and footbridge to get to the station and the train for my homeward journey after an enjoyable walk.

YouTube title
Bourne End to Henley Thames Path, Michael Parkinson

I started walking towards Marlow from the railway bridge at Bourne End and after a couple of miles I reached Spade Oak Meadow where a lady and her husband asked me for help. They introduced themselves as Jerry and Peter and explained the problem, There was one of the many gates in front of us and Jerry was worried that there was a herd of cows in the next field so she suggested that we should walk together to minimise the danger. We chatted as we walked and I learned that they were American and visiting England for two weeks because Peter was giving some lectures on Ancient Greek Armour at Imperial College in London and they were combining business with pleasure. Jerry explained that there are more people killed or injured by cows than by bulls and that they had walked the Hadrian's Wall walk the previous year and she was aware that it was a serious threat. We walked together and the cows walked away from us, Jerry and Peter can be seen and heard shouting goodbye at 2minutes 13 seconds into my video. There was a bridge which carries the A404 road over the river just before Marlow where the Thames Path leaves the side of the Thames for a short distance. I had to walk across a railway bridge incorporating a footpath to proceed along the opposite side of the river and then the walk was through pleasant scenery and at the side of the river passing many locks and weirs before I arrived at Hurley and later at Hambledon Mill. Temple Island which has a large marker indicating the end of Henley Regatta course was next in view. I walked along lovely meadow land before reaching Henley Bridge and finding my way to the Railway Station for my homeward journey. This was another very pleasant section of the Thames Path.

YouTube title
Henley to Reading Thames Path, Michael Parkinson

I started this walk from Henley Bridge and knew that I had to crack on because my objective was to walk the 15 miles to Reading in one day. The first part of the walk along side the river was thronged with many people but it was back to peace as I approached Marsh Lock, Shiplake and on to Sonning Bridge, the walk was marred because I had to make many detours away from the side of the river. There was a large house that had a miniature railway which came out of the front entrance and along the side of the Thames Path for a while. After passing the grounds of Reading Bluecoat School and then walking through very pleasant meadow land there were signs that Reading was not far away. The walk from the outskirts of Reading to the junction of the start of the Kennet and Avon Canal is pleasant with wide areas of grass and recreational land along the way. When I reached the junction of the canal and the river I had to cross a footbridge to keep on the Thames Path and reached Caversham Lock. It was not long before I got to Reading Bridge and was pleased to walk over the bridge and up to the railway station for my journey home.

YouTube title
Reading to Goring Thames Path, Michael Parkinson

It was a lovely summer day on 12 August 2015 as I walked from the centre of Reading going past the two large bridges and along the wide path towards Tilehurst where I had to clamber up a set of steps and cross a bridge over the station and along roads for a while before regaining the path at Mapledurham where the lock keeper allowed me to record his voice but not vision as he told me about the lock and documentation that boat owners must have. It was lovely to be walking along a grassy path at the side of the river again with open countryside on both sides and many types of boats going by, this continued until I reached Pangbourne meadow where many people were enjoying themselves at what is obviously a popular place owned and well maintained by the National Trust. I had to leave the meadow, cross a road bridge and walk up a hill and saw a relic of the past because motorists are still having to pay at Whitchurch Toll Bridge where I videoed the old sign with the charges, it would have been a halfpenny for me but it is now free for pedestrians.

The Thames path goes through the churchyard at Whitchurch and surprisingly the Church was not locked so I videoed inside a little before walking through the village and back to the Thames path which has steep ups and downs as it goes through a wood where there were glimpses of the river through gaps in the trees. It was beautiful and peaceful and motivated me to recite a few lines from the Patience Strong poem 'If you stand very still' but you would have to go to YouTube to hear that. Soon after the path rejoined the side of the river a train was going over a bridge on it's way to Goring Station where I eventually arrived and was pleased to get on trains home via Reading, Paddington, St Pancras and East Midlands Parkway before driving home after a tiring but very interesting day.

YouTube title
Goring to Wallingford Thames Path, Michael Parkinson

The walk from Goring is quite and peaceful with lovely views over river, weir, countryside and locks and continues through Streatley where, like Goring, the path runs through the churchyard. There were a few diversions away from the river as I approached Moulesford where, again, I walked past the Church and followed more diversions before arriving at Cholsey and eventually reaching my destination at Wallingford. I then walked into the centre of Wallingford and got on the 134 bus to Goring Station for my homeward journey.

YouTube title
Wallingford to Shillingford Thames Path, Michael Parkinson

Wallingford was once bigger than Oxford, my guidebook informed me, and it was very impressive as I started my walk from the bridge with the tall church spire in the background. I passed Benson lock and had to cross the river using a path constructed over the weir and was glad to get away from the noise of the cascading water as I reached the other side. There were lovely views over the river on the approach to Shillingford where I had to leave the path and walk across a bridge over the river and arrived at the Shillingford Hotel which has a Mediterranean style swimming pool complete with sun beds. There are picnic tables on a wide expanse of grass between the Hotel and the river. As I was videoing the scene I heard a man saying, 'do you want to film me?' I looked at him, accepted his offer and learned a lot about him. He had been a stone mason and, according to what he said, owned two barges and a ship. I loaded this as a separate video to YouTube because if you wanted to describe the most eccentric character on the river you would be hard pressed to come up with anyone more fitting then this man and the conversation is amazing. I would not dare put in print some of the things he said.

YouTube title

Stonemason Thames Bargeman talks to Michael Parkinson

As I was videoing near Shillingford Bridge from the Thames Path in August 2015 this man asked if I wanted to film him which I immediately did. He told me about the importance of a 'keystone' in bridge construction, scarring on the stonework and much more. He then went on to tell me about his barges and his ship and to my amusement told me about his exploits with his crew of twenty women and the missile on the top of his barge. If you want a laugh and are not a prude have a look and listen to this video, I can't watch it without laughing out loud. This man is so eccentric that he made me feel normal.

YouTube title

Shillingford to Culham Bridge Thames Path, Michael Parkinson

It was spring 2016 as I walked past masses of blooming Wisteria and buttercup laden Oxfordshire meadowland at the start of this walk near Shillingford Wharf. I continued through this wildlife corridor until I reached a sign which informed me 'having gently meandered through meadows and woodland, the river Thame meets the mighty river Thames at this point. Imagine past activity, boats and barges shipping goods from Dorchester, maybe flour from Overy Mill, willow from the osiers for baskets and reeds for thatch from the Hurst Meadow. Once an important local transport route, this stretch of the Thame is now part of a carefully managed wildlife corridor'. A wooden bridge enabled me to walk over the Thame and I paused to video the scene as it flowed into the Thames.

More enjoyable scenery and graceful Chestnut trees preceded the peace being shattered by the sound of a transport helicopter flying overhead, probably from the Military base at Abingdon. I walked through a kissing gate and crossed over a bridge at Day's Lock and walked over another bridge which crossed the weir. Peace and rural splendour prevailed again until I arrived at brick built Clifton Hamden Bridge. Soon, the path was alongside Clifton Cut which was dug in 1822 to bypass a straggly line of the Thames. Clifton lock was at the end of the cut where the path was at the side of the Thames once more. Peace prevailed again and I walked past the water input for Didcot Power Station before arriving at Culham Bridge which I crossed on my way to the railway station for my return home.

YouTube title
Culham Bridge to Oxford Thames Path, Michael Parkinson

**Dedicated to the memory of Ellis Downs.
Floral tributes to him can be seen on 3 minutes 40 seconds into this
video.**

This section of my walk started in a surprising way. I had travelled by rail and bus to Wallingford, then taxi to Culham and chatted with the driver telling him that I was going to walk along the Thames path to Oxford. On arrival at Culham Bridge the driver turned into the car park at the side of the river and I jumped out being keen to start my long walk. The driver made no attempt to take the money I was offering but continued to tell me about his other work which involved lecturing in local colleges. At that point a lady asked the taxi driver to move because she wanted to get out, he asked me to wait because he wanted to tell me something. I was a bit rude because I just thrust a note at the driver, told him to keep the change, and walked quickly away to start my walk. I videoed the bridge and the lock before proceeding along the path and videoed a fork in the river where I commented 'the river looks quite wide here'.

I walked on, across a small wooden footbridge and eventually encountered a carpet of floral tributes with notes to someone called Ellis Downes. I just videoed but was speechless, with shock, I think. A prominent note simply said

'RIP Ellis, Missed by all at college' another said 'nothing is so precious as the MEMORY that lives on'. I realised that a tragedy must have happened and noticed a burnt circle in the grass where there had been a fire and that the water appeared very fast flowing. In a subdued frame of mind I continued my walk past Abingdon where I had to use a footpath constructed over the weir and eventually passed Radley Rowing Club and saw many boats moored on the other side of the river as I approached Oxford and made my way to the Railway station for my homeward journey.

The following day I learned of the tragedy that had occurred. On Saturday 7 May 2016, in the evening of a hot day, a group of young people were enjoying themselves at the side of the river, 16 year old Ellis Downes stripped to his boxer shorts and swam to the other bank of the river where he laid down for a while saying he was tired. His friends offered to drive round to the other side of the river to collect him but Ellis got into the water to swim back, sadly, he did not make it despite efforts from his friends. Ellis, who was studying forestry and land management at Abingdon and Witney College's Common Leys campus, developed a passion for hunting and country sports from a young age when his dad took him out into the fields. When I read all about this I realised what the taxi driver had been trying to tell me and felt ashamed because I had just rushed away.

14 Thames Path Walk, Oxford to Source

TWO GIGGLY GIRLS, A BULL in a field, a horse muzzling my shoulder, a copulating couple and an interview with two visitors from Switzerland were just a few of the things that happened as I walked from Oxford to a field near Kemble in Gloucestershire on the final section of my walk to the source of the River Thames.

YouTube title

Oxford to Bablock Hythe Thames Path, Michael Parkinson

Osney Bridge in Oxford was the start of this walk on 6 July 2016 and I soon had to cross a wooden footbridge as the path continued along Fiddlers Island before crossing Medley Bridge to reach the South side of the Thames and passing Godstow lock and the ruined Abby. I walked past Kings and Eynsham locks and under Swinford bridge and had to walk along roads for a while before being at the riverside again before crossing the river by using the walkway on the lock gates and another one over the weir at Pinkhill. I then walked across a meadow before going along a road to my destination, the Ferryman Inn at Bablock Hythe. This was a pleasant walk through nice countryside with the Thames looking much narrower than I had noticed before.

YouTube title

Bablock Hythe to Tadpole Bridge Thames Path, Michael Parkinson

The path was really narrow as I started this walk through ideal quiet country surroundings and Northmoor lock looked immaculate as I chatted to the keeper before making my way further along to Newbridge which despite the name is one of the oldest bridges on the river. I continued through ideal surroundings and whilst going over a wooden stepped bridge I videoed along the river to show just how narrow it is. Yet another bridge and weir greeted me as I approached Chimney Meadow before arriving at Shifford where I crossed the river yet again before walking alongside Shifford cut and over the delightfully named Ten Foot Bridge. I arrived at Tadpole bridge and went to the Trout

Hotel to get a taxi to Swindon Station. This was a lovely walk, so peaceful, that even the whistling of the birds sounded noisy at times.

YouTube title
Tadpole Bridge to Lechlade Thames Path, Michael Parkinson

I went down the steps at Tadpole bridge and walked along the North bank of the river until I arrived at Rushey lock where the path crosses the lock and weir on the South bank, after a while I passed Old Mans Bridge but did not need to walk over it as I continued to walk past Radcot lock and weir and on to Radcot bridge. I had to climb up the steps on to the road and cross the bridge and down the other side to continue along the North side of the river where the Thames path was a grassy carpet and took me to Grafton Lock and further on was Kelmscot village. Then I walked over a small wooden bridge before arriving at Buscot, crossing the weir, and noticed a sign that indicated two miles to Lechlade. I followed a sign which indicated the way to Lechlade avoiding the bridge and steps. This took me to a road where I turned left and saw a house with a stream running underneath it. A huge sign shouted 'Gloucestershire' at me and a smaller one whispered 'Lechlade on Thames' where I walked underneath Ha'penny Bridge, up the steps, along the road, and walked into the centre of Lechlade for a taxi to Swindon and trains home after a truly magnificent day.

YouTube title
Lechlade to Cricklade Thames Path Bull, Michael Parkinson

This walk started in great style as I went from Ha'penny bridge and videoed two giggly girls who told me which way to go at the Roundhouse Bridge. This was up the road and through Inglesham and then a long walk on roads and fields before getting back to the side of the river at Hannington Bridge. I continued until I reached another diversion on roads into Castle Eaton where a man told me which way to go for Cricklade. I followed his directions and walked along a series of paths sometimes close and at other times away from the Thames and across many bridges where the river sometimes was filled with reeds and sometimes running water. I knew that there was a main road just before Cricklade and was pleased to hear the sound of traffic going along it so knew that I was close to my destination and my taxi back to Swindon Station. I walked up to a gate with the sound of traffic even louder and then saw a prominently displayed sign **BULL IN FIELD.** What was I to do? I decided to walk along the edge of the field because there were no cattle visible at that point, soon there was a style so I thought that would take me over the barbed wire fence and into the nettles and reeds at the side of the river, not very inviting, but an escape route if a Bull came into sight. I walked a little further and, to my dismay, saw a huge bull in the field to my right. The Bull turned his head and started to walk in my direction. I turned and walked, very fast, back to the gate, which I went through and reviewed my situation. If it were not for the Bull I would have been at the main road and soon into Cricklade where I had arranged to phone the taxi company to give my position so they could collect me, of course they could not pick me up from the middle of a field. It had been about two hours since I had seen the man at Castle Eaton and even if I got back there it would be too late to get my train back home but decided this was the best option. On my way back I saw a row of small cottages in the distance and decided that there would be a road so walked towards them. I managed to get through a hedge, on to a narrow road, and walked to the cottages. I knocked on the front door of a cottage and explained my predicament to the lady who came to the door. I asked if I could use her post code to call my taxi. She obliged but after about 20 minutes she had to speak to the taxi driver who phoned to say he could not find the address. The lady was lovely and I was so grateful for her help. I got to Swindon and was relieved to get to London and my train from St Pancras with a couple of minutes to spare. This was the worst experience that I endured on the whole of my walk.

YouTube title
Bull obstructs Thames Path, Cricklade by Michael Parkinson

After the incident with the Bull I recorded my spoken story, added some video clips and loaded it to YouTube. I reported the situation to Wiltshire Council who responded with an official service request and these words, *'Thank you for your report. If there is a bull in the field which is permissible under the legislation this sign would not be illegal. Please can you confirm if a bull was present in the field the sign was displayed. Regards'.*

I did confirm that there was a bull present and though I accept that the landowner was within his rights I would hope that something could be done to prevent the situation affecting other people.

YouTube title
Cricklade to Water Eaton, Bull gone, Thames Path, Michael Parkinson

On 10 August 2016 I walked from the point where I had abandoned my walk the previous week because of the Bull and was pleased that there was no sign on the gate or cattle in the field. There were three styles that had probably been erected as refuge from a Bull and I spotted three young deer just across the very narrow river before seeing two bigger styles and then a wooden footbridge festooned with signs indicating, Wiltshire County Council Public Bridleway, Thames Path National Trail and Thames and Seven Way. So all these well signed walking routes were either leading into or away from the field where a bull is legally permissible. I crossed the bridge to the South side of the river and passed a pipe bridge to my right and walked under a large concrete road bridge and through a lovely meadow which included a cricket pitch before arriving at Cricklade Church. This was only a short walk but I felt compelled to find out if the Bull was still there and not miss any of the Thames Path out.

YouTube title
Cricklade to Ashton Keynes Thames Path, Michael Parkinson

The River Thames flows through the centre of Cricklade with many small bridges allowing access to houses on the main street. I followed a well signed route through a series of gates and bridges before arriving in a meadow where I chatted to a couple from Switzerland who had come to England to walk the Thames path from the source to London. Of course they were walking the opposite direction to me. As I was videoing I felt something pushing against my shoulder and looked round to see a friendly horse muzzling my shoulder, and videoed a group of them as they shared the path with me until I went through a gate near their stables. There were a number of gates and small bridges as I continued along the river which was partially choked with reeds and arrived at North Meadow which is a well looked after Nature Reserve. I did not have to cross the river at the next bridge but continued to a larger one which had once carried a railway but is now a bridleway and took me to Elmlea Meadow and the Cleveland Lakes. There was a small stone bridge surrounded by reeds as I passed some large lakes and reached Thamesmead and Manor Brook Lake before turning towards Ashton Keynes where the very narrow Thames was flowing freely under many small bridges. Walking through Ashton

Keynes Millennium Green I then walked along a road called Happy Land into the centre of Ashton Keynes which, just like Cricklade, has many little bridges crossing the very narrow Thames and leading to stone cottages.

This was a fantastic walk, full of interest, with lovely views of the continually narrowing river.

YouTube title
Ashton Keynes to Ewen Thames Path, Michael Parkinson

Raymond, my friendly taxi driver shouted encouragement and wished me good luck as I started this walk from a small bridge over the shallow and narrow Thames at Ashton Keynes, he had taken me to and from Swindon railway station for my last few walks and had gone out of his way to make sure he was dropping me at the correct places. I was soon walking along narrow paths and tiny bridges as I set off past the vicarage along a tree lined route that took me to kissing gates and eventually to Somerford Lagoon on the left side of the path and the now slowly trickling Thames on the right. This formed part of Cotswold Water Park and I crossed over the Thames yet again at Lower Mill before passing the Lower Mill Estate and had to walk on roads for a while until I reached Somerford Keynes where there is a very small stone bridge over the Thames. I walked along paths in Neigh Bridge Country Park and crossed over another small wooden bridge and walked over a stone bridge at Old Mill Farm where the lady from the farmhouse gave me guidance for the next part of the walk which was the most rural and lonely sections that I had walked along. I passed a wind pump and was then walking along the edge of fields to my left and the reed shrouded river to my right as I approached the village of Ewen.

As I clambered over a style I noticed something in the distance in the corner of the field that I was walking towards and decided that it was probably a sheep because it was white. As I got closer it became obvious that what I had seen from a distance was in fact an almost nude couple who were locked in a compromising position. I certainly did not take any video footage but needed to walk close to the couple because they were directly in the line I had to walk. As I approached, I said 'it looks as though you are having more fun than I am' the lady replied 'are you walking along the Thames path' I said 'Yes' and she said in a friendly and conversational manner 'you need to go round to your left because this is a dead end' I said 'thank you' and swung round to my left. I had received many directions along the walk but these were the most unusual circumstance.

I continued my walk and soon saw the first weir on the Thames which is opposite a garden wall near Ewen and the water level appears to drop about twelve inches as it goes over the waterfall. As the path reached Ewen bridge I had to go up a steep slope on to the road and took some video of the scene looking down from the bridge with just a trickle of water flowing. I walked up the hill to the crossroads in Ewen where I finished this section.

YouTube title

Ewen to Source Thames Path, Michael Parkinson

This eagerly awaited final part of my walk started at Ewen in Wiltshire where I walked along the Thames path for a short distance before walking along a road and onto a path to my right, where there was a little wooden foot-bridge, I continued along a path and reached a position where the riverbed was just a bit soggy and demonstrating athleticism defying my age I leapt over the Thames. However a little further on there was actual water again but on reaching Kemble Bridge the bed appeared to be dry. The path I was on stopped at Kemble Bridge and started again on the other side and after a short distance I had to cross a small footbridge which had no sides or handrails. I then walked up a field following the course of the river which was only detectable because the grass was long and lush where the water would have been. I continued to walk along the bed and arrived at the first bridge on the Thames where it was totally dry. Continuing to follow the course I had to go through two gates to cross a farm track and followed the course further up the hill where I crossed the A433 Tetbury Road with gates and steps on each side. I negotiated yet another gate as I walked up another field before arriving at the heap of stones marking the source.

There is a stone plaque engraved with these words:-

THE CONSERVATORS OF THE RIVER THAMES
1857 - 1974
THIS STONE WAS PLACED HERE TO MARK THE
SOURCE OF THE RIVER THAMES

There is a finger post with two signs:-

THAMES PATH Public Footpath
Thames Barrier London 184 miles 294 km

My research shows that the Conservators of the River Thames ceased to have any responsibility after 1974.

I was not surprised that there was no water from Kemble Bridge to the Source but have noticed that someone whose YouTube name is KembleSteve has loaded a video to YouTube showing it flooded in January 2013. I contacted KembleSteve and he has given permission for me to include the name of his video in this book, the title is *Thames Source Flooded Jan 2013*.

I continued to Kemble Station where I started my journey back to Nottingham, tired but happy that I had achieved my ambition of walking to the source.

15 Blackpool Tower Ballroom Phil Kelsall

MOST PEOPLE HAVE HEARD OF Blackpool Tower and the famous ballroom which sometimes hosts Strictly Come Dancing but not many know that anyone can go into the ballroom and dance on that famous sprung floor. Joan and I first went there with the family in the early 1980s and were impressed with how lovely everything was. We have enjoyed a few days in Blackpool most years since and the ballroom has not changed much over all those years. Phil Kelsall still plays the famous mighty Wurlitzer although he has less hair than his publicity pictures show. Reginald Dixon retired as organist of the Blackpool Tower Ballroom in 1970 after 40 years service. His replacement, Ernest Broadbent had to retire because of ill health after 7 years so Phil Kelsall was appointed in 1977 and was awarded the MBE for services to music in 2010.

Joan and I had learned to dance the waltz and a few sequence dances with me benefiting from Joan's expertise in not only dancing well herself but pushing and prodding me in the right direction for much of the time. We had enjoyed dancing at the Calverton Miners Welfare and other places in Nottinghamshire but when we danced at the Blackpool Tower Ballroom it was brilliant. Our favourite dances were the Mayfair Quickstep, Melody Foxtrot, Tango Serida, Saunter Together, St Bernards Waltz, Square Tango, Barn Dance, Waltz and a few others. In our advancing years we are not physically capable of dancing as we used to do but we still enjoy spending a day in the ballroom listening to the music, watching the other dancers and staggering round a bit ourselves. Just being in that place is magic for both of us and, unlike Strictly Come Dancing, no one is thrown out because they are not good enough. In recent years I have loaded a few videos to YouTube that illustrate the atmosphere, colour, music and enjoyment at the ballroom. The first is a couple of 79 year olds who astonished us with one of their 'rock n roll' moves. They were sitting next to us and as they came off the floor the Lady said 'tell your friends that I am nearly 80' the video, loaded in October 2012 is called *Rock n Roll Blackpool 79 years young*.

On one occasion in 2013 there had been heavy overnight rain and the dancers were carefully avoiding cloths and a bucket that that had been positioned to catch water from the leaking roof, I videoed the scene as Phil played a Lilac Waltz medley with the title *Phil Kelsall Blackpool Wurlitzer Lilac Waltz*

Medley. Something unusual happened another day because there was a film crew recording an episode of BBC CBeebies accompanied by loads of school children. I had to be careful not to video the children but captured a short clip of Edward Grimes and presenter, Katy waltzing on stage next to Phil Kelsall as he played 'Pal of my cradle days'. The title is *Jedward CBeebies, Katy, Waltz, Phil Kelsall, Blackpool Tower.*

However, you do not need to dance because watching dancers of varied ability and listening to organists playing the mighty Wurlitzer and other organs gives hours of pleasure.

Another thing that gives pleasure to many people is afternoon tea which has become so popular that the tables encroach well over the dance floor and people sitting at them enjoy their tea and cakes and a romantic escape to a bygone age. The final video was loaded from our last visit to the ballroom in October 2017 and shows how many more tables are set out for tea with the title *Blackpool Tower Ballroom, Tea, Spectators, Dance, Phil Kelsall*

Phil who was awarded the MBE in 2010 has brought his Technics SX FA1 to Nottingham on three occasions to perform concerts for me at the Nottingham Arts Theatre, the first occasion was on 15 June 2009 when he did two shows in one day. The next show was on 11 July 2010 when he performed in the afternoon before the Billy Fury Dance Show in the evening.

Something unusual was included on 17 April 2011 when Phil performed his basic concert at the Nottingham Arts Theatre but some of the tunes were accompanied by 15 dancers from the Rollo Academy of Performing Arts who are based in Nottingham. The choreography was done by Sam Rollo the principal of the Academy and the dancers enjoyed performing on stage with Phil. The audience and I enjoyed something a bit different though it took a lot of organising.

I sincerely hope that Joan and I will continue to attend the Blackpool Tower Ballroom for some years to come.

16 Joanna Forest, Feel your boobs

IN SEPTEMBER 2017 JOAN AND I enjoyed a week at Brighton, the main reason for our visit was that Sussex were playing Nottinghamshire in a four day County Championship Cricket match at Hove. Before we went I scoured the entertainment available and noticed that there was a concert at the Little Theatre in Brighton on the evening of 20 September. There was to be a soprano singer by the name of Joanna Forest so I booked two tickets. I did not know what to expect because I did not know anything about Joanna. We arrived at the theatre about half an hour before the start and I asked the lady at the box office if I could video some of the concert fully expecting a blunt refusal. She replied 'I don't think so, but I will ask the performer' she telephoned someone and to my surprise the answer was 'yes, provided that I did not annoy any of the other patrons'. I was escorted into the auditorium and told what I could and what I must not do. We were given a programme but I did not have time to read it before the start of the show.

I really liked Joanna but was shocked when she informed the audience that whilst she was on a performing arts course at Italia Conti in London, at the age of 21, she had undergone operations to remove breast cancer. I was amazed that she had fought back and eventually continued with her singing career and here she was performing a show completely on her own. At the end of the show Joanna chatted to many people whilst I spoke for a long time with her husband, James.

When I returned home and loaded the videos to YouTube Joanna and I became facebook friends and I used that media to ask if I could include a chapter about her in my book and the reply came within five minutes:

> *'That sounds great - good luck with it and you absolutely have my permission. xxx'.*

Joanna Forest became one of the youngest women in the UK to be diagnosed with breast cancer at the age of 21. This is her story of what happened and how she went on to be a volunteer for Coppafeel breast cancer awareness charity:-

My ambition was always to be a successful solo performer. I'd been training since the age of 11 and appeared in the West End professionally. At the age of 21, things were looking good. I'd just starred in Michael Palin's debut play, The Weekend, alongside Richard Wilson. Getting cancer that year was not part of the plan.

So much goes through your head when you find out you have cancer and are told you need treatment but even at 21 I don't think you are old enough to fully comprehend what it might mean. My first worry was that I would lose all of my hair. Anyone who knows me knows I have really thick hair (in one interview it was even described as 'epic' hair), so the thought of that going was a real concern. How would I continue working if this was the case?

Chemotherapy and radiotherapy were rotten and made me sick. I hated it. When I showed my radiation scar to my husband, James, many years later, he cried. But it was the physical surgery which has had the most lasting impact.

I initially had a lumpectomy that removed a discreet portion of breast tissue and left me with a large scar. Following that, I had a segmental mastectomy (which I have never previously told anyone about), which removed loads of tissue, lymph nodes and lining over the chest muscles.

I was eternally grateful for the operation eradicating the cancer, of course, but I was still very sad about my physical appearance, especially given my career ambitions as a performer. I felt weak and was anaemic for years, but never wanted to tell anyone why and I worried that people would think I was not up to the job, especially as my acting agent at the time told me not to talk to anyone about it for fear it would stop me getting roles.

'After being told by my agent to keep my cancer to myself, here I was openly talking about it to a group of strangers and really helping young girls like me.' My confidence was absolutely shot to pieces. I didn't want to see anyone, talk to anyone about it and the last thing on my mind was that I would have the mental strength to stand up on a stage by myself and sing. When I saw my idols looking so beautiful in their gorgeous dresses, I didn't think I'd be able to do it. So I kept it all buried deep inside me.

Eventually, knowing that I would find it almost impossible to sing on my own, I realised the only thing that would get me on stage would be to do something with other people. So I got an audition for the part of Wendy in Peter Pan, starring Shane Richie as Captain Cook.

At the audition I was so, so nervous but I won the part. The costume allowed me to not get completely undressed in front of others and I loved it so much I went on to perform 13 seasons in the role.

The other jobs I had in this time were as the voice of a child's toy, voicing one of the Powerpuff Girls for Cartoon Network, lots of plays for the Shaw Society, an independent film called Crab Island, where I played a blind girl, and a controversial appearance in a Yorkie ad with its now-dropped 'It's not for girls' campaign.

My favourite role was playing the role of Tommy Stubbins alongside Tommy Steele in a year-long tour of Dr Dolittle The Musical, where I made some amazing friends.

I loved doing it but I knew deep down that I found a comfort zone I was too scared to break out of. Hiding behind a role became rather easy, but deep down I always knew that I wasn't really fulfilling my dreams. My confidence to perform solo was still at a real low.

It was when I came across the CoppaFeel! breast cancer awareness charity that everything changed. For the first time, as a 'boobette' volunteer, I was challenged with standing up by myself, as myself and telling an audience about my cancer experience.

After being told by my agent to keep my cancer to myself, here I was openly talking about it to a group of strangers and really helping young girls like me. My confidence then started to come back and in 2013 I met my husband, James, who asked me what I really wanted to do.

I told him that I wanted to sing as a solo artist and he urged me on to finally take control and chase my dream. I knew I'd have to free up Christmas and wave goodbye to Neverland. Not having that comfort blanket was terrifying but if I wanted to establish myself as a singer, I had to take big steps.

My first performance as a soprano solo singer was at a packed-out Freedom Bar in Soho at 1am in front of about 500 musical theatre graduates who were up for a huge night. Full of nerves, but supported by James, I sang Nessun Dorma. It seemed to go down really well, with the packed crowd joining in with the 'Vincerò!'s at the end.

I came off to warm applause and cheers and felt so emotional that I had done it. More importantly, I had the bug to do it again, and again, I then did it again, a few weeks later with Paul Potts in a duet at The Palace Theatre, in a huge concert for CoppaFeel!.

The whole experience taught me that going through something like cancer can be terrifying and it can take away all your confidence but it can also encourage you to fulfil your dreams.

Joanna Forest's debut album Stars Are Rising was released on Arts Records on 10 March 2017. These are the video names that I have loaded to YouTube of Joanna performing in her one lady show at the Little Theatre, Brighton. Throughout her show she spoke to the audience as though every one of them was her closest friend.

I dreamed a dream, Joanna Forest at Brighton
Time to say goodbye, Joanna Forest at Brighton
Oh Mio Babbino Caro, Joanna Forest at Brighton

17 Cricket, Notts and England

JOAN PRESENTED ME WITH A membership of Nottinghamshire County Cricket Club for my 60th Birthday in 2000, I had been a junior member as a lad and had attended a few games over the years. As the season progressed I thoroughly enjoyed my time at Trent Bridge and on three occasions Joan came with me, and to my surprise, enjoyed it. The following year we took out a Married Couple Membership and both enjoyed the cricket and started to make friends amongst some of the members. Most people think that cricket is boring and it can be slow at times but the spectators often enjoy chatting to each other and we became part of a group that enjoyed the ambience and friendship of people with varying knowledge and interest in the game. There were a few jokers amongst us and we enjoyed our first season as joint members and have renewed our membership every year since.

One of the friends in our group is Charlie, he has an infectious laugh, loves to get people helping with a crossword and has played amateur cricket so his opinion on the technical aspect of cricket is invaluable. However, it is not just his cricket brain that is useful, he, Joan and some others can rabbit on for ages about the best method of hanging washing out.

A big difference between cricket and football is that members get to know the players and there is a bond between them, here is a story that illustrates what I mean. Near the start of 2010 season I had dropped Joan off outside the ground (she was going to the shop opposite to buy a few things) whilst I parked the car and met her inside. When she arrived she told me and our friends that a Notts cricketer who she did not know had carried her bags from the gate and up the steps into the pavilion for her. She described the player but no one could identify him. At the start of the next game she noticed the player was Steven Mullaney who had just moved from Lancashire to play for Notts and amongst our group, he became known as 'bagman'. Steven was appointed captain of Nottinghamshire in 2018.

There is a reciprocal arrangement whereby members of other counties can sit in the membership areas at other grounds so we meet and chat to members of other counties. Joan and I have a great affinity with Sussex County Cricket Club because we had enjoyed a few holidays at Hove and often went to the Sussex ground. Recently we have stayed in Hove and attended the whole of some four day games when Notts are the visiting side so we have friends there as well.

Many books, full of facts and figures, have been written about cricket but I just concentrate on the spectators aspect and this is evident in videos that I have loaded to YouTube. The first of these was at Hove on 2 June 2013 when Nottinghamshire fast bowler Harry Gurney took a hat trick (that is when a bowler takes three wickets with consecutive deliveries). I moved quickly to video Harry leading the Notts team from the field and the title is Cricket *Hat Trick Bowler, Harry Gurney, Nottinghamshire.*

At the end of June 2013 as preparations for the England v Australia test match were progressing a story broke which was publicised on BBC TV plus national and local newspapers.

This was part of the BBC version of the story:-

Schoolchildren who won a competition to sing a song at the first Ashes Test match of the summer have been told to change the 'cheeky' lyrics. Nettleham Junior School, near Lincoln, won a contest to perform in front of a 20,000-strong crowd at Trent Bridge.

But organisers have now asked for a 'more welcoming' tune to be sung.

The chorus has the line: 'You can keep your koalas and your kangaroos / you can keep your coral reefs and even the sunshine too / but you'll never get the Ashes back'. Head teacher David Gibbons said: 'The children had written their original version, which was a little bit cheeky.

The Star newspaper was more direct:

School's pro-England Ashes song changed.

Schoolchildren who won a competition to sing a song at the first Ashes Test match of the summer have been told to change the 'cheeky' lyrics. But killjoy cricket chiefs banned them from singing it to 20,000 fans during the first match at Trent Bridge in Nottingham next month because it takes the 'mickey' out the Aussies.

The cheeky chorus went:

'You can keep your koalas and your kangaroos. You can keep your coral reefs and even the sunshine too.

You can keep Harbour Bridge and give Neighbours the sack. Because Australia, you'll never get the Ashes back.'

The song, written by pupils at Nettleham Junior School near Lincoln, also mocked legendary Aussie spinner Shane Warne, 43. A lyric from the cheeky song:

'We would even suggest that Shane Warne is recalled but he is too worried about going bald.'

Notts County Cricket Club bosses thought the song was hilarious and chose it as the winner of their contest to find an Ashes' anthem.

But the English Cricket Board feared it could upset the visitors.

School head David Gibbons said the original was seen as being 'too pro-England'.

The children will instead sing a song about 'following your dreams'.

Joan and I had tickets for all five days of the test match and I was interested in the story so contacted Notts CCC and was told that the decision to ban the children from performing the song inside the ground was taken by the ECB (England and Wales Cricket Board) who have total control of the ground during test matches even though the game is played at Trent Bridge. Furthermore the children would be allowed to perform their winning version of the song outside the ground but not inside. I was given permission to approach Nettleham School on a personal but not official basis. I contacted the school and was invited to go in and video the children singing the song for my YouTube channel. Joan and I went into Nettleham Church of England Aided Junior School and I videoed various attempts at their song but it did not look good from a lighting aspect inside so teacher and guitarist Thomas Leach suggested that we go outside. I happened to have a cricket ball in my car so gave it the girl in the centre who managed to use it without dropping it, this YouTube video shows what they did *Cricket, Australia You'll Never Get The Ashes Back, Nettleham School*. Nottinghamshire had Australian batsman David Hussey playing for them at the time, I told him the story and showed him my video of the children performing the song, he thought it was great and 'no way' would his fellow countrymen be upset by it. Whilst writing this chapter I have discovered another video that the school put on YouTube themselves, the title is *Uptown Nettleham*. What fun, and they even involved the lollipop lady. It has been a privilege to be involved with such a progressive school.

Of course Trent Bridge is a famous Test Match ground and on 11 July 2013 I videoed Saun Ruane singing Jerusalem as the England team and the not out overnight Australian batsmen Steve Smith and Phil Hughes entered the field at the start of the second day of a Test Match. Hughes went on to score 81 not out and took part in a record breaking last wicket partnership of 163 with Ashton Agar who scored 98 on his debut. This was the final test match played at Trent Bridge by Phil Hughes who can be seen entering the field at

1minute 04 seconds, he died on 27 November 2014 after being hit by a cricket ball whilst playing for South Australia against New South Wales. My video is called:-

Jerusalem, Phil Hughes Tribute, England v Australia 2013 Trent Bridge Test Match

The fortunes of both sides fluctuated in that match because England had scored 215 in their first innings and had Australia in trouble at 117 for 9 but the dramatic last wicket partnership took their score to 280, a handy lead of 65 runs. England then scored 375 in their second innings leaving Australia requiring 311 to win. When Australia reached 80 without losing a wicket Joan and I thought that England would lose but Australia subsided to 231 for 9 still 80 short of victory. The last wicket partnership put on 60 before lunch was taken so they just required another 20 runs after lunch with England wanting just one wicket for victory. I don't know who stage managed it but singer Sean Ruane lifted the crowd and perhaps the England players with his rendition of 'You Raise Me Up' followed by 'Rule Brittania' and finally 'Land of Hope and Glory' my video title is:-*You Raise Me Up, Rule Brittania, Eng v Aust, Trent Bridge 2013*

After lunch the packed Trent Bridge crowd witnessed the arrival of Australian batsmen Brad Haddin and James Pattinson followed by the England Team. The umpires entered the field and acknowledged the singer. The crowd watched in silent anticipation as each ball was bowled Australia scored 5 more runs before James Anderson took the wicket of Brad Haddin (caught by wicket keeper Matthew Prior for 71) to win the game for England by the slender margin of 14 runs. It was a thrilling end to a great match.

On 5 August 2015 the most amazing first morning of a Test Match occurred at Trent Bridge. It was the first day of the fourth test match of the series, England were playing Australia, England won the toss and elected to bowl in overcast conditions which were just right for bowling. When the first wicket fell in the first over I was pleased but not over exited until a second wicket fell in the same over, at that point I got my iPhone from my pocket and videoed my comments and the crowds reaction as Australia were all out for 60 before lunch. Stuart Broad, the Nottinghamshire and England fast bowler took 8 wickets for 15 runs in nine overs and three balls and England were batting before lunch, just as the sun came out and conditions helped the batsman. England were 274 for 4 by the end of the day with Joe Root 124 not out. I edited my video clips in the evening and put a video on YouTube with this title:-*Cricket England skittle Australia 60, Broad 8 for15, Michael Parkinson.* At the time of writing (Feb

2018) this has had over 26,800 views. England went on to win the game and regain the Ashes.

Another form of cricket which has grown in popularity is T20Blast where both sides are allowed only 20 overs and it does not matter how many wickets they lose, just runs scored. It usually provides instant excitement and Joan likes it more than I do. In August 2017 Nottinghamshire or Notts Outlaws as they are known in that form of cricket were playing a quarter final game at Trent Bridge against Somerset. The game was being shown on Sky TV and whilst the match was in progress one of the Sky team spoke to Joan and asked her to speak to them whilst being filmed, on camera they informed her that she had been selected as 'spectator of the match' which would give her two free tickets for the finals day at Edgbaston. Two semi and the final are played on the finals day so there are three games in one day. Notts Outlaws won the game we were watching at Trent Bridge so booked their place for finals day. If you want to see the Trent Bridge crowd enjoying that victory go to YouTube *Hi Ho Silver Lining, Sung by Trent Bridge T20 Cricket crowd*

Joan is the lady sitting down wearing the Yorkshire tea shirt. I don't think that anyone can look at that video and say, 'cricket is boring'.

As were going out of the ground the Chief Executive and her assistant spoke to us and told us that they would give us free tickets for the luxury bus to take us to Edgbaston in Birmingham for finals day. The weather was good for the big day and the luxury bus took us to the ground. It was a fantastic day out and Notts managed to win their semi final match against Hampshire so had to play the winner of the other semi final (Warwickshire) in the final.

In the interval before the final the crowd were treated to entertainment provided by the Sky commentary team who organised 'Freddie' Flintoff as Elvis Presley and David Lloyd (Bumble) as Johnny Cash. The song they were singing was Sweet Caroline and all was going well until Andrew Flintoff fell backwards over a large speaker. He just did a summersault and carried on, much to everyone's amusement, he then got security staff excited by going into the crowd who loved it. I loaded a video to YouTube which features the crowd singing and enjoying the fun:- *Freddie & Bumble, Sweet Caroline, Edgbaston T20 Final 2017* It has attracted over 10,000 views (Feb 2018).

Notts Outlaws beat Birmingham Bears in the final to win the T20Blast title 2017 and this time the celebration song was 'Hey Jude' my video title is:-
Cricket Notts win T20 Cup at Edgbaston 2 Sep 2017

Towards the end of 2017 season a game at Trent Bridge finished early so Joan and I went to the Lady Bay Sports Ground where Notts and Leicestershire seconds were playing. We knew many of the young players involved and they told us what the match situation was and where we could get a cup of tea. We overheard a conversation between two young players in which one of them had received a letter terminating his association with Notts, evidently because he was not good enough. I felt sorry for the young man and realised he is just one of many young people with skills and ambition at cricket, football, athletics, performing arts and many others who do not quite make it. I have seen many examples of this and wonder how many fall by the wayside for every one who achieves success.

18 The Seekers Judith Durham

JUDITH DURHAM AND THE SEEKERS were booked to perform at the Nottingham Concert Hall on 25 September 2013 and Joan asked me if I wanted to go as my Christmas present. It was billed as 'The 50th Anniversary Farewell Tour' when we went to get tickets all the front stalls were sold and the best available was described as an open box at the side of the stage so we got two tickets there. I had seen Judith and the Seekers at Bournemouth in 1965 whilst Joan and I had attended her solo performance in Nottingham a few years before, so we were both looking forward to the show.

The Seekers had planned to tour Australia before coming over to Britain for the remainder of the tour and after they performed the first night at Melbourne on 14 May 2013 Judith was in her Hotel room and realised that she could not remember how to turn the TV set on. She was not in pain but did not feel right and was unsteady on her feet so phoned her manager who came to her room. He soon realised that something was wrong so took her to hospital where a scan was conducted and a large brain haemorrhage was diagnosed. When we heard the devastating news on radio our thoughts were not about her forthcoming show but whether she would live because it was reported that one in three people do not survive a large brain haemorrhage. After a few weeks it was announced Judith's singing voice was intact but her memory and ability to read and write had gone so she had to go into a special hospital for a three month rehabilitation programme. It was evident that the swift actions of her manager Graham Simpson had probably saved her life. Some weeks later, ticket holders were given the opportunity to have their money back or to retain tickets for a possible new date though this was not certain, we elected to retain them. Some months later it was announced that the 50th Anniversary Tour had been reconvened with the first show in Australia on 3 November 2013 and that Nottingham would be part of a 15 concert UK tour on Thursday 1 May the following year. The UK performances had been carefully programmed to allow Judith maximum rest for travel between venues so the itinerary was:-

April 24, Cardiff, St David's Hall
May 1, Nottingham, Royal Centre
May 4, Liverpool. Philharmonic Hall
May 7, Brighton, Brighton Centre

May 10, Gateshead, The Sage
May 13 and 14, Glasgow, Royal Albert Hall
May 18, York, Barbican
May 20, Belfast, Waterfront Hall
May 23, Bournemouth, International Centre
May 26, Birmingham, Symphony Hall
May 29 and 30, Manchester, Bridgewater Hall
June 2 and 3, London, Royal Albert Hall

I wonder if any readers attended one of those shows?

Before Joan and I went to the concert I made sure that my iPhone was fully charged but did not expect that members of the audience would be allowed to video. We found that our seats were at the side of the stage in a little separate section with office style seats on casters and a high wooden partition behind us. This was the meaning of the 'open box' that we had booked. When Judith Durham, Athol Guy *double bass* Keith Potger and Bruce Woodley *guitars* walked on stage they were given an emotional standing ovation that went on for five minutes, this was before they had spoken or sang a word. I wondered how they were going to get through all the songs if that continued. When they started to perform it was evident that the three men in the group were keeping a close eye on Judith and if she had to move about the stage one of them always escorting her. As the show progressed Joan pointed out to me that some people in the audience were taking video and I was in a good position because there was no one behind me. I videoed Georgy Girl and put it on YouTube with this title:-*The Seekers Georgy Girl, Golden Jubilee Tour, Nottingham Concert Hall 2014.* 'The Carnival is over' was the final song in the show and was given a standing ovation by the audience who realised that the Carnival, *is,* over because surely, the Seekers will never perform at Nottingham again. As the group left the stage, Athol, Keith and Bruce were looking after Judith as they took their farewell bows, ending perhaps, one of the most emotional shows I have ever seen. The title of that video is:-*The Seekers, The Carnival is Over, Golden Jubilee Tour, Nottm 2014,* that video has had nearly 8,000 views and it is just one of many that were taken during their final tour. Just read the comments on that video to see what it meant to so many people, even at the final two performances at the Royal Albert Hall in London people were allowed to record video and they can be seen on YouTube by many Seekers fans who were not able to get tickets.

19 Scarborough Spa Music

WHEN I WAS A CHILD most family holidays were at Bridlington in Yorkshire where we would spend time on the beach, go on the Yorkshire Belle for short sea trips past Flamborough Head or walk along the cliffs, but I liked it best when we went to the Floral Hall where the Owen Walters orchestra played. Scarborough is about twenty miles up the coast and they have had an orchestra for many years as well. Probably the best known violinist and leader of any seaside orchestra was Max Jaffa who retired in 1986 after 27 years with the Scarborough Spa Orchestra. Max performed many concerts for the BBC as part of a trio with Reginald Kilby *cello* and Jack Byfield *piano*.

I found out about the Scarborough Spa Orchestra by hearing an interview with them on BBC radio in 2003. I suggested to Joan that we should go to Scarborough to try out their concerts and we enjoyed it so much that we have gone back every year since. The orchestra consists of ten musicians and some of them play three different instruments (but not at the same time). They play nine concerts a week starting in June and going through until Mid September and if the weather is good, morning concerts, they call it 'Music in the Air' are performed in the Suncourt which is outdoors but sheltered from the wind by a series of stone pillars and glass panels allowing views over the promenade and sea. If the weather is inclement, the morning concerts take place in the Grand Hall where the evening concerts take place. If you have never been to an orchestral concert before the Scarborough Spa Orchestra is a great place to start because they play a varied selection of music which I would describe as popular light classical and they have an extensive repertoire designed that if a person attends every concert for three weeks, they would not hear the same tune played twice. However, one concert each week is based on requests from the audience so you would probably hear a few repeated in that performance. Here are playlists from a couple of old programmes:-

Monday 1st August
11.00am Music in the Air (Morning)

1	Old Faithful	Holzman
2	Rendezvous	Alleter
3	Russian Rag	Cobb

4	Dream Princess	Ancliffe
5	Tik Tak Polka	J. Strauss II
6	Bing Crosby Hits	
7	Barwick Green (from 'My Native Heath')	Wood
8	Lady Be Good SelectionGershwin	

Interval

1	Children's March	Finck
2	Melody in FRubenstein	
3	Dance of the Icicles	Kennedy Russell
4	Florentiner March	Fucik
5	Noel Coward Melodies Selection	Coward

Wednesday 3rd August
11.00 am Music in the Air (Morning)

1	Liberators March	Ancliffe
2	Runaway Rocking Horse	White
3	Brother Can You Spare a Dime?	Gorney
4	Romanesca Tango	Gadé
5	I'm Getting Sentimental Over You	Bassman/Washington
6	Melodie d'Amour	Englemann
7	Making Whoopee	Donaldson
8	Embraceable YouGershwin	
9	New Moon Selection	Romberg

Interval

1	Light Horse March	von Blon
2	St Louis Blues	Handy
3	Butterflies in the Rain	Myers
4	Georgia on My Mind	Carmichael
5	Tea For Two Cha Cha	Youmans
6	Oliver Selection	Bart

7-45pm Evening Summer Serenade

1	Crown Imperial	Walton
2	By the Beautiful Blue Danube	J. Strauss II
3	Dobra Dobra (violin)	Skalka
4	Horse Guards, Whitehall	Wood
5	Adieu	Elgar
6	Westminster Waltz	Farnon
7	Fragrance	Ancliffe
8	Peanut Polka	Farnon
9	Viennese Memories of Lehar	

Interval

1	Brighton Sea Step	Hurst
2	Over the Hills and Far Away	Curzon
3	Elfentanz	Lehar
4	Thunder and Lightning Polka	J.Strauss II
5	By the Tamarisk	Coates
6	Souvenir d'Ukraine	Ferraris
7	Always	Berlin
8	THE SPA TRIO; I Know Two Bright Eyes	arr Byfield
9	Pal Joey Selection	Rodgers

I think this should give an idea of the varied selection of music played in the Scarborough Spa Concerts. Here is a tip, type a title from this list in YouTube and see what happens. I finished up at a New Year Day Concert from Vienna with the Vienna boy's choir and Chinese subtitles. They had a few more musicians than the ten in the Spa Orchestra though.

The Musical Director and pianist is Paul Laidlaw, Paul introduces and tells the audience interesting stories about the music, he uses a digital piano for outdoor concerts and an acoustic concert grand indoors. During concert intervals Paul and most members of the orchestra go out onto the promenade and are happy to speak to any audience member.

Children are catered for with a 'Teddy Bears' Picnic' concert each week, these are aimed principally at pre-school children and toddlers, but many adults join the audience in large numbers to enjoy the music with a rather different scene. They are devised and presented by Kathy Seabrook who is the flautist with the Orchestra, Kathy is well known throughout the area, and beyond, for her outstanding work with young people. When we attended one of these concerts it was interesting to watch Kathy trying to encourage the children to be interested but at the same time discouraging them from swarming over the stage.

I took a few video clips to show what happens when it rains just before a planned outdoor concert and they have to quickly move inside, YouTube title, *Scarborough Spa Orchestra, Suncourt to Grand Hall, Rain*

Scarborough is the only seaside place in England to still have their own professional orchestra. Joan and I stay at the Red Lea Hotel, on Prince of Wales Terrace and use the South Cliff lift to go down to concerts, with views over the sea towards Caton Bay coupled with using the lift, it is a pleasant experience. Here are a few testimonials taken from the website:
www.scarboroughspa.co.uk

I have reproduced these exactly as they are with no editing:-

'Thanks to you all for the pleasure your musical talents have given us this summer.'

'I love the music and wonderful variety performed by extremely talented musicians. Long may you continue to entertain us. Thank you so much. The Spa Orchestra is a big highlight in our week's holiday.'

'It is always a pleasure to sit back and relax to beautiful music well played. May I thank the Orchestra for their marvellous playing.'

'Thanks again for a great 16 weeks of wonderful variety of music and the Teddy Bears' Picnics. Watching the parents and grandparents joining in with the children learning about music in a fun way is just great.'

'The entire Orchestra is a joy to be listening to and watch. If possible, it is getting better year by year. Paul telling us about the numbers being played is good and such fun as his sense of humour is so great.'

'Thoroughly enjoyed the concerts this season. A wonderful selection of music as always.'

'Another brilliant season, as always. Nowhere else could you get such a wide variety of music, and the fun and enjoyment that the Orchestra seem to have.'

'A fantastic and very enjoyable season.'

'I've been listening to Spa Orchestras since 1959. I know I'm not alone in saying that the variety of sound, choice of music, standard of performance...I could go on...is the BEST it has ever been!!'

'Just like to say how lucky we are to have your fabulous Orchestra in Scarborough.'

'It's been a superb season. Well done to everyone.'

'Your choices of music to be played at morning and evening concerts are just right – such a wide variety, and truly something for everyone. Keep up the good work!'

'It's been a good season. Thanks go to Paul and the way he chats with people – whatever he may be feeling. Many thanks to all.'

'A very big thank you to everyone connected with the Spa Orchestra. The wonderful atmosphere you all create is something very special.'

'Just keep up the wonderful work you all do in giving so much pleasure. Thank you.'

'Wonderful... you chaps are the best! Thank you for a truly delicious and rich Season – and for making it happen here in Scarborough: we're so lucky to have you. All good wishes!'

'I absolutely love the Scarborough Spa Orchestra! I tend to come over once or twice a year on the summer season when I'm home from college and I always have a nice time. I also attend the concert held each New Year and find the music there absolutely beautiful. Although I'm only 19, I love the music played by the orchestra and am so grateful that I have the chance to listen to it. Considering the variety of music played you wouldn't think it was such a small orchestra. Every member does a good job I'm so glad that Scarborough still has a seaside orchestra.'

Another favourite performer at the Scarbough Spa is Howard Beaumont who was appointed resident organist in 1989 and plays for dancing in the Ocean Room and afternoon concerts in the Suncourt. He came to Nottingham Organ Society in January 2013 and performed an unusual piece showcasing two different organ styles, the YouTube title is *Bach to Beatles Howard Beaumont*. When the weather allows, Howard performs open air concerts at Scarborough, here he plays his signature tune and talks about being there when Sunderland won the FA Cup *The Best Of Times, Howard Beaumont, Scarborough*.

If it rains Howard moves inside where he plays a Kawai organ. This YouTube title is a tribute to Gracie Fields *Goodbye, Howard Beaumont, Organ, Scarborough*.

There is a variety of music in the Suncourt, The Stringrays Rock n Roll band, gave me permission to video them as they performed in August

2014. This is the title of a YouTube video *Stingrays Rock n Roll, Matchbox, Scarborough Spa*.

Kenny Stamp played in the Suncourt on a Sunday afternoon in 2013. He busks in his home town of York to raise money for St Leonards and in 2012 donated £2000 to the Hospice. This is the YouTube title *Besame Mucho, Trombone, Scarborough*.

Jayne Anne Strutt has a YouTube channel bearing her name, she combines music with scenery and I invited her to submit something for this book, here it is:-

The Way Not Taken – My musical soundtrack – Jayne Anne Strutt.

When Michael asked if I would like to contribute to his great literary epistle it made me wonder how on earth I could fit in to his ambitious plan.

Perhaps the best way to start is to share our commonality which is undeniably a love of music; although the Thames walk and Michael's various travels would also qualify. My contact with Michael came through a mutual love of an old seaside tradition kept green on the 'North Yorkshire Coast' by the legendary Scarborough Spa Orchestra which in 2012 celebrated its centenary. They still actually play the soundtrack we grew up with from that lovely era of so called 'Light Music'. The music may be 'light' in that it instantly brightens up and/or mellows one's outlook, but it is by no means 'light' in terms of musical talent. Many brilliant musical hacks who wrote much of this material for radio and television; including Trevor Duncan and Ronald Binge, to name just two, were exceptional composers in their own right, in fact I consider they are from a great unsung army of 'unsung musical heroes'.

On the subject of 'unsung heroes', probably the best example is Mr Eric Fenby, Yorkshireman, modest music teacher and amanuensis to one Frederick Delius. Without his unique sacrifice back in the nineteen twenties which took the young Fenby to France as a musical assistant, much of the finest work of the then blind and paralysed composer would never have emerged. Then those of us who respond to this chromatic magic would perhaps have never fallen under the spell and thus we would have ended up so much the poorer aesthetically.

It was Eric Fenby's moving story, set out in his book 'Delius as I Knew Him', describing in detail this unique event in musical history, that inspired and brought me to Scarborough in the first place. Then there was Ken Russell's biographical 'BBC Monitor Series' film about Delius 'A Song of Summer'. This was probably the best of Ken Russell's filmic creations and left me in no doubt that Delius was indeed a very rare musical genius. It also demonstrated that Eric Fenby was the finest example of how the ordinary can become the extraordinary and yet at the same time enable another individual to flourish by completing his life's work. It was no surprise that Mr. Fenby himself was inspired by the 'Scarborough Spa Orchestra' where he was once allowed to conduct, and that according to the plaque dedicated to him in the foyer of the Spa Complex ...'he went on to find a unique place in the history of music'.

One of my favourite pieces of music is 'On Hearing the First Cuckoo in Spring' by Delius. This was the only example of 'love at first sight' (so to speak) I've actually experienced, and it's very funny that still in my teens a 12/6p L.P. by the 'Concert Arts Orchestra' would shape much of the rest of my life. I was indeed smitten and have never changed much musically or emotionally. We all benefit by having something to aspire to, and this music resonated deep within, it also lifted an often morbidly pessimistic soul to a new high and inspired a will to find out more about this love of my life. At once I planned a trip to the Deluis home at Grez-sur-Loing, I'd only just passed my driving test and this was to be my ambitious goal, a solo pilgrimage to Paris and then South East on to Grez. Of all things in my life before and after this was the most amazing experience, exploring Paris was fantastic, although I was financially broke! But at Grez I was so privileged to be invited into Delius' house and even to have tea in the garden, my car parked beneath what was Delius' music room. With a rather shaky hand I took reels of 'Super Eight' cine film which has been carefully edited and now appears with Delius' music in various forms on my YouTube channel, 'The Way Not Taken'. As you will see most of my videos (though not all) feature some form of 'Mother Nature', it is then of no coincidence that Frederick Delius is also well known to be the 'true apostle of nature' musically.

Please do find this tiny corner of the world-wide-web 'The Way Not Taken' which is well away from the madding crowd.

I do hope there will be something inspirational there for you too.

I wish Michael well with his publication for which I am pleased and honoured to contribute.

Jayne Anne Strutt

Thank you Jayne. In my opinion, you are part of the Scarborough Music Heritage.

20 Disneyland Paris

IN DECEMBER 2016 MY GRANDDAUGHTER Claire put a message on Facebook that she wanted someone to go to Disneyland Paris with her. I saw her a few days later and she said that no one had responded. I knew that my wife Joan would like to go and we found that my daughter Julie wanted to make the four up so we started making plans. We agreed that we wanted to travel by train and Claire found a good deal whereby we could stay four nights for the price of two in a Disney Hotel if the booking was made before the end of January 2017 and five day passes for the Park were included in the deal. This appeared too good to miss so we selected our dates and Claire made the booking for the first week of July at Hotel New York which is situated in the Disneyland grounds. We had to wait until four months from the date of return travel to make our Eurostar train booking which I did in person at St Pancras Station. We decided to travel on the 1258 Eurostar to Lille and change to another train to Marne La Vallee (the Disneyland Station) and booked the direct train from the Disney Station to St Pancras for the return journey. Six weeks later I made the return train bookings by East Midlands Trains from Nottingham to St Pancras. (There is a direct Eurostar service to Paris Disney but the departure time was too early in the morning for us). So everything was booked and we were all looking forward to our treat.

We set off from Nottingham on Monday 3rd of July, went through the well organised Eurostar departure system at St Pancras and boarded the train bound for Lille, and Brussels, we had to change at Lille for the TGV to Marne La Vallee. I gave the other three members of our party a scare because as soon as we got on the train I got off and went along the platform to video the train and engine. On the way along the platform I had a few words with a Eurostar hostess and told her what I was doing, she said I had time to go along to the engine but to get on the train when I had done that because it may go a few minutes early. I got back on the train and it started to move about ten minutes ahead of schedule, I immediately got a text message from Claire 'where are you, the train is going'. I walked along through about eight coaches and I was pleased to see the others and they were pleased to see me. We had a wait of two hours at Lille so we ventured out of the station for a little walk and I enjoyed videoing people playing a digital piano at the station. Video clips of the hostess, engine, that journey and Disneyland is on YouTube *St Pancras Eurostar and TGV to Disneyland Paris via Lille*

A nice touch was that on arrival at the station we were able collect our entrance tickets to the park and put our cases into the Disney Express counter for delivery to the New York hotel so we enjoyed a walk through the park and savoured the delights of Disneyland on the way to the Hotel. When we arrived I had a sleep whilst Joan unpacked and after we had all rested for a while we went into the park that night. We had a meal at 'King Ludwig's Castle' and walked through to the other section of the park for the firework display, Joan and I went back to the hotel then but the youngsters stayed out late.

The next day we explored the park and I videoed all the Forest of Enchantment show, which is on YouTube as *Disneyland Paris, Forest of Enchantment Part 1 or part 2* That evening we went to the Rainforest Cafe. This was set out as a tropical rain forest with animated animals, sounds of thunder claps and sudden rainstorms. There were singing birds, trumpeting elephants, chest-pounding gorillas and schools of brightly coloured fish in a lushly landscaped jungle of tropical vegetation, banyan trees, waterfalls and a starry night time sky. The waiting staff all joined in the theme of the place and this turned out to be our favourite evening eating venue, it was worth risking being eaten by an Elephant because the food was good.

Another day we went on the 'Walt Disney Studio Tram Tour, Behind the Magic' an amazing experience that demonstrated how film makers set up some of the scenes, my YouTube video *Walt Disney Studio Tram, Paris, Earthquake, Fire, Flood, Screams.* Another exciting, noisy and interesting show was the 'Action Stunt Show Spectacular' which had cars whizzing about in all directions with very talented drivers and some inside information about how they do some of the stunts that are seen in car chases on film.

It was nice to go on the more sedate Disneyland Railroad on our way to my favourite ride which was probably designed for children, a gentle boat trip called 'It's a Small World' with colourful characters and illuminated displays accompanied by recorded voices of children singing. My video is called *Disneyland Paris, It's a small world, Michael Parkinson's favourite.* We had a walk around some of the park again that night and I loved the colours, music and sights of the place. Something I really enjoyed about the parks was the different styles of music which appeared in unexpected places, an example of this is the Gota Lejon Band who I videoed whilst they were playing at the bandstand one morning.

YouTube
Disneyland Paris, Gota Lejon Band from Sweden, July 2017

They are a marching band from Sweden who led the parade at night and on the evening of the last full day we got in a good position to watch the parade and enjoyed it, my video is *Disneyland Paris Parade, July 2017*

The weather had been beautiful and we enjoyed Disneyland finding something for all ages to enjoy. On the last day we checked out of the hotel in the morning and left our luggage which was transferred to the station for us to collect from the Disney Express counter 40 minutes before the departure of our train. They have a well organised system of tickets and receipts so that you get your luggage. Therefore we were able to enjoy our last day around the park, luggage free. Joan and I did our own thing, leaving the youngsters to enjoy the more boisterous things that they enjoyed.

It was chaotic when we went to the station for our Eurostar train back to St Pancras, very hot and a long wait to get on the train but such a relief when we were able to take our seats for the homeward journey. Whilst we had enjoyed our adventure at Disneyland it was nice to get on the familiar but slower East Midlands Trains service back to Nottingham and home. It had been a fantastic, expensive, enjoyable, entertaining but tiring few days and we all loved it.

21 | Eric Coates
Viola to Composer

ERIC COATES WAS BORN ON 27 August 1886 at Watnall Road, Hucknall in North Nottinghamshire, to mother Mary and father Harrison, the local doctor who, in 1888 had a large house built for the family at the top of Tenter Hill (later renamed Duke Street), this property has a Blue Plaque with these words:-

THE ERIC COATES SOCIETY ASHFIELD DISTRICT COUNCIL
The Uncrowned King of Light Music, In this house the Famous Composer
ERIC COATES Lived, Learned to play the violin and Wrote his Early
Musical Works.

Eric was the youngest of three girls and two boys, although another girl died at three months old, his brother's name was Gwyne and his surviving sisters were Gladys, Dorothy and Meta. Eric was exposed to music as an infant because his father was the choirmaster of the local church, his mother played piano and his sisters were interested in music. He was given a small violin and lessons when he was six years old and immediately impressed his family by playing tunes that he heard or melodies he wrote himself. He used reams of music paper writing out his childish thoughts and experiments on orchestration and when he was taken to see 'Florodora' at the Theatre Royal, Nottingham in February 1901, at the age of 14, he was impressed by the tuneful melodies of Leslie Stuart, particularly 'Tell me pretty Maiden' this motivated him to arrange his own orchestration including a special cello part. He got family members and local residents to make up an orchestra but the first 'try out' in the drawing room was a disaster as aunt Eliza could not master the special cello part. After three attempts young Eric lost his temper, used bad language, received boxed ears from his father and was sent to bed. This YouTube video, taken from a film made in 1930 shows what influenced young Eric *Tell Me Pretty Maiden (1930)*

I feel a great sense of kinship with Eric because I was born at Arnold just five miles from Hucknall and he, like me, enjoyed cycling along the byways around Newstead, Papplewick, Linby, Calverton, Oxton, and further afield to Southwell and Newark.

From the age of 12 Eric received two lessons a week on violin from George Ellenberger in Nottingham at which his mother accompanied him on piano. He also had one lesson a week for harmony from Ralph Horner in West Bridgford and this formed the foundation for composition, an important factor in his later success as a composer. His father not only paid for the music lessons but also bought him a first class travel season ticket between Hucknall and Nottingham. Eric did not go to school, instead, he and his sisters and brother were given lessons by a visiting governess named Miss Hobbs whom he did not like because she was teaching general education and not his beloved music. The next few years were packed with tuition, practice interspersed with playing in concerts with string quartets and amateur orchestras and he was encouraged to play viola instead of violin. During holidays Eric attended concerts at the Albert Hall in Nottingham and sometimes spent four shillings and threepence on a return train ticket to attend concerts in London. Eric had progressed to the stage where he received fees for some of his performances, insignificant compared with what his father was paying out in tutor fees and travel expenses. A huge decision had to be made about the career that Eric should embark on with a bank manager friend of his father strongly advocating that he should be a bank clerk. Eric told his father that he hated that possibility and fortunately another friend suggested that he should be a student at the Royal Academy of Music in London. Eric's father arranged that he would go to the Academy for one year subject to him passing a scholarship test and, if he had not made progress by the end of that year he would have to take up a position with the bank.

In autumn 1906 Eric made his appearance at the Royal Academy of Music, at that time on Tenterden Street, Hanover Square and he had to pass a practical test before being accepted on a scholarship. He played some of his own compositions on viola to the principal Sir Alexander Campbell McKenzie who decided that he would take composition as first study with Frederick Corder, viola as second with Lional Tertis and piano as third with Hartley Braithwaite. With what turned out to be amazing accuracy Sir Alexander told Eric that he would start as a viola player but would end up as a composer. Eric's family found him lodgings with an Aunt who lived at Kilburn, forty minutes ride by horse drawn bus from the Academy. He bought (with a cheque from his father) a huge rather ugly viola which caused derisive comments from fellow musicians because of the size but they all admired the beautiful distinctive tone. Eric diligently attended studies at the Academy, wrote copious amounts of music, and as Liononal Tertis told him, practised slow bowing for hours on end. He soon discovered that paid work, at night, was available as a viola player in theatre orchestras and claimed to have played in probably every theatre around London. The system was called being a 'deputy' (that meant deputising for the musician who held the viola desk but could not make it that night). The prospect of having to take work as a bank clerk motivated him to succeed as a musician but a problem emerged which was to cause tremendous suffering and affect his career. It started as a dull ache in his left arm and fingers of that hand and was later diagnosed as neuritis.

During June 1907 Eric was invited to play viola in the Hambourg String Quartet for a working tour of South Africa. This meant relinquishing his scholarship at the Academy but he was allowed to continue his composition studies. He had intensive electrical treatment on his arm before visiting South Africa and good news awaited him on his return. Two of his songs had been well received at a concert at the Queen's Hall and there was an invitation to go into Boosey & Co where he was informed that his song arrangements had sold for £5 down and a threepenny royalty after one hundred copies had been sold. Eric then made contact with poet/songwriter Fred E. Weatherly and they agreed to collaborate with, of course, Eric providing the music and the first product was 'Stonecracker John' which was eventually published by Boosey and sold thousands of copies. Eric became a member of the Queen's Hall Orchestra in 1910, the conductor was Henry Wood and the hall was situated on Portland Place so Eric had his bicycle sent to London and used it to travel between lodgings, that he had moved to in Portsdown Road, and the hall. That at least was a regular source of income, fortunate because an important episode of his life commenced on Saturday 4 March 1911. Eric and a friend attended a concert at the Royal Academy of Music where they had both been students and chatted whilst looking at the programme before the start about what sort of person billed as the 'Reciter' was going to be, deciding she would be awful and at best, a comic turn. The programme merely stated, new student name Phyllis Black would recite Coleridge's 'Kubla Khan' and Tennyson's 'The Mermaid'. Phyllis walked on stage, a charming little girl wearing a lovely white dress with two fair plaits which fell below her waist and she looked no more than sixteen. Eric was captivated and decided that he wanted to write music to 'The Mermaid' so managed to meet her a few days later, and found that they shared much in common with their love of music combined with poetry. It was love at first sight, but there was a problem, it was the day before Phyllis's 17th birthday and Eric was 25. Her family were furious, Eric was summoned to their home where the matter was discussed and the young couple said that they wanted to be married. The next time they met Phyllis told Eric that her family had decided that she was not to meet him again because she was too young, they laughed and made up their minds to see each other every day which they secretly did. Phyllis must have gone to Nottingham to meet Erics's mother resulting in this undated letter, which I have been given permission to include:-

Dear Mrs Coates,

Before Phyllis returns I would like to thank you for entertaining her so kindly. I quite think Eric will have told you all the incidents that led to his intimate relations with Phyllis.
As she is so young and not 'out' in the strict sense of the word my husband and I could not agree to an engagement for the present. We therefore bound them to wait at least twelve months during which time they would get to know each other better.
Eric is very impulsive and we should like a more tried acquaintance before the more serious step is taken.
Please do not think that we do not like Eric. It is simply that we would have been much happier if Phyllis had been of an age to know her feelings better. It is easy to mistake infatuation for love.

With kind regards,
Yours sincerely,

Annie B Black.

The situation went on for months but, according to Eric, in early 1912 they went to a shop in Regent Street and he bought an engagement ring but they desperately wanted to get married. The Black family had a house at Elstree near London and a cottage in Northern France and at the end of 1912 they moved Phyllis there to be away from the persistent advances of the young composer. In January 1913 Eric went to the cottage in France taking a contract that he had just been given for principal viola in the Queens Hall Orchestra as evidence of his improved prospects. Phyllis, her parents and Eric discussed the fact that the young couple wanted permission to be married. Eric told them about the orchestra contract and that he had more songs coming onto the market. The discussion was not going well and the young couple threatened to elope culminating in Phyllis saying, 'you know mother, if you do not let us be married now, one day you will go to my room and find that my bed has not been slept in.' There was a long silence and suddenly, 'very well children'. Letters were despatched immediately to Paris for her trousseau and the couple were despatched back to London to search for a flat. They were married at New Jerusalem Church, London on 3 February 1913.

They moved into a top floor flat on Abbey Road, North London and were very happy together only being separated when Eric was at the Queens Hall and Phyllis was involved in her stage career. In the summer of their first year of marriage they enjoyed a long holiday in Devon preceding the Promenade concert season, Eric's first as principal viola. They continued to enjoy life with Eric spending much of his time composing between concert engagements and in summer 1914 went on holiday to Wales but on 4 August war broke out and they went back to London to find their world shattered. Promenade concerts and all Eric's engagements had been cancelled causing he and Phyllis to let their accommodation out and live in a bedsitter in Hampstead which, though small, did include a small piano. Eric was declared medically unfit to serve in the forces. After a few weeks promenade concerts started again and there was a boom of musical entertainment in London.

In 1915, songwriter Fred Weatherly was instrumental in setting up the Performing Rights Society in Britain, this organisation was important to Eric because it enabled composers to obtain copyright protection and financial rewards from sheet music sales and gramophone recordings, which were becoming more popular at that time. There was huge opposition to the PRS as it is now known and many bandmasters sent letters to Eric stating that because he was involved, they would not play his music but Fred told Eric just to hang on and things would be all right in time. Eric did just that and in 1917 was rewarded by a payment of fifty pounds for the first three years of his music being performed. Another development that helped Eric was that, in 1916 the 'New Queen's Hall Light Orchestra' with fifty musicians, was formed, conducted by Alick Maclean, who had been Director of Music at Scarborough Spa. Alick included an Eric Coates composition 'Wood-Nymphs, Valsette' in a concert, it was popular with the audience and was soon played widely throughout the country. Readers can listen to it by typing this heading on YouTube *Eric Coates – Wood Nymphs (Valsette)*. Eric had been composing orchestral music for some years without it being performed so this was a big breakthrough for him. Eric and Phyl decided to move closer to central London and got a flat only three minutes walk from the Queen's Hall.

In 1919 Henry Wood decided to remove Eric from the Queen's Hall Orchestra because he had been missing too many rehearsals and performances due to the neuritis, which was causing acute pain in his left arm.

Eric welcomed the opportunity to concentrate on composing but the loss of income caused financial problems. Eric went to Scarborough in the Summer of 1919 to conduct some of his own compositions with the Spa Orchestra and went back for a few days every year until 1935. Phillis earned money by following her theatrical career but they were compelled to move to cheaper accommodation as income from Eric's compositions was sparse. On 17 April 1922 their son Austin was born and three months later Phyllis was asked to perform with Noel Coward in his play called 'The Young Idea' and became a much sought after performer in the West End until throat trouble brought her career to an end.

Because they had young Austin, Eric and Phyl found a small house in Hampstead Garden Suburb and but did not have the money to buy it so Doctor Coates provided the capital in the form of a loan. Eric composed a Phantasy 'The Three Bears', young Austin had asked him to set it to music, and conducted the first performance at Eastbourne. Eric and Phyl discovered the joys of dancing and often went to the Savoy Hotel Ballroom where their favourite dance was the Charleston. In 1930 they achieved Eric's ambition by getting a luxury top floor apartment in Baker St because he liked to be in the centre of London for composing. They also got a house near the coast in Sussex for holidays and relaxing. The first thing he wrote at Baker St was called 'By the Sleepy Lagoon' which became popular in the 40s. In 1933, Eric was working on a composition based on views across London from his window of Covent Garden, Westminster and Knightsbridge when Columbia Gramophone Company told him they wanted to record a transcription of three of his songs. He saw this as an opportunity to get his London Suite recorded as well though the recording manager was not keen on the idea. When the Abbey Road session started Eric got the song transcriptions done quickly and the first two movements of his London Suite went well but a technical problem prevented the final Knightsbridge movement being done in the allotted time. Eric appealed to the musicians of the London Philharmonic Orchestra to just give him a few minutes more so the 'Knightsbridge March' which was to become, the biggest seller that Columbia ever achieved, was recorded.

One Saturday evening, a few weeks later, Phyl shouted Eric to come quickly because of something on the radio, he recognised it as part of his Knightsbridge March, they looked at the Radio Times and noticed the announcement of a new weekly feature entitled 'In Town Tonight' they listened for the half hour duration of the programme when more of Knightsbridge was played. They were then deluged with telephone calls, people had phoned the BBC and been told it was by Eric Coates so had phoned through to his home number. Twenty thousand letters arrived at Broadcasting House within the next two weeks, they wanted to know the name of the composer and the title of the signature tune. Eric received numerous requests to conduct Knightsbridge played by a variety of orchestras and bands but had to refuse most of them. In the Autumn of 1950, Eric was invited to tell the story of Knightsbridge on the 500th edition of the programme. Time has moved on and now (2018) there are scores of versions on YouTube.

During the 1939/45 war Phyllis and Eric decided to stay in their top floor Baker Street apartment, Phyllis went to a Red Cross Depot where she used a sewing machine to make hospital supplies and suggested that Eric should write something for the workers. He came up with something that Phyllis called her signature tune and after some deliberation they called it 'Calling all Workers'. This was later, adopted by the BBC, in October 1940, as the signature tune for 'Music While You Work' which had many thousands of broadcasts, going out twice a day during and after the war, until 1967, a good version of this can be seen, with wartime pictures, on YouTube *Calling all workers – Eric Coates*

Soon after this Chappell & Co informed Eric that his Valse serenade 'By the Sleepy Lagoon' composed in 1930, had been published in America as 'Sleepy Lagoon' and was selling in tens of thousands of copies. This went on to become a number one song hit in the USA and was sold all over the world. On 29 January 1942 the BBC broadcast the first 'Desert Island Discs' programme with 'Sleepy Lagoon' as the signature tune and it is still being broadcast today, I estimate that over 3,200 episodes have been broadcast as I write in 2018 and Eric Coates appeared as a 'cast away' on the programme in 1951.

In November 1940 Eric accepted an invitation from Jack Hylton to conduct a series of London Philharmonic Orchestra concerts at various music hall venues in Northern England and Scotland.

In May 1941 a government representative called to the Baker Street apartment with the news that they were commandeering part of the building to house staff involved in the war effort and they had 14 days to get out. Phyl and Eric were upset but managed to find a nice house in Buckinghamshire. They were not keen on the prospect of winter there so moved to Hampstead. Eric started work on his Three Elizabeths Suite but having pencilled the sketches he needed peaceful surroundings to do the orchestration so they moved to a small hotel in the Vale of Evesham where he managed to finish the composition.

Eric conducted the BBC Symphony Orchestra playing the first performance of the Three Elizabeths at Bedford on Christmas Eve 1944 with the performance being broadcast by the BBC in the 'Music For All' series. Eric and Phyl liked the hotel in Bedford that they had booked for two nights and arranged to live there for three months.

Eric was appointed a director of the Performing Rights Society and travelled to America in that capacity where he conducted the Columbia Broadcasting System orchestra in New York. Eric was asked to provide a rousing march for the Associated British Picture Corporation film 'The Dam Busters' which was released on 16 May 1955. The music he provided has achieved international acclaim as 'The Dam Busters March', it has been included in many concerts and has been played by orchestras, brass bands, rock bands, pianists, organists and even bagpipes at the Highland Military Tattoo. It has been included in advertisements, words have been put to it and there are many versions on YouTube.

Eric Coates died on 21 December 1957, having achieved his ambition to become a composer. he wrote a biography, published in 1953, called 'Suite in Four Movements' and I have taken some information from this most informative book with permission and help from Harry Smith, curator of Eric Coates memorabilia and from the Eric Coates Society.

The Eric Coates Society organise a concert every year, two of the performers in October 2012 were:-

Haruko Seki piano, who promotes the music of Eric Coates in the UK and Japan, she can be seen on YouTube with these titles:

Sleepy Lagoon Eric Coates Haruko Seki piano and

Bird Songs at Eventide, Eric Coates Haruko Seki piano

Laura Roberts, principal soloist with the Cantamus Girls Choir, Mansfield, sang the premier performance of 'Tit for Tat' which was gifted to the society having been found in the possessions of a deceased person the previous year. William Lyle had written the words with music by Eric Coates, who, possibly gave it to someone whilst at the Royal Academy of Music in 1906 the YouTube title is, *Tit for Tat, Eric Coates Words, William Lyle*

The Torkard Ensemble performed in the October 2014 concert and although the instrumental section only included nine musicians they raised their standards to perform the Dam Busters March.You Tube title, *Dam Busters, Coates, Hucknall Torkard Ensemble.*

The Torkard Singers performed my favourite Eric Coates song in the second half, the YouTube title is, *Bird Songs at Eventide, Hucknall Torkard Ensemble.* The Eric Coates Society concert 2016 included the Southwell Minster Girls Choir who sang 'Children's Hymn', the words and music had been composed by Eric in response to a request from the Baptist Church on Watnall Road,

Hucknall, for their anniversary on 25 of May 1947. This was close to where he was born and spent his childhood, he explained 'I have written this hymn specially for children, it is quite short and somewhat on the light hearted side, I don't think that children want to sing anything too serious. The words are my own and are meant to be a picture of my early days in Hucknall when I used to wander about the dusty lanes on my bicycle before motor cars came along to spoil the peace of the countryside' the YouTube title is *Children's Hymn, Words & Music by Eric Coates*

The Eric Coates Society has more information and welcomes new members: **www.ericcoatessociety.co.uk**

22 Thursford Christmas Spectacular

IN OCTOBER 2010 JOAN AND I were in the Blackpool Tower Ballroom and Phil Kelsall told us that he would be going to Norfolk on the following Monday to start rehearsals for the Thursford Christmas Spectacular. I was promoting a concert for Phil at the Nottingham Arts Theatre the following spring and was typing 'he had performed at Thursford for 29 consecutive years' so decided to phone and ask about it. They put me on to a member of staff who told me 'you must see it to believe it' and they had just had two tickets returned for an otherwise sold out season. Joan said 'lets try it' so I bought the tickets and we arranged to stay at the Blakeney Hotel, about ten miles from Thursford, for a few days in December. It was a pleasant drive there, we enjoyed looking round the surrounding area and on Wednesday evening we went to Thursford and from the moment we arrived in the huge car park it was magic. There was music, coloured lights, illuminated trees and everyone appeared so happy but not me when Joan wanted me to pay for us to go into Fantasy Land before the show started, 'that's for kids' I moaned. It was brilliant and I soon lost my grumpiness as we walked around a sea of colour, displays, life size toys, traction engines, music, and exhibits. Best of all was being amongst many adults, taken back to the wonderment of childhood. When we went into the show we found it was not an ordinary theatre but a converted and enlarged traction engine shed with a long but not deep stage down one side and blocks of seats situated so that none are far from the stage. We were sitting towards the back and as the show developed we felt involved because the singers moved slowly around the gangways through the audience, sometimes moving and singing, sometimes stopping and singing to individual sections of the audience. Our eyes were glazed with emotion as we watched and listened to those trained voices, some standing very close to us. They were constantly on the move, alternating between on stage and amongst the audience. The music and song selection varied between Christmas and general themes and I noticed over 30 lovely dancers, who did the most amazing moves. The musicians changed from classical, ragtime, traditional jazz, brass band and other styles providing music for various acts. There were transitions from one scene to another with such quick changes in style that it was difficult to believe that the same people were playing serious music at one time and minutes later, playing whilst jumping around like pop groups. They played their part (and instruments) in achieving a magnificent show. There was song, dance, comedy, juggling, readings and more in a programme that varied between slow and sentimental to fast and furious. Phil Kelsall, usually plays at the Blackpool Tower Ballroom with not a sheet of music in sight but here he is on stage for nearly the whole of the performance, studiously concentrating on a huge score and unobtrusively playing accompaniment or backing except in a solo spot which he played in his own flamboyant style with no time to look at music, if he had any. The building houses a few traction engines, antique fairground organs and an old fashioned carousel that is included in the show for a few minutes adorned with pretty dancers. White doves did a fly past at the end, stage managed in silence so that I could hear the beating of their wings.

The brochure describes it, *an extravaganza of non-stop singing, dancing, music, humour and variety. It's a fast moving celebration of the festive season featuring an eclectic mix of both seasonal and year round* favourites. We agreed so decided to go again the next year but booked for mid November because we wanted to do some walking around Blakeney marshes and it had been bitterly cold in December 2010.

The show in 2011 included an unusual routine where the dancers, wearing soldiers dress uniform complete with helmet plumes, performed marching routines, backed by appropriate music, culminating in them forming a close order line along the stage and slowly falling backwards until all of them were lying flat on their backs. A large mattress was carefully positioned so the end ones could fall on to it. It must have taken a huge amount of time and expertise to perfect and I understand that it did not always work right and they had some injuries. I learned that the whole auditorium is converted back to a display area for the steam engine and organ collection exhibition which runs from April until September for the summer season. Robert Wolfe is a firm favourite as resident organist amongst summer visitors and plays two concerts each day on the Wurlitzer organ. Then they have to move everything out again for the Christmas Spectacular, that must be a huge operation.

We booked again to attend in mid November 2012 having decided that it was more enjoyable to go earlier in the year and we arranged to stay at the Blakeney Hotel again, like the Christmas Spectacular, it was becoming something to look forward to. John Cushing, the Director and Producer included some interesting facts in the programme:-

The Thursford Christmas Spectacular is the largest Christmas show in England with an audience of 130,000, and theatre seating for 1420 at each performance. Our shows are always a sell-out and have now become known as a Norfolk phenomenon that has put this village, near Fakenham, firmly on the entertainment map, and generates at least £10m to the local economy from the spin off for accommodation, restaurants and shops. The show has a £3m budget and is a three hour fast moving celebration of the festive season featuring an eclectic fusion of the seasonal and with chart topping pop favourites being sung alongside traditional carols, and is the largest show of its kind in the country if not Europe, with a cast of over 130 professional singers, dancers and musicians the range covers everything from solo singers to full four part choral numbers, solos and amazing dance routines.

In mid November 2013 we went again to Blakeney and were booked into the Thursford Christmas Spectacular and an interesting thing happened one morning whilst we were walking on the marshes at Cley next the Sea, about two miles from Blakeney. We approached a man who had set up a large tripod holding a camera and telephoto lens. Being careful to walk and speak quietly I asked him what he was photographing and he told us that it was, a Marsh Harrier, whereupon Joan got her new iPad out and took some video of what looked small in the distance with the naked eye. We chatted with the man who told us that he has loads of pictures on his website but to my shame I can't remember what it was. We said our farewells and continued with our walk which took us to the Norfolk Wildlife Trust Cley Marshes Visitor Centre where we enjoyed a lunch. Joan and I are moderately interested in bird watching but are not as devoted as most of the people we meet on the marshes. After lunch we walked along another track and spotted a large wooden building with small openings for birdwatching so we went in and noticed about ten people inside. They all had sophisticated camera equipment and were peering intently through the look out openings. There was some quiet conversation and it became evident that they were looking for something specific which they had travelled great distances to see. I asked what it was and got the answer Marsh Harrier whereupon Joan got her iPad out and showed them the video she had taken in the morning which she then enlarged. They were amazed because none of them knew what an iPad was and they could not believe the quality of her video which of course captured movement whilst their expensive cameras only captured still pictures. It was a surreal situation because some of the people had been in that hide for hours and Joan who knew very little about it had not only seen it directly overhead but had the video to prove it.

We enjoyed the Thursford show as usual and loaded this video to YouTube:-
Thursford Christmas Spectacular Entrance 2013

We had found the best way to book our tickets for the Spectacular was online and did that on the first possible day, Christmas Eve 2013 for the following November 2014. The following autumn we enjoyed our stay at the Blakeney Hotel and enjoyed the Christmas Spectacular as usual. Just before Christmas that year national radio and newspapers reported that The Duke and Duchess of Cambridge had taken their Son, Prince George, round Fantasy Land and mingled with other visitors at Thursford on Saturday 20 December. They did not demand special treatment and the Prince of Cambridge waited in line with his mum and dad to be given a toy by Father Christmas. 'George seemed to have a lovely time,' said Geraldine Rye, Thursford Christmas Show's general manager. When I saw him, he was walking around. 'It was a private visit and they were not given any special treatment' she added, 'we only knew shortly beforehand that they were coming; young George enjoyed his visit with his parents and reportedly gazed in awe at the animated reindeer, penguins, polar bears and elves set among twinkling lights'. I am impressed that Prince George was taken to Thursford and was able to enjoy a normal visit with his parents, he would have been 17 months old at the time. The title of my YouTube video is, *Thursford Christmas Fantasy Prince George visited 2014*

We went again to Blakeney and Thursford in November 2015 and even though this was the fifth show we had seen it was like a new experience because each year the show is completely different. When it was over and most of the audience had gone I took some video of the carousel and the 140 foot wide stage continuing to the end where the Doves had finished their 'Flight for Peace' and gathered prior to being collected by David Sherwood, their keeper. George Cushing had started the whole thing off by assembling a collection of road rollers, traction engines, fairground organs and even the mighty Wurlitzer organ, originally as a private collection. Most of these would have been scrapped if George had not bought and restored them. I learned that it takes 25 men eight weeks to erect the set for the show and six weeks to dismantle it ready for the Steam Engine Exhibition which starts in April. The name of my YouTube video is *Thursford Christmas Spectacular, wurlitzer, doves at end of show*

A funny thing happened as we set off for Blakeney in November 2016 for the 40th year of the Christmas Spectacular. Joan packs the case and likes to keep it flat and puts it in the boot of the car just before we set off. We had left our home after breakfast and were approaching Melton Mowbray when she suddenly shouted 'stop, I've not put the case in' so I had to take my first opportunity to turn round and go back to collect it. I can't say anything about her because she is proof-reading this book for me. Our stay at the Blakeney Hotel was lovely as usual and we enjoyed our marshland walks. John Cushing marked forty years of the Spectacular by explaining how it developed in his programme notes.

Forty years ago, in 1977, a lucky connection with a friend in Cambridge introduced me to the choir from King's College. On the last Sunday before Christmas they came to Thursford to lead our carol concert, and imagine my surprise when 500 members of the public turned up as well.

There was just one spotlight on the choir. Today there are thousands of lights and the latest LED systems; the generator we have on standby is powerful enough to supply a whole town if we had a power cut.

In 1978 we ran the concert twice. The music and entertainment spread its magic fast, and we used local amateur choirs and musicians to meet the demand. By 1982 we were in show business. Our little concert had become a totally professional show with dancers and military musicians. We expanded the seating to today's capacity where we run two shows a day for six weeks to full houses of 1400 per show. In the early days we didn't advertise much, we had no budget, but you can't beat word of mouth! When I look in the car park and see the names where thy have come from on the back of the coaches, I am truly humbled and astonished. People make the journey here from all over the UK and Ireland, many returning year after year, old friends, and we are so grateful for your support.

This support extends beyond not just Thursford, as so many local hotels and restaurants benefit from the overnight stays and shopping you all do whilst visiting our tiny village. It is estimated the visitors that come for the show bring as much as £10m to our local rural economy and we never stop striving to improve and update our entertainment for you. It was always my ambition to have all of my father's steam collection on display, and we have expanded the building to take Santa's Magical Journey around the steam exhibits, a wonderful dreamlike tour attracting 13,000 children with their families each year.

As Producer and Director, I work closely with my incredible hands-on team of 30, now joined by my sons Charlie, 26 and George, 24, who have grown up with the show and are closely involved in management and promotion and are both passionate about its future. Behind them and close to me is my wonderful wife Barbara whose support is everything to me and puts up with me no matter what.

I am so proud of this show, and best of all is the chance it gives me to employ so many incredible young performers. In these 40 years we have worked with over 6,000 of them, and many have gone on to great roles in the West End. We are lucky to receive accolades from the top of the entertainment world: I have seen no lesser man than the great Cameron Macintosh quote: 'Any cast member who has appeared at Thursford is good enough for me.'

I was 12 when I put on my first play, a production of Aladdin at Gresham's school where I was pupil and though that is a long time ago, I remember the thrill of making a show with talented players to present to a receptive audience. It is my privilege that I have never stopped doing that, and I have loved every minute of it. I hope you will enjoy the next three hours, and allow my journey through show business to become your journey to Christmas joy. I have been so lucky to find a career that brings harmony and happiness and I am delighted to share the celebration of dancing, singing, music, colour and laughter to you all.

Some say that Christmas would not be the same without the Thursford Spectacular. On this our 40th year, we sincerely hope you will agree.

Merry Christmas to you all, John Cushing

I think John has written an enlightening article which answers many of the questions that occurred to me when I phoned the Thursford office seven years ago and asked 'what is it'? The answer I was given is perfect 'you must see it to believe it'.

We made our annual pilgrimage to Norfolk in November for the 2017 performance and I had formulated an ambition to walk to Blakeney Point so on a cold, windy morning we got on the Coasthopper bus at Blakeney and I got off at the next village, Cley next the Sea, and Joan, being the sensible one, stayed on the bus to Cromer where she had a look around before getting the bus back to Sheringham and later the bus back to Blakeney and the comfort of the hotel. In the meantime, I walked from the bus out to the shingle beach, turned left and passed many people enjoying sea fishing. It was not easy walking along the shingle but the tide was out and I found it easier to walk near the sea where there was some flat sand. I trudged back across the stones and along a path in the dunes to look at the first place of interest, the watch house, a disused coastguard station, purchased by the National Trust in 1932 and leased to the Girl Guides Association. This is just visible from the Blakeney Hotel and I had often seen it in the distance and wondered what it was like. I continued walking towards the point where there is a restricted zone and signs forbidding walkers to encroach on the territory reserved for the vast number of seals. However, well before I reached the zone there were many seals on the beach, they obviously can't read. I walked away from the shingle and back along the dunes where there are some small wooden shacks with tiled roofs and chatted to a painter who told me that they belonged to London University and that in the summer many students used the huts as a base to study the area. I felt privileged to be walking in the designated Blakeney National Nature Reserve which has been managed by the National Trust since 1912, and lies within the 'North Norfolk Coast Site of Special Scientific Interest'. The only other building at Blakeney point is the Coastguard station comprising a new part, painted royal blue which includes a museum and the much smaller, original station. There is a notice and mark, half way up the window, indicating the level of the water in December 2013 when all of the area was flooded right up to the Blakeney Hotel which had to be evacuated. Having seen the coastguard station from Blakeney, over the years, I was proud that I had achieved my objective of walking to it. I walked past the coastguard station and looked over the estuary, now known as the River Glaven, which can become blocked by the advancing shingle causing flooding of Cley village, the marshes nature reserve, and the reclaimed grazing pastures. It was windy with squalls of rain on my return journey but I soon got back to the sea fishermen and past the Allan Williams Turret towards the windmill near the road. The bus had just gone so I walked back along the path past a sign with large letters boasting Cley Harbour, but it did not look much like a harbour to me. The path continued through the village and I walked back along the road being happy to reach the Blakeney Hotel and Joan who made me a nice cup of tea. After a little rest I went into the leisure area and enjoyed a hot shower, the steam room, jacuzzi, sauna and swim. Later, as we enjoyed dinner in the elegent dining room, we swapped stories about our enjoyable day. My video of the walk is on YouTube as *Norfolk coast walk Cley-Blakeney Point-Seals-Cley*

The next afternoon we drove to Thursford well before the performance because I wanted to video the coaches which arrive from a variety of places, Scotland, Isle of Wight, Devon, Nottingham, Sheffield, Essex, West Yorkshire, Burton on Trent, Loughborough, West Midlands, Cumbria, Peterborough, Northumberland, London and more. I have been told that I am unusual because I videoed coaches, but they illustrate to me, the attraction of the Christmas Spectacular, that encourages people from so many places to this tiny village. The YouTube video is called *Thursford Christmas Spectacular, 28 Coaches*

Online booking for the 2018 Spectacular started on the 18 December 2017 so I made sure to book our tickets on that day to get the position we wanted and then phoned the Blakeney Hotel to book four nights in our favourite room. This will be our ninth consecutive year and we look forward to it as much as ever.

23 Nottingham Organ Society

THE FAMILY WENT ON SUMMER holiday to Brighton twice in the early 1950s and the highlight for me was being taken to see organist Douglas Reeve playing at the Dome. On one occasion he and his wife Joyce, a singer, performed an old song called 'The Volunteer Organist'. This had a profound effect on me that I have never forgotten. Although Douglas died in 1982 he can be seen on YouTube with the title *Douglas Reeve - Selection*.

I went to a Nottingham Organ Society concert at the Bonington Theatre, Arnold, Nottingham in July 2008 and enjoyed it so much that I joined and have been a member ever since. The society was founded in 1967 to cater for people who are interested in organ music other than that heard in churches or classical. The club organises two functions each month at the theatre which has comfortable raked seating with good lighting and technical facilities. First, and usually on the first Monday each month, they welcome some of the top national and international performers of electronic organ music. They have a social event usually on the third Monday of the month when a Technics organ and a Steinway baby grand piano are available for members to play.

The society own a system of cameras and screens that are set up at concerts enabling members of the audience to see the performers fingers on key boards or feet on pedals to overcome the age old problem that usually only half of the audience can see such things at most piano or organ concerts. The system is controlled from a seat at the back of the theatre by a technically minded member who sets everything up and takes it down for each concert. One of the things I really like about being a member is that just before the date of the monthly concert I receive by post a copy of the Society's magazine 'HARMONY' which gives details about the next performer and events with news items, articles and a few jokes thrown in, this is all organised by members and committee members. There is a large free carpark and I enjoy seeing a variety of organists who travel sometimes great distances to entertain us at Arnold. Here are details of just a few organists and my suggested titles though there are many more on YouTube.

YouTube title
Dirkjan Ranzijn, Party Time, Paloma Blanca, Dog in Audience

On this track you will see Dale the guide dog who enabled his master to attend concerts before he sadly passed away. I loved the comment that a person from abroad made 'why got dog inside hall'.

Dirkjan Ranzijn was born at Alkmaar in Holland in 1968, as a youngster he was taken to musical theatre and circus performances and his earliest memories are of deciding that he wanted to perform on stage but had no idea in what capacity. He took every opportunity to sing and act in school productions but when he was ten years old he was given a Bontempi keyboard for Christmas and after a few days he was playing 'Jingle Bells' and tunes he had learned by ear. His parents got a tutor who said that Dirk needed a full organ so a Thomas organ was bought and he received lessons from a number of teachers. He performed a charity concert at the age of sixteen, and on leaving school at 18 embarked on a two year course involving acting, music and all aspects of stage presentation gaining his diploma two years later and has worked as a professional entertainer ever since. Dirk has released 26 solo albums, appeared extensively on Dutch television and performed in many countries, he is a passionate amateur photographer, his main interest is the world of the circus and for 20 years has been photographing hundreds of Circus Shows, his work has been used many times on the Internet in books, souvenir brochures, flyers and more.

In the meantime, Dirk's 26th solo album has been released and is already a great success. In 2012 Dirk had his big break through on Danish television in a very popular Evening Show, this led to his own 2 hour TV show and a one hour documentary about his life and work in the Show Business. In 2015 Dirk was the 'Orchestra' during 6 Saturday Evening shows on Dutch Television. All together his television career spans over the 25 tv shows.

Dirkjan combines playing the organ with impishly likeable presentation and sometimes tells a story, you can see what I mean on this YouTube video *Dirkjan Ranzijn, Sexy Camilla story, Nottingham Organ Society*.

YouTube title
Robert Wolfe, Tiger Rag, Nottingham Organ Society

At the age of 11, Robert Wolfe was given a small single keyboard as a Christmas present and quickly amazed his parents by immediately playing by ear and by the age of 14 was playing a Compton theatre organ at a pub in Hertfordshire. He took his own Hammond electric organ and performed in pubs and clubs in and around his hometown of Luton.

On a visit to the Thursford, near Fakenham in Norfolk, young Robert asked and was granted permission to play the Wurlitzer, obviously doing well because he was asked back occasionally. The family went on holiday to Blackpool and visited the Tower Ballroom where Robert was infatuated with a desire to emulate the organists playing the mighty Wurlitzer. Two years later, at the age of 16, he achieved his ambition and joined the team of organists at Blackpool. Three years later, in 1981, John Cushing offered him the position of resident organist at the Thursford Experience. This was a big decision for Robert, why would he leave the most famous venue in the country for the rural tranquility of Norfolk? He accepted and from spring to autumn, seven days a week, Robert has become a favourite with crowds who delight in his warm personality, his unique musical combination of meticulous accuracy and interpretative sensitivity. Robert's music has often been broadcast on BBC Radio 2 and he has been featured on TV including playing the Thursford Wurlitzer live for The National Lottery, with an audience of around 20 million. During the winter months he performs concerts in the UK, USA and Canada. He has produced many CDs and DVDs and it was a sell out when he performed for the Nottingham Organ Society on 2 December 2013.

YouTube title
Mark Thompson, Theatreland, Jack Strachey, Nottingham Organ Society

Mark Thompson was an early starter compared with Dirk and Robert and has been playing electric organ from the age of seven and joined the Technics Academy at the age of nine quickly advancing through the grades and doing well in local competitions.

He moved to the Yamaha School of Music and began playing concerts at the age of fifteen and in 2002 won 'Young Theatre Organist of the Year' competition. He soon became an established performer on the organ circuit, plays in 60s and 70s band, 'Wallstreet', playing keyboards and providing backing for vocals. He works as musical director or rehearsal pianist for many North East musical theatre societies and in the orchestra for their shows. Mark also works as vocal coach, accompanist or MD for many North East stage schools and for musical theatre colleges in Blackpool and Leeds. Mark also plays cocktail piano at hotels, restaurants and weddings across the North East. He often plays with a jazz band 'The Fab Dakers Boys' at Newcastle United's football ground on match days and he regularly performs in 'The Ratpack Vegas Spectacular' show at theatres around the country.

In 2012 Mark was appointed Musical Director for The Gala Theatre's pantomime 'Sleeping Beauty' in Durham, with a total of 60 performances in which he played keyboard, conducted and managed to perform a role as well. He has done this every year and for the 2017/18 production of Robinson Crusoe the number of performances has risen to 73.

Mark obtained a mathematics degree at Durham University in 2007 but his career as a professional musician means that he has not needed it. At Nottingham, he set a fun competition for the audience but readers can join in so perhaps you would like to write your answers down and compare them with what Mark tells you at the end. The YouTube title is *Mark Thompson, Guess the Shows, Nottingham Organ Society*. I am sure you will enjoy his Geordie accent.

YouTube title
Theatre Organ Medley. Tim Flint, Nottm Organ Society

Tim Flint was born in Belper, Derbyshire in 1964 and started playing the organ at the age of twelve, after showing a great interest in music at school. He started on a very small chord organ and had lessons from a local organ teacher. Tim was a very fast learner, and his teacher suggested that Tim really needed an instrument with two manuals and pedal board.

His teacher took pupils to give performances at disabled centres or senior citizens homes and Tim was always there, not only showing a flair for playing, but also communicating with his audience. Tim made excellent progress and after about 18 months his teacher said that he really couldn't do any more for him. So he had to be self motivated developing his own style and after a couple of 'proper jobs' he decided to turn professional. He has established himself as a favourite on the organ circuit and has played at most of the organ societies and festivals in the UK and overseas. Tim is an examiner for the Independent Contemporary Music Awards and also teaches his own pupils on a one to one basis.

Tim has made CD recordings and in 2001 started organising his own organ and keyboard festivals, which he is calls 'Superior Hotel breaks with Tim Flint and Friends.' Tim performed at the Nottingham Organ Society in February 2014.

YouTube title
12th Street Rag medley, Nicholas Martin organ

Nicholas Martin first started playing the piano at age eight. Even at this tender age he knew music was to be the foremost interest in his life! His career in music began in 1981 when he became one of the youngest resident organists, at seventeen years old, to play the Wurlitzer at the famous Tower Ballroom in Blackpool. The next year he was heard playing the Wurlitzer by Nigel Turner (a Northamptonshire entrepreneur) who, in 1983, offered him a position of resident Wurlitzer organist at 'Turner's Musical Merry-Go-Round' a new entertainments centre at Northampton. He remained there for the next twenty-one years playing on the former Paramount Newcastle Wurlitzer organ on which he recorded several best selling albums. Turners closed in 2004 and Nick became Musical Director at Wicksteed Park, Kettering, Northants, where he remained for four years. Since then Nick has been a touring musician performing to the many organ and keyboard societies and clubs that are situated around the country. He also has made 31 annual visits to Florida to perform at the famous Kirk of Dunedin Community Church. He performs concerts and plays for dances using his own Technics organ/keyboard or happily visits venues where they have a theatre organ in situ. Amazingly there are still many Wurlitzer, Compton and Christie theatre organs in various halls, churches and even private residences, where popular recitals are held.

Another facet to Nick is his extraordinary commitment to charity work. The registered charity 'Miracles to Believe in', which he and his wife Marianne helped to establish in 2001, has become a real-life passion for the Martin family. 'Miracles' is a charity that helps children afflicted by the disability autism - which both of Nick's sons have. For his devotion to fundraising for 'Miracles' he was awarded the BEM. in the Queen's New Years Honours list (Dec. 2014). One of his sons often accompanies Nicholas when he visits Nottingham Organ Society and members make him welcome. Sadly the other son is not able to come to the Bonington. I marvel that Nicholas follows his career and obviously, with tremendous support from his wife, supports 'Miracles to Believe In'.

YouTube titles
Klaus Wunderlich Medley, Claire Greig, Wersi, Nottm Organ Soc
and, with on screen words
Minors of the ABC, Children's picture club

Claire Greig was born and still lives in Derby, at age 5 her parents took her to Pontins 'Middleton Towers' on holiday where she received free organ lessons and returned home full of enthusiasm to learn the organ. She was enrolled into group class at a music school over the next 3 years she moved quickly through the grades and by the time she was 8 years old had managed to pass the first five grades. At this point her parents decided that she needed private tuition and enrolled her with a very good local professional organist. About the same time the organ was changed to a Wersi Beta with a full set of drawbars and programmable rhythm unit. This enabled her to play lots of different types of music and she started to learn to program rhythms to fit the various pieces of music. Continuing with the higher organ grades which also now included theory of music, which she found quite difficult at times because of her young age, she was entered for and passed the Associate Diploma (with Hons) at the age of eleven.

By this time Claire had started secondary school, she joined the school Wind band playing flute and piano. She worked her way through grades on flute at school but wanted to concentrate on organ exams. Next in line was the Licentiate Diploma and this was followed by the Fellowship Diploma which she passed with Honours at the age of sixteen. During these years she had played at Derby organ society and been involved in a number of charity concerts and made annual visits to the National Organ Festival which led to her first festival booking at the age of seventeen. She started playing on the organ circuit in mid 1998 and has played at many of the clubs and societies throughout the UK and Channel Islands. At 21 she embarked on a BA (hons) degree course in Derby moving on to a Masters degree at Chester University where she completed her studies in 2008. This was an MSc in Exercise and Nutrition Science. In 2009 Claire got married to Andy and although she is now officially Mrs Barrett she has kept her stage name as Claire Greig. I have enjoyed Claire performing at Nottingham Organ Society on many occasions and particularly like her conversational style introductions.

YouTube title
Brett Wales plays live at Wersi Summerfest 2009

Brett Wales was raised by his grandparents, Marianne and Alwyn, who owned an Elka 707 organ, one day, when Brett was three years old, Alwyn got home from work to find him playing the organ with his left hand and keeping time to the rhythm unit. Grandad asked Bret if he could involve his right hand which he immediately did, he was obviously an infant prodigy and thanks to continued support from his grandparents coupled with hard work and dedication has become a top class entertainer and recording artist. He is the President of Nottingham Organ Society and hosts music festivals in exclusive hotels. He lives only a couple of miles from the Bonington theatre.

YouTube title
Rock n roll Chris Stanbury, Nottingham Organ Society

Chris Stanbury performed at Nottingham Organ Society on 5 March 2018, Classically trained on organ and piano but is equally at home when playing jazz and pop music, Chris holds various prestigious musical qualifications from the London College of Music including Bachelor of Music and Master of Music degrees. Studying at music college opened many doors to the music industry and Chris's dedicated and easy-going manner has enamoured him to audiences and music professionals alike. Somehow, Chris combines his successful performing career with that of a music examiner for the London College of Music and is a committed and passionate teacher. Chris' examining work takes him all over the world 'I love teaching and helping my students achieve' says Chris, 'Seeing a student's progression, no matter what their age or ability, is very rewarding'.

24 Royal Academy of Music

I WAS WALKING ALONG MARYLEBONE Road at lunchtime one day in 1999 when I noticed a rather impressive building and went across the road to investigate. It was the Royal Academy of Music and there was a notice advertising a lunchtime concert at 1-10pm so I went in, enjoyed the concert and felt privileged to be inside such a famous place. I was given a programme of events and found many things that interested me so attended more concerts, competitions and even a masterclass over the next few weeks. I found that I could become a 'Friend' of the Academy for a nominal fee and enjoyed going to 'Friends' events. One day, a fellow friend asked me if I wanted to go to the rehearsal of the string orchestra which he had done before, he took me along to Duke's Hall and my friend asked the conductor, David Strange, if it was all right for us to be there and David made us very welcome. Subsequently I attended more rehearsals and enjoyed witnessing an aspect of music I had not appreciated before. One thing that impressed me was the ability of the students to start playing from anywhere in the score by David saying something like 'from 2 before 110' or 3 after 165. The string orchestra is formed from first year students from all around the world and it was interesting witnessing them being moulded into an orchestra.

I was intrigued how David handled a situation that happened one day. At rehearsals the students would place their belongings on the audience seats, instrument cases, bags and coats were all strewn about and suddenly a mobile phone ringtone started just as David was explaining something to the orchestra. A very embarrassed young lady got up from her position in the orchestra, walked past the conductors rostrum and switched the offending noise off. As she walked back past the conductor she apologised but David was very pleasant to her, saying 'what is that lovely ringtone, sounds like a glockenspiel to me'. I thought that was a clever way to deal with the situation because the student was visibly upset and he handled it with compassion. When it came to the actual performance in that same hall but with a large audience and members of the orchestra dressed in concert gear, I enjoyed it more than a normal concert because I could appreciate the work that everyone had put in.

I noticed a common theme in most of the concerts that I had attended either in Nottingham or at the Academy. It was that musicians very rarely spoke introductions to the audience, sometimes there would be a string quartet for instance, they would perform, acknowledge applause, and go off stage without one word and I believed that was wrong.

On one occasion I attended a lunchtime concert performed by a piano trio at the Academy and was impressed by the visual communication between the violinist and the pianist. I spoke to them and their tutor after the concert and asked if I organised a concert for them in Nottingham, would they speak introductions to the audience'. They agreed, so we discussed a possible programme and I said that I would look at what I could set up in Nottingham.

Having never promoted a concert before it was a challenge and I quickly got estimates for hiring various venues and investigated costs of travel expenses, fees to performers, insurance and came up with a proposition to put to the musicians. One of my stipulations was that I wanted them to play a programme of popular music that would attract an audience. (I had seen examples of musicians playing difficult, challenging, pieces that were difficult to play but not good for an audience to listen to). After consultation with Mitra and Haru we devised a programme and they recommended Felix Tanner, viola, Jonathan Byers, cello and Roger McCann, double bass as the other musicians to make up a piano quintet. The Djanogly Recital Hall, part of the Lakeside Arts Centre at Nottingham University is one of Nottingham's most prestigious venues for a string Quartet concert and I found that I could hire it out of University term time but they would not sell tickets for me so I spoke to the box office staff at Nottingham Royal Centre about the problem. To my amazement and delight the box office manager told me that they wanted to try out a new computer system that would allow them to sell tickets for an event such as mine and they offered to sell tickets with no commission charge in return for them using it as a trial. It must have been beginners luck because the ticket sales were good, helped by people seeing my flyers and being able to book at the Royal Centre box office.

I discovered that pianist Mitra Alice Tham did composing and arranging so asked her to use these skills to arrange Scott Joplin's 'The Entertainer' for the quintet which was used as the opening to the programme which consisted of:-

The Entertainer	quintet	Tham/Joplin
Havanaise op 83	violin/piano	Saint-Saëns
Salut d'Amour	violin/piano	Sir Edward Elgar
Viola Sonata 1st movement	viola/piano	Paul Hindemith
Vocalise	viola/piano	Rachmaninov

Song without words	cello/piano	Mendelsshon
The Swan	cello/piano	Saint-Saëns
Sonata in G minor, Largo	double bass/piano	Henry Eccles
The Elephant	double bass/piano	Saint-Saëns
Chaconne in D minor	piano	J.S.Bach arr Busoni
Speciality impromptu from audience theme played by Mitra Alice Tham		
Quintet in A major, 'The Trout' quintet		Franz Peter Schubert

The concert was a great success, but I must tell you a little story that happened afterwards. The musicians had travelled from London by train and four of them were accommodated overnight by some friends who had two spare rooms and lived near us at Keyworth, a small place six miles from Nottingham. I had organised drinks/nibbles and performers meeting the audience after the concert so it was fairly late when we all arrived at Keyworth. The couple and the four students were just settling to bed when the students had a whispered conversation that they were hungry and wanted to go out for something to eat. They elected Jonathan to lightly knock on the bedroom door of their hosts to ask where they could go out for a meal (they did not know that the village is so quiet that even the chippy closes at 9pm). There was a step down from the students room and another one up near the door of the hosts and as Jonny walked along in the dark he tripped and fell against the host's door which burst open. He apologised and then asked about somewhere to eat which resulted in the hosts getting up, and inviting everyone downstairs where the lady rustled them some food, so they all had a good laugh and a midnight feast. Joan and I plus our guests had a chuckle when we heard the story the next day when we met on our journey to take them to the train.

The concert earned an excellent review in the Nottingham press and I had some complimentary letters, this is what one of them said:-

Dear Michael

I wish to thank you for the wonderful Haru Quintet Concert, which was a joy to listen to. The music was well chosen, beautifully played and the rapport between the players made it a night to remember. I thought the highlight of the evening was the Piano Variations on a theme from the audience, the inventive and varied styles of expression were a joy to hear.
Signed

Pianist Mitra Alice Tham had demonstrated her special talent of composing impromptu on stage on a given musical phrase. On 30th January 1998 Mitra was specially chosen by the Purcel School, for musically gifted children, to exhibit her special talent on a phrase given by His Royal Highness, The Prince of Wales, during his official visit to the school. Mitra's instant composition was aired on the radio the same evening. For this special private event, she was featured in the London newspapers, her performance being described as 'brilliant and excellent' by Prince Charles. She orchestrated this 'royal' composition and the piece was selected for a special performance at the Royal Academy of Music, London, a few months later.

The musicians sent me a card with these words:-

We very much enjoyed playing in Nottingham. Thank you very much for your wonderful organisation and for the occasion. Best wishes Haru Sekiya

I had a professional video made of the concert and whilst writing this book I have loaded four extracts to YouTube that will show the reader what the performance was like. They are:

Bach/Busoni Chaconne, Mitra Alice Tham, Piano, Djanogly Recital
Piano String Duo Classics, Mitra Haru Jonathan Roger
Entertainer, Piano Quintet arranged by Mitra Alice Tham
Piano instant composition for Iris, Mitra Alice Tham

The audience member who volunteered to provide the theme for the instant piano composition had been a school pianist for many years and ran a choir when she retired. Her name is Iris so I described it as 'Instant composition for Iris'.

I continue to attend events at the Academy and have promoted other concerts and shows, but more of that in another chapter.

25 Phab, Fanfare for Christmas

PHAB IS A NATIONAL CHARITY whose objectives are 'to inspire children with and without disabilities to Make more of life together!'

On Wednesday 15 December 2010 I attended a Fanfare for Christmas concert at St James Church Piccadilly, London, performed by the London Orpheus Choir in aid of Phab. It was presented by Ed Stewart, Phab President who I can remember as 'Stewpot' presenting Junior Choice and many other programmes on BBC radio. The choir, conducted by James Gaddarn, performed a really enjoyable selection of Christmas music accompanied by organist Nicholas Luff. There were readings from celebrity stars, Lionel Blair, Annette Crosbie OBE, Belinda Owusu, David Proud and Richard Wilson who all gave their services free of charge for the charity which was founded in 1957.

I really enjoyed that concert and Ed Stewart gave me permission to video during the 2012 concert with the objective of loading something to YouTube. The choir performed a Gustav Holst arrangement of some traditional and some of his own compositions which he called Christmas Day, I put this on as *Christmas Day-Holst-London Orpheus Choir for Phab*. This was followed by The Shepherds' Farewell to the Holy Family with words and music by French composer Hector Berlioz, my YouTube title is *Shepherds Farewell-London Orpheus Choir For Phab*.

The choir sang 'Ding Dong Ding' words written by G R Woodward who had also written Ding Dong Merrily on High. The YouTube title is *Ding Dong Ding-London Orpheus Choir, St James Piccadilly, Phab*

The Fanfare for Christmas concert on 15 December 2016 was specially significant because it was the first concert since the death on 9 January of Ed Stewart who had supported Phab for twenty five years (since 2002 as President). The choir sang Ed's favourite, In the Bleak Mid Winter with members of his family and people that knew him very emotional. I was not in a good position to video but loaded it to YouTube as a tribute to a man who had done so much for Phab, *In the Bleak Mid Winter, Tribute to Ed Stewart, Phab 2016* The choir finished that concert with a bright and breezy version of Jingle Bells where they sang all the verses, the title is *Jingle Bells, London Orpheus Choir, St James Piccadilly*.

The Diamond Jubilee Phab Concert at St James Piccadilly on 14 December 2017 included Carols and Festive Music with Celebrity readings by Anita Dobson, Nerys Hughes, Christopher Timothy and Mik Scarlet, vice president, whose story is an inspirational one.

Mik Scarlet has been disabled since birth, following a battle with childhood cancer, and was one of the first disabled presenters in the UK. He was also the first disabled actor to appear in a UK soap when he acted in Channel 4s Brookside in 1990. Mik is a broadcaster and journalist, with TV credits for BBC, ITV, C4, C5 and Sky. He has been working in the media for over twenty five years, starting as a kids TV presenter on Channel 4's Emmy Award winning Beat That, before becoming a reporter for BBC 2's current affairs show From The Edge. Mik writes for magazines such as PosAbility and the Huffington Post and is an occasional panelist for Channel 5s The Wright Stuff and reporter for BBC 2s Victoria Derbyshire. He also runs a successful access consultancy. I have only tipped at the iceberg so for more detailed information about Mik go to his website: **www.mikscarlet.com**

John Corless, the Chairman of Phab introduced new President Anita Dobson who made a speech in which she paid tribute to Ed Stewart. The YouTube title is:- *Anita Dobson, New President of Phab, intro, John Corless*

The London Orpheus Choir conducted by Jack Apperley performed The Shropshire Carol which can be seen on YouTube with this title:- *Truth sent from above, 'The Shropshire Carol' London Orpheus Choir*

Fanfare for Christmas finished with Twelve Days of Christmas including a lively performance from organist Ian le Grice, YouTube name:- *The 12 Days of Christmas, London Orpheus Choir, Phab, Fanfare*

When I first went to a Fanfare for Christmas concert it was because I just happened to be in London and found out it was on, but now Joan and I travel specially from Nottingham for the concerts which we really enjoy.

I decided to find out what Phab does and to include a short report in this chapter, it is like trying to put a mountain in a tea cup because they do so much so I invite readers to look at these two websites **www.phab.org.uk** or **www. phabkids.co.uk** However, with their permission, I include some information and comments that I picked up from their sites:-

The first Phab project began in 1957, and for nearly 60 years the charity has encouraged and supported children and adults with and without disabilities to make more of life together. There are over 170 Phab clubs with 8,000 members in all age ranges from under 8s to over 80s right across England and Wales. Phab is very fortunate to have the support of some amazing volunteers who give their time and effort not only during the weeks away, but also at the required training sessions and huge thanks goes out to every one of them! We are most grateful to our Marathon runners, cyclists and all those who raise funds to support both the Phab Projects and 170 Clubs across England and Wales with over 8,000 members. Most of the children and young people have physical, sensory or learning disabilities. Some have complex needs requiring the support of a dedicated carer or two Phab volunteers. Those disabilities can include cerebral palsy (including quadriplegic cerebral palsy), learning disabilities, social anxiety, global development delay, visual or hearing impairment, Downs Syndrome, autism, ADHD, Asperger's, Duchenne Muscular Dystrophy, epilepsy, speech and language difficulties, scoliosis, arthritis, Type 1 Diabetes, hydrocephalus and behavioural difficulties.

Comments This is what the children said:

'I liked feeding the animals at the farm and I held a piglet in a blanket!', Hannah aged 15 with severe learning disabilities and a wheelchair user

'I paddled all the way on the canoe and won the prettiest feather award and had an ice cream. And I think I can make my own drinks completely now too.' Erin aged 14 with severe learning difficulties

'Thank you for taking me on the Phab Project – I felt proud and brave when I went down the tube slide.', Keileigh aged 8 with learning disabilities

'I loved every second of today and being out of my wheelchair, going on the zipwire and big swing.', Isla aged 15 with cerebral palsy and oxygen dependent

'I am proud that I did rock climbing and I made new friends and got myself dressed.', David aged 11 with cerebral palsy

'We had a party and I danced and jumped and found it all very funny!', Sarah aged 15 with severe learning disabilities and epilepsy and a wheelchair user

'I was proud I had made new friends and I was good at the water fight.', Sol aged 12 with learning difficulties

'I got stronger and I'm not scared to say no anymore.', James aged 18 with Global Development Delay and Autistic Spectrum Disorder

'I was brave and went ghyll scrambling and got to the top.', Christopher aged 8 with learning disabilities, severe verbal dyspraxia and Global Development Delay

And this is some of the feedback from families:

'A great chance to do things as a family that we wouldn't be able to do and meet some other families in similar situations.', parent of a 9 year old on Family Weekend

'Tom and Harry had lots of fun but came home with skills that will last them a lifetime.', parent of 9 and 10 year old brothers with Autistic Spectrum Disorder, absence seizures, dyspraxia and speech disorder

'People are made to feel special and important. Sarah told me that she felt safe and cared for.', parent of 16 year old with Micro Deletion Syndrome and mild learning disability

'The morning after Kelly came home she prepared and served her own breakfast and buttered her own toast. We watched in amazement as she asked nobody for help.', parent of 16 year old with severe learning disabilities, delayed development and non verbal

'The Course Leader and all the volunteers made my son feel immediately at home and welcome when we arrived which inspired such confidence in us as parents.', parent of 17 year old with Downs Syndrome and Autistic Spectrum Disorder

'Thank you so much for the photos of Sam. I am going to put them in a frame so he can remember how brave he was.', parent of 8 year old with severe learning disabilities

When I read these comments I realise why so many people give their time, their talents and their money to support such a worthy cause.

26 London Concerts

LONDON IS A FANTASTIC PLACE if you like attending music concerts and I have been enjoying them since 1999 but go on day trips from Nottingham so like to attend concerts in the daytime or early evening. St James Church, is just one minute walk from Piccadilly Circus, along the south side of Piccadilly, and they have lunchtime concerts starting at ten minutes past one on Monday, Wednesday and Friday of most weeks. The lunchtime concerts have solo piano, various stringed instruments or voice accompanied by piano. Sometimes they feature harp, wind instruments, piano quintets, string quartets, wind octets and I have seen choirs who are visiting from abroad. The performers can be established musicians or students of music schools and academies from London or further afield. I have spoken to other audience members who travel great distances to attend and some who come from America for extended visits because they know how good the London concert scene is. From 2013 I have been given permission to video some of the concerts provided the performers agree and have loaded videos to YouTube, here is an example where the pianist demonstrates something extra ordinary:- *Fazil Say-Black Earth, Belle Chen Piano, extended technique.* This has received over 4400 views (February 2018) and has been 'shared' by the composer, Fasil Say who lives in Turkey. Two comments were:-

> *This is a very traditional sort of prologue that Turkish bards use with Baglama (a very traditional yet popular stringed instrument) which requires quite a local spirit. Belle Chen feels it as if she was born in Turkey. This is beyond beautiful. Thanks very much Michael and Belle reminds me of what it means to be ALIVE. I am touched and inspired. THANK YOU!*

This was a fine example of how a young performer used the opportunity of her St James concert to demonstrate her talent and initiative. Of course St James is a Church and on one occasion they had a display of carved wooden figures, 'The Sculpture of the Nativity' had been created from a tree that stood in the courtyard of St Jame's Church, Piccadilly for over 90 years. The Catalpa Tree (Indian Bean Tree) survived the bombing of 1940 which almost destroyed the Church and eventually fell down in 2010. This much loved tree was carved by the Artist Clinton Chaloner during 2011 and 2012 in a stable at his studios in North Wales and was dedicated on Advent Sunday at a special service in 2012. This is the YouTube title *Nativity Wood Sculpture, St James, London.* They sometimes have evening events as well and they usually finish early enough for me to catch the 10pm train from St Pancras. I have attended performances of 'The Messiah' and 'Fanfare for Christmas' amongst other evening concerts.

A strange sequence of events occurred in July 2014, I had learned that a pianist by the name of Maria Marchant was to perform in a lunchtime concert at St James and had contacted her beforehand to obtain permission to video her performance. I forgot to take my iPhone with me when I left home in the morning. Joan realised what I had done and got a taxi to take it and her to the station near Nottingham but got caught in traffic so had to give up. I realised what I had done on arrival at the station and agonised about what I would say to Maria. I attended the concert but was too embarrassed to speak to her so explained what had happened to the concerts officer on my way out. The following day I received a message from Maria, who had been informed what happened, inviting me to video her performance the following week when she would be performing the same programme at St Martin in-the-Fields Church in an evening concert. After some deliberation it was arranged that Joan and I would go specially to Maria's concert provided that she had permission for me to video inside the church, which was granted. On the day of the performance Joan and I arrived very early whilst Maria was rehearsing and were introduced to her Mother. Some time before the concert was due to start Maria finished rehearsing and the four of us discussed what to do in the time available. We decided that the ladies would go out for a bite to eat and a drink whilst I stayed in the Church because I wanted to retain my optimum video position and make sure that no one interfered with the tripod I had set up, or the piano. There were many visitors looking round the Church and soon a crowd of them came to me asking about the pianist they had heard rehearsing, I was able to answer their questions (only because I had studied the programme from the previous week concert). It was nice that most of them said they would come back for the concert and I enjoyed relaxing in the lovely Church. Maria Marchant performed her concert to a huge audience and gave me permission to load two videos to YouTube, they are:- *Debussy, Berceuse héroique, Maria Marchant piano* and *Chopin Raindrop Prelude 28, Maria Marchant.* A few days later a huge bouquet of flowers were delivered to our door for Joan from Maria, what a lovely ending to a story that started so badly.

St Martin in-the-Fields church is another place that hosts many concerts and exhibitions being ideally situated for tourists on one side of Trafalgar Square whilst close by the National Gallery also have occasional concerts.

Tucked away on Marylebone Lane, just off Oxford Street is the rather grandiosely named Steinway Hall which is situated in the showroom of Steinway Pianos. They put on free lunchtime or evening concerts which give established performers or budding stars of the future a chance to perform to an audience. Sometimes the pianist allows me to video but with the proviso that they decide what can be loaded to YouTube. Here is one from 2013 with the title *Chopin Barcarolle Alvise Pascucci Piano.* On one occasion a young lady travelled from Italy, performed the concert at Steinway in London and flew home the next day and gave permission for every piece she played to be loaded to YouTube, here is just one of the nine that I recorded *Chopin Scherzo 3 Op 39 Giulia Rossini Piano.* The nine vidoes have had well over 9,000 views (February 2018). On another occasion I recorded a young pianist who played something written by a living composer. I was surprised that I enjoyed it and contacted the composer, Graham Fitkin, who gave permission to load to YouTube the title is, *Graham Fitkin, Fervent, Yoshio Hamano, piano.* This video has achieved nearly 5,000 views (February 2018). I believe that the combination of sound and vision created by a pianist is an art form, here is an example of what I mean from another concert at Steinway, *Chopin Rondo E-Flat Major, Natalia Sokolovskaya piano* Natalia gave me permission to load all of the programme she performed on that evening so there are seven more of her videos on YouTube. I have also attended lunchtime concerts at St Bride's Fleet Street, St Georges, Hanover Square and St Pancras Church, Euston Road.

I have been writing about formal concerts but sometimes an informal performance just happens somewhere. On 5 April 2017 I was rushing from the train at St Pancras station and had gone past the electric piano (donated by Elton John) when I heard a female voice singing so turned round and went back to see someone not only playing the piano but also accompanying herself on the piano. I listened to the end and asked if she would perform the song again whilst I video recorded it. She did, her name is Melisa Camba singing 'You Will Be Found' from the Broadway Musical 'Dear Evan Hansen'. Whilst she was performing in the busy concourse at the station with noise and people moving around I appreciated what talent she possesses. The YouTube video title is: *You Will Be Found, Melisa Camba, St Pancras Station London* this video has had over 1500 views, 66 likes, and some lovely comments, I include one here:-

From Duddu Rocha, No matter where she is right now, I am sure Melisa will remember this day forever. Undoubtedly, she is a great singer and the song is incredible! I already knew the song, but I felt like I had just heard it for the first time. But for me, the very touching thing in this video, it is that you, Michael, stopped, recorded and talked to her. This is exactly what this song is about. Thank you for doing that for her. Faith in the humanity restored.

I don't know the person who made the comment but what a lovely thing to write. I contacted Melisa whilst writing this book and this is her reply:-

Hello Michael

So great to hear from you! I hope everything is going well.

I am doing very good! I'm actively working at the Philippine Opera Company (my 3rd year) and Playbill Theatre Arts in Manila - trying my best to balance teaching and performing. Currently I am preparing for three productions - 1 in March (Philippine Opera Company's Love Sings) and 2 in April (UST Conservatory's West Side Story and Dulaang UP's The Kundiman Party). Also, I am currently in rehearsal with Artists' Theatre Company's Marco Polo the Musical which will open in Berlin this October 2018 and hopefully back in London the following year. Simultaneously with work, I am preparing for my post graduate studies this September as well. I have narrowed down my options to 2 schools: Mountview Academy of Theatre Arts (London) and New York University. Hope to make a final decision by April. I truly miss playing in St. Pancras. I really hope and pray to be back real soon.

Again, thank you for reaching out! Have a blessed day!

I sincerely hope that Melisa makes it into the entertainment industry but of course she is one of many people with the same objective.

Other venues where I have enjoyed excellent performances are:-

The Royal Academy of Music, Marylebone Road, they publish a comprehensive diary of events giving details of everything from lunchtime concerts, competitions, masterclasses, musical theatre, orchestral concerts, opera scenes and full scale operas. Some are free, others have moderate charges and they make visitors very welcome.

The Royal College of Music, Prince Consort Road, London SW7 (situated behind the Albert Hall). They also publish a diary of events and do similar things to the Academy.

Trinity Laban Conservatoire of Music and Dance is situated in the Old Royal Naval College at Greenwich and some of their concerts take place in the beautiful Old Naval College Chapel.

27 Scottish Army Invade Trafalgar Square

ON 14 AUGUST 2013 I had gone to London for my weekly visit and was travelling on a number 91 bus which goes from St Pancras Station to Trafalgar Square. As the bus approached the final destination I noticed a large amount of people most of whom were wearing blue and white clothing, flags and banners were being waved and footballs were flying high into the air. At that point someone on the bus said, 'they are Scottish football supporters because England are playing Scotland at Wembley tonight.' My intention had been have a quiet walk across the square on my way to the lunchtime concert at St James Church in Piccadilly but there was nothing quiet anywhere near that day. I got off the bus and mingled with the supporters who were well behaved apart from clambering over anything they could to wave their flags from as high as possible. I noticed a couple of men equipped with bagpipes and got interested when they were joined by a drummer in full regalia so I jostled for position to video as they prepared to play.

They started with 'Scotland the Brave' and then 'The Rowan Tree' as the crowd moved closer and a man stood next to me who was videoing his wife and children dancing and thoroughly enjoying themselves. I assumed that they were visitors from abroad but have never found out. What I do know, is that they added to the atmosphere of many people enjoying themselves in the sunshine and I exchanged a few friendly words with the father.

The National Gallery balcony, filled with spectators, formed a good backdrop to the video, whilst the Blue Cockerel sculpture, situated on the display plinth (42 seconds), could have been placed there for the occasion because it blended with the colours of the scarves and shirts of the supporters. I asked and got permission to load the video to YouTube and called it *Scottish Army Invade Trafalgar Square, Bagpipes & Drum*. There have been nearly 25.000 views (March 2018) and many comments, some informed me that the pipers names are, David Braidwood and Wee Bruce Miller Hamilton (Hammy) Burr and the drummer was Gordon Brown. Scotland were ahead twice in the game but England fought back to eventually win 3-2. It was a great day out for the estimated four thousand members of the 'Tartan Army' and tourists who happened to be there in Trafalgar Square that day.

One of the problems with YouTube is that occasionally people think it clever to add foul language or abusive comments on and this happened because the family that were near to me were black. The owner of the channel has three options, they are:

1. remove the comment.
2. report spam or abuse.
3. hide user from channel.

I had to exercise my right to use these options for three comments on this video and after a lot of thought I added this carefully worded comment of my own, which was:-

I enjoy good natured banter between supporters of teams and nationalities. I am an Englishman who enjoyed mingling with the Scottish fans and the tourists in Trafalgar Square who all were enjoying the music and atmosphere. However, please keep the comments within the YouTube boundaries of decency and racial respect. I have had to remove three comments which violated these rules, this is a shame because the writers meant well but they did not word their comments nicely. Michael Parkinson

28 Victorian Ballads to Limericks

THIS CHAPTER TELLS THE STORY of a VHS film I made in 1999, my idea was to combine victorian ballads with poetry written at that time and read in vision. Included here are:-

Seen but not heard - Miss Hayley Griffin
Christmas Day in the Workhouse - George R. Sims
Exam Nerves - Miss Hayley Griffin
The Old Soldier's Granddaughter - Richard Phipps
Billy's Rose - George R.Sims
Selwyn McGrigger - Richard Phipps
Limericks - Miss Hayley Griffin

One day in 1994 I was helping a lady who was moving from her bungalow into a nursing home, I was aware of stressful circumstances for her, to dispose of treasured possessions and move from a home into two rooms is a traumatic experience. Amy told me to bring boxes of books from the loft to be thrown away but gave me her favourite. It was 'The Dagonet and Other Poems' by G R Sims, published in 1903 and contained two of my favourite ballads 'Christmas Day in the Workhouse' and 'Billy's Rose'.

About two years later I developed an idea that I wanted to make a film of someone reading the two victorian ballads interspersed with modern written poetry. I collected some of my favourites that were published in the Nottingham Evening Post, my idea was to call it 'Then and Now.' The paper printed a few poems in each edition and one of my favourite contributors was Richard Phipps who went on to win the Evening Post Poetry award for 1998. I met Richard, we discussed my idea and he gave me permission to use any of his work. On 9 February 1998 a poem was published in the paper which had been written by a 17 year old girl who was confined to a wheelchair.

YouTube title
Hayley Griffin, Seen But Not Heard

Seen But Not Heard

Why do you look at me like that?
Why do you point and stare?
Why do you whisper behind my back
And pretend that I'm not there?
My feelings are as yours are
So why do you treat me thus?
Now that I'm stuck in this chair
Why do you make a fuss
If you're wondering what happened
And why I'm sitting here
Why don't you come and ask me?
I'll try and make it clear.
Why do you treat me in this way
And talk as though I can't hear
Ask my Mother the questions
That asking me you fear
I can do the same as you can,
I can laugh and smile and talk
I am just as you are inside
But outside my legs cannot walk,
This does not make me different
And you shouldn't treat me so
It's not my fault and I don't like
The fact that my legs won't go

Miss Hayley Griffin

I contacted the Post and told them about my film plan, they notified Hayley who telephoned me saying she was interested but was preparing for exams at the Nottingham Girls' High School so would be unable to do anything until later in the year. I mentioned my plan about her reading the two ballads and to my amazement she said in a matter of fact way 'I know them,' I then discovered that her mother was a teacher of English and had been reading the ballads to her and getting her to read them out loud since she was three. Hayley contacted me later, and we got on with the project, she had an excellent reciting style which you can watch and listen to:-

Christmas Day in the Workhouse

It is Christmas Day in the workhouse,
And the cold, bare walls are bright
With garlands of green and holly,
And the place is a pleasant sight:
For with clean-washed hands and faces
In a long and hungry line
The paupers sit at the tables,
For this is the hour they dine.

And the guardians and their ladies,
Although the wind is east,
Have come in their furs and wrappers,
To watch their charges feast:
To smile and be condescending,
Put pudding on pauper plates,
To be hosts at the workhouse banquet
They've paid for, - with the rates.

Oh, the paupers are meek and lowly
With their "Thank'ee kindly, mums"
So long as they fill their stomachs,
What matter it whence it comes?
But one of the old men mutters,
And pushes his plate aside:
"Great God!" he cries, "but it chokes me!
For this is the day *she* died."

The guardians gazed in horror,
The master's face went white;
"Did a pauper refuse the pudding?"
"Could their ears believe aright?"

Then the ladies clutched their husbands,
Thinking the man would die,
Struck by a bolt, or something,
By the outraged One on high.

But the pauper sat for a moment,
Then rose 'mid a silence grim,
For the others had ceased to chatter
And trembled in every limb.
He looked at the Guardians ladies,
Then eyeing their lords, he said,
"I eat not the food of villains
Whose hands are foul and red:

"Whose victims cry for vengeance
From their dank, unhallowed graves"
"He's drunk!" said the workhouse master.
"Or else he's mad and raves."
"Not drunk or mad," cried the pauper,
"But only a hunted beast,
Who, torn by the hounds and mangled,
Declines the vultures feast,

"I care not a curse for the guardians,
And I wont be dragged away.
Just let me have my fit out,
It's only on Christmas day
That the black past comes to goad me,
And prey on my burning brain;
I'll tell you the rest in a whisper,
I swear I wont shout again.

Keep your hands of me, curse you!
Hear me right to the end.
You come here to see how paupers
The season of Christmas spend.
You come here to watch us feeding,
As they watch the captured beast.

Hear why a penniless pauper
Spits on your paltry feast.

"Do you think I will take your bounty,
And let you smile and think
You're doing a noble action
With the parish's meat and drink?
Where is my wife, you traitors-
The poor old wife you slew?
Yes, by the God above us,
My Nance was killed by you!

"Last winter my wife lay dying,
Starved in a filthy den;
I had never been to the parish,-
I came to the parish then.
I swallowed my pride in coming,
For, ere the ruin came,
I held up my head as a trader,
And I bore a spotless name.

"I came to the parish, craving
Bread for a starving wife,
Bread for the woman who'd loved me
Through fifty years of life;
And what do you think they told me,
Mocking my awful grief?
That 'the House was open to us
But they wouldn't give out relief.'

I slunk to the filthy ally-
'Twas a cold, raw Christmas eve-
And the baker's shops were open,
Tempting a man to thieve;
But I clenched my fists together,
Holding my head awry,
So I came to her empty-handed,
And mournfully told her why.
"Then I told her 'the house' was open;

She had heard of the ways of *that,*
For her bloodless cheeks went crimson,
And up in her rags she sat,
Crying 'Bide the Christmas here, John,
We've never had one apart;
I think I can bear the hunger,-
The other would break my heart

All through that eve I watched her,
Holding her hand in mine,
Praying the Lord, and weeping
Till my lips were salt as brine.
I asked her once if she hungered,
And as she answered 'No'
The moon shone in at the window
Set in a wreath of snow.

Then the room was bathed in glory,
And I saw in my darling's eyes
The far-away look of wonder
That comes when the spirit flies;
And her lips were parched and parted,
And her reason came and went,
For she raved of our home in Devon,
Where our happiest years were spent.

"And the accents, long forgotten,
Came back to the tongue once more,
For she talked like the country lassie
I woo'd by the Devon shore.
Then she rose to her feet and trembled,
And fell on the rags and moaned,
And, 'Give me a crust - I'm famished-
For the love of God!' she groaned.

"I rushed from the room like a madman
And flew to the workhouse gate.
Crying, 'Food for a dying woman!'
And the answer came, 'too late.'
They drove me away with curses;
Then I fought with a dog in the street,
And tore from the mongrel's clutches
A crust he was trying to eat.

Back, through the filthy by-lanes!
Back, through the trampled slush!
Up to the crazy garret,
Wrapped in an awful hush.
My heart sank down at the threshold,
And I paused with a sudden thrill,
For there in the silvery moonlight
My Nance lay, cold and still.

Up to the blackened ceiling
The sunken eyes were cast-
I knew on those lips all bloodless
My name had been the last;
She'd called for her absent husband-
O God! had I but known!-
Had called in vain, and in anguish
Had died in that den - *alone*.

"Yes, there in a land of plenty
Lay a loving woman dead,
Cruelly starved and murdered
For a loaf of the parish bread.
At yonder gate last Christmas.
I craved for a human life.
You, who would feast us paupers,
What of my murdered wife?

There, get ye gone to your dinners:
Don't mind me in the least;
Think of the happy paupers
Eating your Christmas feast;
And when you recount their blessings
In your smug parochial way,
Say what you did for *me,* too,
Only last Christmas Day"

George R. Sims

YouTube title
Christmas Day in the Workhouse, Victorian Ballad, Hayley Griffin

Hayley wrote a poem called Exam Nerves and we got permission to use a classroom at the school she attended, with friends setting the scene.

YouTube title
Exam Nerves, Hayley Griffin, Nottingham Girls' High School

Exam Nerves

Restless fingers
Tapping feet
Pencils sharpened
Start off neat
Scribbling pens
Silence weighs
Ripping paper
Panic phase
Heads bowed
Knowledge brimming
Lucky mascot
Time slimming
Blank mind
Ticking clock
Sheet of paper
Answers not
Raised hand
Paper please
Stomach tightens
Hands freeze
Clock ticks
Or tick clocks
Mental anguish
Brain blocks
Last word
Wrist flops
Jelly brain
As clock stops

Miss Hayley Griffin

The Old Soldier's Granddaughter

Where are you going to Granddad
All dressed up in your Sunday best?
I've noticed that you've had a haircut and shave,
While your grey flannel trousers are pressed.

You look very smart in a collar and tie,
With your blazer all buttoned up tight.
Just look at the shine you have on your shoes,
You must have been cleaning all night.

Why do you have medals attached to your chest,
And a beret to cover your head?
Tell me what is that flower pinned to your lapel,
And why is its colour so red?

My dear little child I'm going to honour,
A debt I incurred long ago.
To young friends that I knew when I was a boy,
Names of Billy and Kenny and Joe.

While as to my dress, well I have to look smart,
For friends who were special as they.
And the beret I wear, is the one we all wore,
As we left for the front line that day.

The medals they earned, where the flowers grew wild,
As a bloom it seems simple and yet,
I wear it with pride, for the young men who died,
As a sign that I didn't forget.
And why is it Granddad you're looking so sad?
Why is that tear on your cheek?
Why is it your voice has a different sound,
It quivers whenever you speak.

That's something my dear that is hard to explain,
To someone so tender in years.
I was thinking of pals that I knew long ago,
And the memory brought to tears.

Can I come with you Granddad to visit your friends?
I promise I wont be a pest.
And can I have a flower exactly like yours,
To pin on the side of my chest.

Good day to you Bill, how are you doing?
Heres my little granddaughter called Paige.
How are you Ken, say wotcha young Joe,
You don't look a day older in age.

Who are you talking to Granddad?
There's nobody here only me.
Forgive me my child, I forgot you were there,
I was talking to my memory.

R. G. Phipps

Richard Phipps wrote the above poem that Hayley performed with an officer who was awarded the Military Cross in the second world war.

YouTube title
The Old Soldier's Granddaughter, Hayley Griffin, Richard Phipps.

George Robert Sims was born on 2 September 1847 and died on 4 September 1922 he was a very successful writer of poetry, ballads and plays. This ballad illustrates the way he drew attention to the plight of poor people and the cruelty that children had to endure.

YouTube title

Billy's Rose, Victorian Ballad, read by Hayley Griffin, G.R Sims

In July 2004 Charlotte Griffin and Marcos Langon, both aged 13, danced to Hayley's reading of this ballad, choreographed by Amanda Hall, at the Nottingham Arts Theatre as part of a Michael Parkinson Show. This can be seen on YouTube with the title *Billy's Rose, Danced, Charlotte/Marcos Narrated, Hayley.*

Billy's Rose

Billy's dead, and gone to glory - so is Billy's sister Nell:
There's a tale I know about them were I a poet I would tell;
Soft it comes, with perfume laden, like a breath of country air
Wafted down the filthy alley, bringing fragrant odours there.

In that vile and filthy alley, long ago one Winter's day,
Dying quick of want and fever, hapless, patient Billy lay
While beside him sat his sister, in the garret's dismal gloom,
Cheering with her gentle presence Billy's pathway to the tomb.

Many a tale of elf and fairy did she tell the dying child,
Till his eyes lost half their anguish and his worn, wan features smiled
Tales herself had heard hap-hazard, caught amid the Babel roar,
Lisped about by tiny gossips playing round their mothers' door

Then she felt his wasted fingers tighten feebly as she told
How beyond this dismal alley lay a land of shining gold,
Where, when all the pain was over - where, when all the tears were shed -
He would be a white frocked angel, with a gold thing on his head.

Then she told some garbled story of a kind-eyed Saviour's love,
How he'd built for little children great big playgrounds up above,
Where they sang and played at hop-scotch and at horses all the day,
And where beadles and policemen never frightened them away.

This was Nell's idea of heaven - just a bit of what she'd heard,
With a little bit invented, and a little bit inferred.
But her brother lay and listened, and he seemed to understand,
For he closed his eyes and murmured he could see the Promised Land.

"Yes" he whispered "I can see it - I can see it sister Nell;
Oh, the children look so happy, and they're all so strong and well;
I can see them there with Jesus - He is playing with them, too!
Let us run away and join them, if there's room for me and you."

She was eight, this little maiden, and her life had all been spent
In the garret and the alley, where they starved to pay the rent;
Where a drunken father's curses and a drunken mother's blows.
Drove her forth into the gutter from the day's dawn to its close.

But she knew enough, this outcast, just to tell the sinking boy,
"You must die before your able all these blessings to enjoy.
You must die," she whispered, "Billy, and I am not even ill;
But I'll come to you dear brother, - yes, I promise that I will.

You are dying, little brother, - you are dying, oh, so fast;
I heard father say to mother that he knew you couldn't last.
They will put you in a coffin, then you'll wake and be up there.
While I'm left alone to suffer, in this garret bleak and bare."

"Yes, I know it," answered Billy, "Ah, but, sister, I don't mind.
Gentle Jesus will not beat me; He's not cruel or unkind.
But I can't help thinking, Nelly, I should like to take away
Something, sister, that you gave me, I might look at every day.

"In the summer you remember how the mission took us out.
To a great green lovely meadow, where we played and ran about,
And the van that took us halted by a sweet bright patch of land,
Where the fine red blossoms, grew, dear, half as big as mother's hand.

"Nell, I asked the good kind teacher what they called such flowers as those,
And he told me, I remember, that the pretty name was rose.
I have never seen them since, dear - how I wish that I had one!
Just to keep and think of you, Nell, when I'm up beyond the sun."

Not a word said little Nelly; but at night when Billy slept,
On she flung her scanty garments and then down the stairs she crept.
Through the silent streets of London she ran nimbly as a fawn,
Running on and running ever till the night had changed to dawn.

When the foggy sun had risen, and the mist had cleared away,
All around her, wrapped in snowdrift, there the open country lay.
She was tired, her limbs were frozen, and the roads had cut her feet,
But there came no flowery gardens her poor tearful eyes to greet.

She had traced the road by asking - she had learnt the way to go;
She had found the famous meadow - it was wrapped in cruel snow,
Not a buttercup or daisy, not a single verdant blade
Showed its head above its prison, then she knelt her down and prayed.

With her eyes upcast to heaven, down she sank upon the ground,
And she prayed to God to tell her where the roses might be found.
Then the cold blast numbed her senses, and her sight grew strangely dim;
And a sudden awful tremor seemed to seize her every limb.

"Oh, a rose!" she moaned, "good Jesus - just a rose to take to Bill!"
And as she prayed a chariot came thundering down the hill.
And a lady sat there, toying with a red rose, rare and sweet;
As she passed she flung it from her, and it fell at Nelly's feet.

Just a word her lord had spoken caused her ladyship to fret,
And the rose had been his present so she flung it in a pet.
But the poor half-blinded Nelly thought it fallen from the skies,
And she murmured, "Thank you Jesus!" as she clasped the dainty prize.

*   *   *

Lo that night from out the alley did a child's soul pass away.
From dirt and sin and misery to where God's children play.
Lo that night, a wild, fierce snowstorm burst in fury o'er the land,
And at morn they found Nell frozen, with the red rose in her hand.

Billy's dead and gone to glory - so is Billy's sister Nell;
Am I bold to say this happened in the land where angels dwell;
That the children met in heaven, after all their earthly woes,
And that Nelly kissed her brother, and said, "Billy, here's your rose"?

George R. Sims

Poetry does not have to be serious, the final piece in this chapter is a story of a boy with huge ears and a bicycle riding fish. The YouTube video finishes with Hayley being naughty with limericks and a song called A Kiss at Midnight.

YouTube title
Fish Riding Bicycle, Hayley Griffin reads Selwyn McGrigger

Selwyn McGrigger

Selwyn McGrigger was sat by the river,
he'd baited his hook with a pound of pigs liver.
While laid by his side was his hot porridge gun.
he was keeping a promise to Gilbert, his son.

For early that day young Gilbert had been,
down to the river to wash his ears clean.
Now stop it you hear, its quite naughty to laugh,
just because Gilbert's ears were too big for the bath.

That's why it occurred every Saturday morning,
the bell in the Town Hall would ring out a warning.
For this was the day that young Gilbert to cheers,
travelled down to the river to wash out his ears.

The traffic was halted, for everyone knew,
the speed he could reach, when a northern wind blew.
With his feet on the crossbar, he passed through the throng,
as the wind filled his ears, and just blew him along.

Then once at the river young Gilbert would float,
on his back, as his ears made him act like a boat.
Where the lapping of waves slowly rocked him to sleep,
so he knew not of the stirrings that came from the deep.

For it seems that the river did hold a surprise,
a crafty old Pike, most enormous in size.
Whom it seems that for months had been trying to find,
a way to enact what it had on its mind.

Then slowly and silently, out of the deep,
it glided past Gilbert, who floated asleep.
Upon reaching the bank of the river the Pike,
leapt out of the water, and stole Gilbert's bike.

And once in the saddle returned with a flash,
to the deep river bed, with an almighty splash.
The noise was enough to disturb the lads sleep,
as he saw his bike vanishing, into the deep.

Young Gilbert got dressed and was shouting like mad,
'That's it, just you wait, I'm fetching me dad.'
As the bubbles appeared, young Gilbert could tell,
that the thief had his bike, and was ringing the bell.

When Gilbert reached home, he was nearly in tears,
as his dad listened to him, inspecting his ears.
'Their still a bit dirty, but don't worry son,
we'll go get you bike, fetch me my porridge gun.'

And once at the river he set out the bait,
then closing his eyes, said 'now Gilbert we wait.
You be the lookout and using your ears,
wake me up son, when the monster appears.'

Well they waited in silence, with never a word,
then out of the depths of the river it stirred.
Ignoring the liver, it rose from its place,
and lay looking at Gilbert, a smile on its face.

Then shaking his father, who woke with a roar,
of anger and rage, at the sight that he saw.
Out there on the river, and riding the bike,
and winking and waving, a large grinning Pike.

Well Selwyn jumped up feeling terribly bold,
grabbed the hot porridge gun, that by now had turned cold.
And aiming the weapon, he smiled as he said,
'I'll fill you with porridge, I'll blow off your head.'

As he squeezed on the trigger, heard only a click,
for the porridge had cooled, and by now was too thick.
It just trickled quite slowly, and fell with a thud,
where it turned hard as rock, as it mixed with the mud.

Then the Pike had hysterics, as it rolled in the swell,
doing wheelies and tricks, as it rang Gilberts bell.
'Ha ha' he retorted and chuckled with glee,
'You can do what you like, you'll never catch me.'

This made Selwyn angry, he beckoned his son,
and explained to the lad, bout what must be done.
Then the pair became busy, and after a while,
Had small lumps of porridge, all stacked in a pile.

The Pike all this time was enjoying the treat,
as he yelled 'look no hands,' while he stood on the seat.
Yes he thought he was clever, but got a surprise,
by a lump of cold porridge, between his two eyes.

Then another lump hit him, and brought him to tears,
as the pair fired lumps from young Gilberts ears.
Then a really large lump, hit him clean on the head,
and he fell from the bike, and was totally dead.

Then tying the fish to the bike by its tail,
they left, using young Gilberts ears like a sail.
Then they lit a big fire, and roasted the beast,
and invited the whole of the town to the feast.

Richard Phipps

The film, 'Then and Now' finished with Joan, Hayley and me having a bit of fun as the closing credits were preceded by Hayley reading two of her limericks:

There once was a doctor called Pitts
Who took a whole body to bits
He said to the Press
That he had to confess
He doesn't know where it all fits!

There once was a chess player called Rook
Who played all his moves from a book
One day he was said
To have played from his head
And then all his pieces got took

29 Southwark Cathedral to Bonington Theatre

IN JANUARY 2017 I NOTICED that Franz Schubert's Piano Quintet in A major D667, commonly known as 'The Trout' was to be performed in the afternoon of the seventh of March at Southwark Cathedral, London. I was interested because I had never been to that cathedral before, and like videoing in such surroundings, so set about asking permission to video for loading to YouTube. The musicians were senior students at Trinity Laban Conservatoire of Music and Dance based at Greenwich. I contacted the Professional Placements Coordinator who authorised me to approach the performers who gave their permission, subject to them approving the recordings before they were made public. The next stage was to obtain permission to video inside the Cathedral and this was granted by the Dean after the authorities had checked my YouTube channel and my credentials. I booked train tickets eight weeks before the day of travel, to get a good deal, and looked forward to the performance. By coincidence, I had already seen three of the performers and knew that they were good. One of the group, cellist Urŝka Horvat was appointed my contact with the players and she proved a capable liaison with excellent communication skills, my experience has been that it is unusual for a musician to respond to emails and supply information but Urŝka managed it.

On the day of the concert I got to Southwark Cathedral well before the start time, having made sure it was the correct one (close to London Bridge Station). The staff were very polite and helpful to me and allowed me to set my tripod up as the musicians began their final rehearsal. The musicians completed the pre performance rehearsal and went off to change into their concert dress. The audience started to arrive and I found that I knew some of them from other concerts that I had attended so all was going well.

At that point a member of the cathedral staff strode to a microphone and announced that police had ordered an immediate evacuation of the cathedral and Borough Market. We were instructed to move to Borough High Street and we were not to take personal belongings with us. We did as we were told though I did grab my coat but had to leave my tripod and other things there. It was a scary experience with crowds of people spilling out of shops, offices and market stalls and being marshalled by police with loud hailers. I walked past the deserted Borough Market where the pigeons were enjoying themselves because the stallholders had just gone and left all their produce uncovered. When I got to Borough High Street I learned that a huge area was being cleared because of a suspect vehicle near the Shard. We heard that many railway stations, and all the bridges in the area were closed. Noisy helicopters were hovering overhead and I just felt as though I wanted to be back home in Nottingham but even if I left my kit in the Cathedral there was no escape so just had to stand and wait. I had been enjoying days in London for many years but had never been involved in an evacuation before. After a couple of hours I heard a policeman giving the all clear so went back to the cathedral where the musicians were slowly appearing from different directions even some audience members came back. The concert was cancelled, so we were all disappointed, that was the end of months of planning by me and rehearsing for the dejected performers. We chatted and double bass player Enzo said, 'perhaps you could organise a concert at Nottingham for us' and I retorted 'it is easy to arrange a concert but not easy to sell tickets for it' and we said our goodbyes.

The papers reported the next day:

London on lockdown, London Bridge evacuated as bomb squad probed a suspicious vehicle, just yards from the Shard with hotels and offices shut down and workers told to stay away from their windows, the bomb squad scrambled the area and evacuated the main railway station and surrounding area. The situation was caused by a car near to the Shard with hazard lights flashing and windows broken.

Whilst it was an unpleasant experience at least it was a false alarm unlike the terrible carnage that occurred on Westminster bridge two weeks later and at Borough High Street, (the exact place that I had stood) three months later.

The week after the cancellation at Southwark I had a chance meeting with David Popple, the manager of the Bonington Theatre at Arnold and told him about the evacuation and subsequent cancellation of the concert. He offered to host a concert for a reasonable fee because he was keen to get music into the theatre so I got to work and promoted a concert for them at the theatre. I had vowed never to promote another concert but this sequence of events influenced breaking my pledge. I negotiated payment and travel fees with the players, got flyers printed and the concert was booked for a Sunday afternoon in October 2017. We put together a full programme which was enjoyed by the audience who were very impressed with the calibre of the performers and were impressed that they had travelled from London to entertain them. I believe it was the first time a piano quintet of international origin had performed at the

Bonington Theatre. They were:-
Francesca Fierro *piano* from Italy
Elena Abad *violin* from Spain
Jordi Morell *viola* from Spain
Urŝka Horvat *cello* from Slovenia
Enzo Manuel Delloglio *double bass* from Italy

This is the programme that they performed:-
Bottesini - Gran Duo Concertante for piano, violin and double bass
Beethoven - 'Eyeglasses' duo for viola and cello
Vaughan Williams - Piano Quintet in C minor
Schubert 'Trout' Piano Quintet in A major
Brahms Hungarian Dance Number 5

The musicians decided that they wanted to be known as the Bonington Quintet.

Three videos have been loaded to YouTube with these titles:-
Vaughan Williams Piano Quintet C minor, 1st mvt Bonington Quintet
Schubert Piano Quintet in A major 'Trout' 1st mvt, Bonington Quintet
Schubert Piano Quintet in A major 'Trout' 2nd mvt Bonington Quintet

30 Promotions, Concerts and Shows

IN 1963 I WAS WORKING as a cutter at a garment manufacturing company in Nottingham and one of my colleagues was Florrie who sang in the Boots Ladies Choir, she told me about various concerts that they gave and I organised one for them at St Mary's Church in Arnold, to raise funds for a youth club that I helped to run. This was my first venture into organising a concert and I had a brilliant idea of asking the Vicar to introduce the choir. He got a huge laugh because he introduced them as the Ladies Boots Choir.

In 2001 I promoted a concert for the Haru Piano Quintet at The Djanogly Recital Hall, University Park, Nottingham. The following year it was the Haru Piano Quartet at the same venue with another performance of the same programme at the British Geological Survey at Keyworth in Nottinghamshire on the following day.

In 2003 the venue was The Nottingham Arts Theatre and the show was called Wine Women and Song. There were only three performers, Anja Rossau *soprano,* James Gower *bass* and David Smith *piano,* the programme included favourites from Opera to Musical Theatre with piano solos. I asked classically trained James Gower if he would sing *Halfway to Paradise,* a song that Billy Fury achieved great success with and surprisingly he agreed. It worked well and the audience warmed to him and the other performers. In complete contrast James performed the following evening in 'Dream of Gerontius' with the Nottingham Back Choir at St Mary's Church in Nottingham.

The Nottingham Arts Theatre was the venue in 2004 for a show called 'A Ray of Sunshine' it featured local singer, Helen Ray who had been awarded 'The Queen's Golden Jubilee award for potential in music' two years earlier. Mellisa Brice *clarinet,* David Smith *piano* and Sagi Hartov *cello* completed the musicians in the line up. We had arranged for Sagi and David to stay overnight with us and called for something to eat on the way home. We stayed in the car, because we dare not leave the expensive cello unattended. When we arrived home Joan gave us drinks and told us not to be too late to bed because I had to be up at 5am to take Sagi to the station for the first train to London. Joan went to bed before midnight whilst the rest of us were winding down and reminiscing about previous concerts. At about 1am David went up to bed but came back downstairs after some time because he could not sleep. We continued to chat for so long that it became not worth going to bed, I eventually took Sagi to the station and helped take his luggage to the train, we shook hands and I was relieved to get home and sleep. We got up late the following morning and after leisurely breakfast I took David to the station at a more civilised time. A couple of days later I phoned Sagi and he told me that, after we shook hands, he put his luggage and cello in the rack, sat down and went straight to sleep, not waking until the train arrived at St Pancras. He immediately thought about his highly valued cello which fortunately was still there, he was a lucky man. The YouTube title is:- *Hershblume, Sagi Hartov cello David Smith piano*

Early in 2004 I chatted to two young ladies at a dance show in London, they were students at the London Studio Centre and told me that they would be performing in a show called 'Godspell' the following year and that the centre put on a show at different venues each year, to give the students experience of a travelling show. I mentioned that I promoted shows and they suggested that I speak to the centre with a view to them performing in Nottingham. I contacted the London Studio Centre which at that time was based in York Way, close to Kings Cross Station. It was a strange situation because they were not allowed to hire a theatre and put a show on but suggested a deal in which I would hire the theatre, do some promotion, and they would provide the show, with a box office split. We agreed a deal and it was fixed that three performances of the Joan Littlewood's 'Oh What a Lovely War' would be performed at the Nottingham Art's Theatre on Friday and Saturday first and second of July 2005 and that I would have collections and raffles for 'Jessies Fund'. I got on with organising and it was the easiest and most rewarding show I have been involved with. The Studio Centre provided loads of publicity material and I organised local display and distribution. The show opened at the Theatre Royal, Margate on 8 and 9 June, moved to the Kenneth More Theatre, Ilford 16 to 18 June, Mumford Theatre, Cambridge 22 and 23 June, Nottingham 1 and 2 July with Pleasance Theatre, London from 6 to 10 July. I was invited to go into Radio Nottingham to speak about the show prior to the Nottingham performances so Joan and I went to the show at Cambridge on 22 June for background information.

It was a brilliant production and we enjoyed it five times. There were 40 people involved including technical crew, musicians and performers. One of the performers was from Ireland, her father travelled to see his daughter in the Saturday night show, but she could not perform because of injuring herself walking into a lamp post the night before, I don't know how she walked into the lamp post though. The performers were all at the end of a three year course and were looking forward to the final week at the Pleasance Theatre, North London but two shows were cancelled and many people could not attend the others because of terror attacks in the area on 7 July resulting in 52 deaths and many others badly injured.

The Djanogly Recital Hall, on the campus of Nottingham University was the venue for a String Quartet Concert that I promoted on 24 September 2006, the quartet were formed at the Royal Academy of Music. The performers were Pedro Miereless *violin* Catrin Wynn Morgan *violin* Felix Tanner *viola* and Ken Ichinose *cello*. I arranged for Peter Palmer, music reviewer for Nottingham papers to introduce the concert and apparently all went well but I found out later that there had been an enormous problem with one of the performers.

I did discover the reason which is too sensitive to divulge.

My next venture was something entirely different, can you believe, Karaoke to Cabaret? This was in the Derek Randall Suite at Trent Bridge Cricket Ground on 11 October 2008 and featured the Keyworth School of Theatre Dance, Helen Vale played a couple of solo spots using electronic violin and backing tracks. The Karaoke was led by Paul and Anne. It was great fun, everyone enjoyed themselves. YouTube title is:- *Le Jazz Hot, Dancers Trent Bridge Cricket* The dancers were interspersed with Karaoke. I donated £420 to Jessie's Fund with enormous help from Joan who donated 60 prizes.

Phil Kelsall, who is principal organist of the Blackpool Tower Ballroom performed afternoon and evening concerts for me at the Nottingham Art's Theatre on 15 June 2009. I received a message from Phil a few days later in which he wrote

Just a note to thank you for making us all welcome last Monday. I enjoyed the venue and Dave (tech) was very helpful and obliging. I hope the audience enjoyed the music and that you managed to pass on a small amount to Jessie's Fund. I would also like to thank you and Joan for taking us all for dinner, which was a kind gesture. We all enjoyed the food and your company very much, Thanks again, Phil

He enclosed a cheque value £50 for Jessie's fund, making a total of £230 for the fund.

Year 2010 was the Phil Kelsall and Billy Dance Shows described in chapter one.

Sam Rollo choreographed dance to accompany Phil playing part of his programme at the Nottingham Arts Theatre on 17 April 2011. Fifteen dancers from The Rollo Academy of Performing Arts had rehearsed in their dance studio to CDs supplied by Phil so the success depended on Phil playing exactly as his recordings, this was something different to the normal and it went well. My Billy Fury Shows at Lytham St Annes and Mansfield were both in October of that year, they are described in chapters 2 and 3.

The Floral Pavilion at New Brighton, the Wirral was the venue for my promotion on 1 April 2012, described in chapter 4.

Mitra Alice Tham *piano* Erika Zeckser Owen *viola* and Hannah Lewis *cello* were the performers in my concert at the Djanogly Recital Hall on 28 June 2012. I asked Hannah to play this lovely piece by Franz Liszt and at the time of writing (March 2018) her performance on YouTube has attracted over 9300 views, the title is *Liszt Liebestraum, Hannah Lewis cello Mitra Alice Tham piano.* Another popular video from that concert starts with Mitra explaining that the tune for 'I'm Always Chasing Rainbows' (sung by Judy Garland in the film, Ziegfeld Girl, 1941) was taken from this piece, the YouTube title is *Chopin Fantaise Impromptu, I'm Always Chasing Rainbows.*

In 2013 I promoted three concerts over one weekend at different venues, Mansfield, Arnold and Ratcliffe on Trent in Nottinghamshire, the performers were a virtuoso violinist, singer Laura Roberts and pianist Chiho Tsunakawa. They performed a song written by Victor Herbert for his show 'The Enchantress'. I loaded it to The YouTube with the title: *Prima Donna, Bonington Theatre, Arnold.* This was going to be the last concert I promoted but events described in chapter 29 dictated that I would do just one more for the Bonington Quintet.

The Bonington Quintet, 8 October 2017 was my final promotion, chapter 29.

3 | Coeliac Disease Gluten Free Diet

FROM CHILDHOOD I HAD BEEN told by my parents that I had Coeliac disease but did not know anything about it and, because I thought I was normal did not bother to find out. I was born in June 1939, three months before the outbreak of the second world war. I have been constantly told that as a two year old baby the health visitor noticed that I was not gaining body weight and suffered incorrect bowel function so I was confined to hospital. Apparently, in those days, hospital visits by parents were only allowed once per week and my mother often said that she used to cry all week because she couldn't see me but when she went to see me she would cry on the way home because I looked so poorly. After many months the doctors decided that I had something called coeliac disease and was allowed home with mother being told that I should eat a lot of bananas but it was wartime and bananas were difficult to get. After some time mother was told to apply for a medical certificate to obtain them but this had to be signed by a hospital doctor. She often told me what happened. The queue to see the doctor stretched from inside the hospital, along the drive and out into Peel Street, mother had arrived at 8am and moved slowly forward until by about 12-30 she was inside the door of the hospital and by 1pm was at the door of the doctor who at that instant was putting his coat on to go out. Apparently his secretary pleaded with him to stay and deal with the few people left because 'they had been queuing all morning' the doctor dealt with a few more applicants and was rude to my mother because he did not think that bananas were important. Mum took the certificate and tramped round the shops but none of them had bananas in wartime England. At that time bread was not known to be a problem.

When I started school at five years of age I was so small that the headmaster wanted to delay my starting for a year so that I could catch up stature but regulations did not allow it. Bullying never happened to me because my size appeared to protect me from physical abuse but I suffered continued humiliation and was repeatedly ridiculed because of my size so grew up with an inferiority complex.

From the age of around 30 I started to suffer many nasty symptoms which I won't describe because you may be about to eat. I started to suffer constant itching on my arms but no one knew why, in my early forties I had many bouts of diarrhoea and vomiting particularly in summer and I suspected it was because of frequent salads. The problems got worse in my mid forties and the doctor ordered nothing to eat for a week and then a slice of toast, but I was as bad again, it continued for five weeks and Joan went to the doctors with me saying she was worried because I had gone down to six stone and was continuing to go to my stressful job. That caused the doctor to say 'maybe I should prescribe nerve pills' and I said 'when I was young I had something called coeliac disease, could it be anything to do with that?' to which the doctor said 'I don't think so as you are mid forties now, but how do you spell it?' He got a huge book out of the cabinet and thumbed through the pages until he found the appropriate one. He read for a while and asked if I was in a private health insurance scheme, and as I was, he made an appointment for me to be checked the following week. The people who administered the test were of the opinion that the medical authorities would not have known enough about it to know what it was in 1941 or to suggest a proper diet. The test proved positive and I was immediately put on a gluten free diet, and joined the local and national Coeliac Society. I was given a leaflet 'Understanding Coeliac Disease' and read that one of the symptoms was itching of arms or legs, I stuck rigidly to the diet and within about three weeks started to feel a bit better. Joan was brilliant, she got rid of everything from the pantry that might tempt me and denied herself luxuries that we had both enjoyed, like an iced bun or a hot dog.

Within a year I had increased my weight to over seven stone and have continued to build my weight and stamina. It was 1994 when I was diagnosed and it was amazing how little the medical profession knew about the disease then compared with today. The Coeliac society has worked to show awareness and they publish a Gluten Free Food Directory each year; the website **www. coeliac.org.uk** will provide information. Most shops have gluten free sections though the products are very expensive compared to normal foods. I eat a banana every day and do not get the itching any more.

The gluten free bread comes in precooked sealed packaging and has to be cooked in an oven before being eaten, this is no problem at home but can be when we go abroad. A friendly holiday representative providing a translation of what was required in Spanish and I printed copies which were helpful when we went on regular holidays to Torremolinos and the Spanish islands. This is the wording:-

Por favor

Solo 5 minutes

El pan al horno
Con el papel de plato

(Will you please cook this special gluten free bread in a hot oven for 5 minutes, please do not remove the foil)

On one occasion we went on our regular holiday to the island of Formentera and forgot to take our printed paper with us but Ian, a friend that we had met on many occasions offered to write something out, he was from Newcastle and had been taking Spanish lessons so was pleased to demonstrate what he had learned. We gave a loaf of bread, wrapped in its foil, and the note that Ian had written to the waiter at breakfast but a member of the kitchen staff brought it back to the table indicating he did not understand. Ian, who was sharing the table with us and his wife Kay, tried to explain in his best Geordie Spanish but loud shouting and waving of arms from the Spanish man ensued. Joan and I were completely perplexed and after breakfast I took the bread and note to reception who called the manager, they were not pleased that we had upset their staff member but took the bread from me and said they would get it done before the evening. When we all met at dinner that evening a rather embarrassed Ian explained that he had got his note wrong and in the discussion at the table the member of staff thought that he was being told to put himself in a hot oven for five minutes, when he found his mistake Ian had gone to the manager and explained so all was forgiven. That was before microwave ovens were invented.

In 2013 Joan and I went on the Eurostar train and booked a gluten free breakfast for me but when it was brought to the table there were two gluten free rolls that had not been put in the microwave. As they advertised that gluten free meals were available we were surprised that they did not know better. On another occasion the Nottingham branch of the Coeliac society organised a Christmas Dinner with food that was obviously all gluten free. The meal started with soup and bread roll and just as we starting to eat an announcement was made that the rolls were not gluten free and they were hurriedly collected in, Joan asked if she could keep hers but the caterers would not hear of it. In conclusion, it is reasonably easy to cater for a gluten free diet at home but is fraught with difficulty elsewhere.

32 Childhood Memories

I WAS BORN IN ARNOLD, Nottingham on 2 June 1939 and had an older sister, Ann and a younger sister, Joyce. Mother's name was Ethel and Dad, Fred, was a professional gardener who worked for the local council and combined gardening duties with part time retained fireman. If there was a fire call in the daytime the siren would sound and the fireman would rush from where ever they were working but at night time he was alerted by a bell in the house. Often on Sunday mornings he would go round checking the fire hydrants, using a fire engine for transport and sometimes took me with him. I loved sitting in the cab of the fire engine and sometimes would get out to help Dad clear the weeds, grass and nettles so they were easily assessable. The family house was situated on one side of Arnot Hill Park with the front gate opening to Arnot Hill road and the back gate opening on to what we called back path, leading into the park. I can vaguely remember talk of a bomb dropping nearby and that Josie Packwood's brother went out of the house and lay under the hedge, I thought that was a strange thing to do and could not understand why. I can distinctly remember big celebrations happening because the band stand on the top lawn of the park was cleaned up and there was to be a band that night. Dad was 'on duty' in the park and I was put to bed but was excited because I could hear the band playing, after a while mother took me out of bed, wrapped me in an eiderdown and carried me down back path to the Council House where huge crowds were gathered and they were all just standing, looking at a huge illuminated sign which said VV or VE, I can't remember which. The band were playing and top lawn, as we called it, was packed with people, it was smashing, I did not know what it was all about but everyone was very happy and I had never seen so many people in the park before, of course I know now that the celebrations were the end of the war in 1945.

I went to Arno Vale Infant School situated about half a mile from our front gate and 'us kids' walked to and from school where I developed a respect for the caretaker and can remember his name, to this day. He was very important to me because whatever big problem happened Mr Varley was sent for. If a child was sick Mr Varley would come along with a bucket of sawdust and a shovel and cover it over, if it snowed Mr Varley would clear a path from the gate to the door of the school and at, milk time Mr Varley would put the crates of milk out and every child would be given a small bottle of milk. If the boiler broke down Mr Varley would tell us to keep out coats on. Isn't it strange what things stick in childhood minds? I was given a three wheel 'bike' and spent hours riding round the park on it, that park gave me so much happiness as a child. But I haven't told you the best bit yet! If you went out on to back path, went up another path, across the drive and across the other side you came to Dad's allotment and on the other side of that was a wooden fence with posts and just two rails, 'us kids' used to scramble under the bottom rail and down an embankment to railway lines which went from Daybrook station to Gedling colliery. We would put a half penny or a small stone on the line and hide in the bushes while a train came past, the engine first with lots of noise, smoke and steam and then the trucks which seemed to go on for ever until the guards van on the end with the guard standing on the open part. We used to wait until the train had gone into the tunnel under Arnot Hill Road and creep out of the bushes to see the enormous flat halfpenny or the little hint of grey powder where the stone had been. Excitement happened one day because one of the trucks caught fire at Daybrook Station and my father was in the fire crew that attended, so he told us all about it when he got home. Whenever Dad got back from a fire, the first question was 'Where was the fire Dad?'

On one occasion myself and another lad had gone to 'hilly fields' after school one afternoon, there was a place with a few bricks situated so that we could gather some twigs and get a little fire going which we did, having done so many times before. We were happily sitting against our fire when we spotted a man running towards us and shouting at us. We did what any small boy would do in the circumstances and ran. The man got to our fire, kicked the bricks away and ran after us again, we gave him the slip and both went home. On arrival at home, I was in trouble because mum and sisters were all dressed up ready to go to the pictures and I was scruffy. Mum said that Dad would be home from work in a few minutes so I was to wait for him. Dad arrived and we were eating tea when his fire bell rang, Dad ran out leaving me worrying about the man that had kicked our fire because he could have scattered the burning sticks. Mum and my sisters got home first so I told them that Dad had gone to a fire. Dad soon arrived and in reply to the usual question said 'hilly fields, some kids lit a fire'. I survived a worrying few days and only told my parents about it when I was an adult. Dad got ten shillings for each callout and when the fire siren sounded which could be heard all over Arnold members of the family used to say, 'another ten bob for Fred'. I liked a story that my father often related:- at Arnold fire station there is a large tower with openings at different heights that were used for training purposes, on one occasion a training exercise was taking place in which the men had to jump out of one of the openings on to a large blanket held by the other men. One of the firemen adamantly refused to jump, he said 'I will not jump unless the flames are licking round my arse' and he never did.

On the right hand side of Dad's allotment was a field that had the two council horses when they were not working. One was called and Punch and the other one, (you've guessed), Judy and one occasion a new horse which was called Blossom was put in the field. A few days later on a Sunday evening the family had been out for a walk and had nearly reached home along back path when an older boy came running up to my father shouting 'there's been an accident, come quick' so Dad went running off with the boy leaving mum to take us home. That was a recurring memory of childhood that often father would have to run off because the fire bell in the house or the siren outside sounded or something had happened in the park. On this occasion we found out the next day that Blossom had tried to jump out of the field over some railings, had not made it, she had got two spikes in her belly and had to be shot, we were all devastated.

On one occasion, I was probably only five or six at the time, mum told me not to go back to school one afternoon because she was taking me out, she took me to the Nottingham Arts Theatre. All I can remember is that there were two grand pianos in front of us and people dancing on stage. I absolutely loved it and always remembered the occasion when I heard that music. A few months before mother died I was sitting with her and that music came on the radio, I immediately said 'this is from that thing you took to me see when you kept me of school', mum was surprised that I could remember the music, she had assumed I had not liked it because 'I sat there and never said a word' she told me there was no dialogue, just dancing to those two pianos. It was strange that she had lived for over 50 years thinking I had not liked it and I had lived with happy memories for all those years.

Time moved on and I got more adventurous, a friend named Anthony Hemm, 'Tant' and I gave ourselves a challenge to climb every tree in Arnold Park during summer holidays. We made great progress apart from me falling out of one and bouncing from the top of a hedge and into a field I was a bit shaken but soon got up the next tree. We managed to do all of them except one, a huge beech tree with a smooth trunk and lower branches about eight feet from the ground, this was situated in a field not far from where he and I lived. One morning Tant turned up at our back door with a canvas bag and said, 'we can climb that big tree today'. He showed me what was in the bag, some huge nails and a big hammer, we got to the tree and put a few nails into the trunk so we could reach the lower branch and the rest was easy, we were soon at the top and feeling very pleased with ourselves. I think we left the nails in the trunk and I can't recall knowing that we had done wrong but a few days later a letter arrived from the council and I was in trouble. Mum told me that the letter said that I had been seen hammering nails into the big tree in the field near back path and if it happened again the family would be thrown out of the house. I was sent to bed and spent all day in my room till Dad came home, he came to see me and read the letter to me and did not shout but explained that it was wrong to hammer nails into trees because it could damage the tree. I certainly have remembered that lesson all my life and have had reason to tell people about it myself. Mother appeared to calm down because she accepted it was the other lad's fault really! Aren't mothers wonderful?

I was given a black and white rabbit that I named Frisky and my friend Stuart Barker had one called Timothy. Stuarts family went on holiday and brought his rabbit for me to look after but a problem developed a few weeks later as Stuart and his father came to see me because Timothy who was supposed to be male was expecting babies so was being renamed Topsy. I was asked if I had put them together and admitted that I had but apparently caused amusement amongst the adults by saying, 'they were only together for a few minutes'.

Stuart's father was part of a group that owned a big shop in Nottingham named Henry Barker, Smart and Brown. He had a car and on Saturday mornings took us to the Metropole Cinema for the ABC minors film club. The cinema was packed for those shows and any member who had a birthday in the preceding week was invited up on stage, I remember there was always a long line of them and we used to sing a song, the words were:-

We are the girls and boys well known as,
Minors of the ABC.
And every Saturday all line up
To see the films we like and shout aloud with glee
We like to laugh and have a sing song
Just a happy crowd are we——
We are all pals together
We're minors of the ABC

Claire Greig gave me permission to use music from her CD First Impressions combined with these on screen words.

YouTube title
Minors of the ABC, Children's picture club

I had a cousin Malcolm who was five months younger than me and lived close by. He and I were great pals but I was envious of him because he played for the school football team. For many years we used to go to Notts County and Nottingham Forest Football matches which we made an all day event. Malc was a Forest supporter and me a County fan, we used to leave Arnold early in the morning, get the bus to Nottingham and walk towards the football ground along the canal banks. There were no floodlights in those days so in winter the games would kick off early so they would finish in daylight I think they used to unlock the gates about two and a half hours before kick off and we were usually there early to get a good position in the 'kids pen' where we stood until the game finished, then we would wend our way back along the canal towpaths to the city centre and our bus back home. In summer we went to Notts Cricket at Trent Bridge where we were junior members for ten bob a season which also gave us entrance to test matches.

My father changed his employment and worked on the surface at the Calverton Colliery so the family moved to a newly built council house at Arnold.

I moved on to Arnold Robert Mellors County Secondary School in 1950, something I liked about the school was that at assembly on Monday they played a piece of music to us and repeated it every day of the week. They also took us on bus trips to orchestral concerts at the Albert Hall in Nottingham. Although I was not brilliant academically I managed to stay in the A stream and there were over 40 lads in the class. I had been given a bicycle by my parents and used to ride around the country lanes around Arnold and ventured as far as Lincoln one day in the school holidays.

My sisters had a friend called Pat Stacey who set up a club for her friends which she called 'The Sheredean Club', she organised little concerts and plays in the family back garden and persuaded her father to provide music. They got ambitious and organised a little show in the hall of Front Street Baptist Church at Arnold, I was asked to operate the curtains, one rope to open and another one to close, so I had to stand at the side of the stage. One of the routines was South Sea Island dancing for which Dad had provided the raffia for the grass skirts. I really enjoyed the show and my close up view of the dancing girls. A full account of the Sheredean club is in the Arnold Library.

When I was in my third year I was appointed a prefect and given the task of making tea for the teachers for the morning and afternoon breaks and was given the prefects prize, probably for making a nice cup of tea. Woodwork was my favourite subject and I won a prize for making a bedside cabinet which I still use today.

In the spring and summer of my last two years at school I got myself a part time job working on a farm for two hours Monday to Friday and fours hours on Saturday. The way it worked would not be allowed today but it did me no harm. At the end of school in the afternoon I would cycle to a farm called Derry Mount, owned by Tommy Hammond who are still well known farmers in the area. I think there were about twenty five of us, girls and boys, and we climbed on to the back of an open lorry and were taken to the field where they wanted us to work. We climbed down from the lorry and did a variety of jobs, sometimes thinning out various seedlings, sometimes weeding along the rows of crops or sprinkling sulphate of ammonia around crops and many other things. I was paid 11 pence per hour so if we were not rained off I was earning twelve shillings and ten pence a week. We got gradual increases so got up to one shilling and one penny per hour by the time I left school.

In the autumn we used to go 'spud picking' and don't let anyone tell you it was called anything different. On one occasion we were taken out to somewhere near Southwell to another farm and the field was massive with probably about 100 pickers working. All was going well but suddenly everything came to a standstill. There appeared to be a problem with the tractor and being a nosy child I went to see what it was. The farmer was doing something with spanners and took a part off the 'spinner' (that was the mechanism that spun the potatoes out). The farmer said he would have to go to Newark to get another one and, looking at me said, 'Do you want to come with me son?' I jumped at the chance and he invited me to get into the passenger seat of a scruffy truck. The farmer did not say much as he drove along the edge of a few fields but drove to a ramshackle looking building, stopped and told me to get out and wait as he jumped out and opened the doors of the building. He drove out in a shiny big Rolls Royce car and opened the door for me to get in. Off we went and eventually stopped outside a large agricultural machinery place and I remained in the beautiful car whilst the farmer went in. He came out after a few minutes with a replacement part in his hand and drove back to the farm where we transferred to the truck and back to the field. So, if you see someone driving along in a scruffy truck be aware that his other car could be a Rolls Royce.

My parents allowed me to keep all my earnings in exchange for forfeiting my pocket money so I was happy, they said that my sisters got their spending money for being good and I said that, 'I was good for nothing.'

When I left school I got a job in the coach building department of a garage and did not like the work much, in 1954, the government brought in a law that every vehicle had to have two red reflectors, one on each side of the back. I fitted many of these and one customer stood and talked to me as I fitted the reflectors to his car. He was a director of a blouse factory across the road and he suggested that I would be better off working in his factory so I accepted his interview offer and went to see him at the factory. I decided to take the job at Claymar Blouses so that is how I got into the rag trade.

At about that time I bought a used James 147cc motor bike and found it much easier than my push bike and soon passed my driving test. I had a cousin, Margaret, who wanted to learn to dance so we went on the motor bike into Nottingham to 'Hanford and Richards' dance studio one night a week and mastered a few basic dances.

I was officially apprenticed to be a cutter but the company paid for me to have driving lessons and I finished up doing more driving than cutting. By the time I was approaching 18 I had to make a decision if I should apply for deferment of National Service until I was 21 or to start my two years National Service at 18 and decided on the latter because I wanted to get it done.

33 National Service

I WAS CONSCRIPTED INTO THE Army as a National Serviceman on 22 January 1959 and was sent to Blenheim Barracks in Aldershot for basic training. I was in intake 482, Royal Army Service Corps, on arrival at the Barracks I was put in a group of men where we went through documentation, medical examination and injections involving walking slowly along as we were jabbed with the same needle. We were escorted to the Quartermaster store and were issued with a full set of kit, someone told me that the store had a motto: 'If it fits, bring it back and we'll change it'. We were given something to eat and taken to a big wooden hut that they called a barrack room, a soldier told us which bed and locker was allocated to each man and then walked out. There was no instruction about what would happen next, we were just left to our own devices. It was probably about 6pm in the evening by then. We chatted amongst our selves and it was interesting finding out about where the other people had come from and their thoughts on the situation we found ourselves in. Some had the attitude that they would not be broken by the army, some were not going to be told what to do, some talked regretfully about having to leave a good job to do national service. It emerged that one chap, who was even smaller than me was a professional jockey, he was a great raconteur and told some interesting stories, then we started telling jokes and had a good laugh. Time slipped by, 8pm, 9pm, 10pm, and at 11pm we decided that no one was coming back so we made our beds up and turned in.

Get up, I heard a voice shout, crash went the barrack door as it was thrown wide open, stamp, stamp, stamp sounded boots on the wooden floor as a soldier with two stripes on his sleeve snarled at every one of us in turn. He told us that our parents had fun having us but he had got us now and it was not fun for him because he hated us. It was 5am, he ordered us to put some horrible big boots on we had been issued the afternoon before.

He chased, harried, insulted and made us run to a big room where a spartan self service breakfast awaited. That's enough of that, I will just describe what happened to me from now on.

If I had committed a bad crime I could not have been treated worse than the six weeks basic training. Well, that is what they called it, I describe it as six weeks of basic humiliation, degradation and mental cruelty. I think the worse thing for me was being drilled on a square with open railings on one side where people going about their civilian lives doing mundane things that I had taken for granted but suddenly could not do. They were walking along the pavement, standing at bus stops, getting on buses and pursuing their civilian lives whilst I was a prisoner in a hostile environment. This must be as unhappy to read as it is to write so I will skip a few weeks.

An officer sitting behind a big desk smiled and spoke to me in friendly terms, 'I am here to help you decide what trade you want to follow during your National Service.' I noticed papers on the desk that I had completed in my aptitude tests the day before. In response to me saying that I would like to be a driver, he said, I think these tests show that you would make a very good clerk. That surprised me because my sisters were both clerks and I accepted that was because they were better educated than me. He continued, we can put you on an eight week clerical training course and they will treat you better than this lot here. I agreed and signed the piece of paper he put in front of me. That was the way the Army worked, the iron fist to the velvet glove.

The great day arrived, I was moved from Blenheim to Willems Barracks situated on the other side of Aldershot, whilst we had to do some foot and arms training the emphasis was on clerical training and would you believe? We had to learn to type! That was fun, about 20 chaps sitting in a room with an instructor telling us all about home keys, which I initially thought was a keyring holding your house keys. There was a desk each complete with a type-writer and a pile of paper, we were shown how to feed paper in. Then for two hours we had to type the home keys, they were:- asdf with the fingers of the left hand and ;lkj with the right hand. The next day we were introduced to g, h and gradually over subsequent lessons, all the letters of the alphabet, eventually we were typing 'The quick Red Fox jumps over the lazy Brown Dog.' This is called a 'pangram' because it includes all the letters of the alphabet.

We were given instruction on understanding Queen's Regulations, phonetic alphabet, filing and office procedures. It was not all work, I spotted a notice asking for volunteers for the Garrison Choir with a practice one evening a week. I applied and was told to report to the Church, not far from the barracks at 7-30pm one evening. There were six of us and the organist played whilst we sang a hymn, he explained that we only had to do one hymn a week and there would probably not be any services so we need not take it too seriously. He told us that we could go if we wanted or stay and listen to him playing. We stayed and enjoyed him playing a lovely selection of light music. His favourite was the Leroy Anderson composition Blue Tango and he played it over and over again, it sounded great on that Church organ. In 2008 I was attending a performance by Len Rawle at Nottingham Organ Society and he mentioned that he did National Service based at Aldershot so, during the interval, he confirmed that he was the organist I had met at Aldershot. Whilst writing this book I sent him a message asking if I could mention him and received this reply:-

Hello Michael, Good to hear from you even if it is yet another gentle reminder of just how fast one's life rushes by. Thankfully my music making keeps me young at heart and still performing. My 2 years National Service was made all the more bearable by a steadily increasing number of opportunities to keep my fingers moving. First up was the piano in the NAAFI then the Garrison Church beckoned followed by officers mess concerts and passing out parade concerts. I then targeted the Ritz Cinema and played for the Saturday children's matinees until my last day's service. Not long after, the manager heard there was an organist keen to play anywhere, the Empire theatre next to the Ritz wanted me to open their Sunday film show. Next up came the Hammond organ at Bordon Camp. So one way and another, National Service provided me with invaluable opportunities. Little did I think such a good grounding would lead to an MBE for services to music - All I have ever done really was to take opportunities as they presented themselves. Although now 80 I have a full 2018 diary with concerts both here and abroad providing some great journeys not to mention catching up with many wonderful friends. I trust you are fit and well and wish you great success with the book. It will be an honour to be a small part of it. Kind regards, Len.

It was lovely to receive this message and interesting that it is 59 years since Len provided such enjoyment for me.

About five weeks into the course we all had to take part in a huge mobilisation exercise which lasted five days and involved being moved by bus, rail and lorry to various places and assuming a new identity that we were given for the exercise, it was interesting but interfered with our clerical training.

We were told that there would be exams at the end of the course and if we got an 80% pass rate we may be rewarded with a special posting to a British Embassy abroad or the War Office in London. Between 60 and 80% would be a pass mark meaning probably Germany. My ambition was to get to the War Office because I had met a man from Nottingham who had been posted there, he was living in civilian accommodation and wore civvies to work, I could not believe his story but my goal was 80%.

The examination at the end of the course took a whole day and included a touch typing exam, two days later the results were put on the notice board, I had achieved 78.3% so had passed but failed to achieve the special posting mark, the notice stated that we had to attend the following day for posting results. We had to stand in a smart regimental line and take our turn for the important posting interview and when my turn came the officer told me that because of the mobilisation exercise the special posting mark had been changed to 78% so I had just crept in. The officer showed me a list and asked my choice, of course, it was 'The War Office' and he said he would do his best. Imagine my delight when I received a notification of posting to the War Office. I had achieved my dream.

I was given a few days leave and a travel warrant to London with instructions to report to the Camp Commandant, Lansdowne House, Berkely Square, London, on a Monday morning. On arrival I was ushered into an office where a man in civilian clothes gave me astonishing information:-

1 I was to work in the Directorate of Military Intelligence, section MI3

2 I was immediately being promoted to the rank of Lance Corporal but as acting rank of Corporal for payment purposes.

3 There was no military accommodation so I would be given a lodging out allowance and would have to find lodgings myself. The man said that he had a telephone number of a lady that provided such accommodation and offered to phone her for me. He did just that and I found that her name was Mrs Patrick who lived on Brondesbury Road, Kilburn and she would provide bed and breakfast for under the lodging out allowance but I had to buy the rest of my meals.

4 I was to be given a travel pass for the journey between central London to Kilburn.

5 I was to attend an induction course at a place called Someries House, starting in about two weeks.

6 I was to provide civilian clothes for work but would wear uniform for pay parade.

7 I was to sign the official secrets act and communication intelligence registration.

8 I was given the rest of the day to get into the lodgings at Kilburn.

9 I was to report in uniform the next day to an office in the War Office building on Whitehall.

If this book was fiction it would be difficult to make all this up but sometimes fact can be stranger than fiction. I set off to Kilburn with the address on a piece of paper and found Mrs and Mr Patrick, they took me to a room on the third floor and showed me my bed situated in a bay window area overlooking Brondesbury Road. I was to share with two other chaps who were in the services. They showed me the large breakfast room on the ground floor and gave me a list of rules.

The next morning I reported to the specified place in the War Office and had to sign various papers abut my conduct and official secrets. I was told about the various departments of Military Intelligence and some were so secret that we were not allowed to mention the name of the department. We had to refer to them as 'our friends'. I was told that my position would be Corporal Clerk and then taken to the office where I had to work. It was situated on the ground floor with windows overlooking Whitehall and about 100 yards towards Trafalgar Square from the Horse Guards.

The War Office was staffed by some military and some civilian personnel and I was introduced to my work colleagues and soon found what a lovely but mixed group of people they were. The civilians were British and the foreign ones had defected or had arrived in Britain by various means, from mainly Iron Curtain countries, they were all linguists or translators. Even now it would not be discreet to put into print what the function of the office was or how they operated. I was told that I could wear civilian clothes from then on but had to keep my army uniform in a large filing cabinet because I had to wear it for pay parade once every four weeks. Pay parade was a crazy situation because all the other ranks took their uniforms into the toilets, got changed, took their civilian clothes back to the office before going to a room where the pay parade took place. I had to move 'in a smart and soldier like manner' to the desk occupied by civilian clothed pay corps staff to receive my pay packet. Then it was back to the office, collect civvies, toilet to change, back to the office and put uniform in cabinet. After I had been there a few months they changed it so that we only had to wear uniform once every third month and eventually we got paid wearing civilian clothes all the time.

Anyway, back to my induction course, it only lasted for five days but on the Friday I received a message from one of my MI3 colleagues, they had put my name in and won the ticket allocated to the Intelligence Directorate for Trooping the Colour: The Queen's Birthday Parade which was to take place the next day. It was of course the parade ground on the edge of St James Park, the date was 11 June 1960. It was a fantastic experience to attend that parade and combined with what I had learned about my new colleagues made me very proud to be British and I still am.

It transpired that the previous incumbent of my job had not been very good so it was easy to impress. The Government Communication Head Quarters, GCHQ, based at Cheltenham, used codebreaking techniques to intercept, translate and print messages which were passed around the MI sections in locked green boxes, (same as the red boxes used for cabinet papers). One of my jobs was to sign for the box brought to MI3, unlock and pass the appropriate papers to the relevant person in the office for extraction of information and then replace the papers, lock the box and take it to the next MI section so I soon found my way around the huge War Office building.

I was told that the BBC Playhouse Theatre situated opposite Charing Cross tube station was a couple of minutes walk away and that anyone could go to the live or recorded shows they did there. It became a regular lunchtime treat, Monday was a variety programme featuring current singing and comedy stars, Wednesday was Bob Miller and the Miller Men big band and Friday was David Eade and the Oscar Rabin big band. All of these programmes had guest artists so we saw most of the stars including Billy Fury. Other lunchtime favourite venues were the National Gallery or Westminster Abbey which was free for visitors in those days. Just behind St Martin in the Fields Church was the Nuffield Centre a place that Lord Nuffield provided for servicemen to relax and they had an arrangement with the London Theatres whereby at 5pm each evening vouchers were issued allowing free tickets for shows, concerts and plays. I had to work until 5-30pm but was allowed to go across to obtain a voucher for a show then went back to the office to make up for lost time before going to a theatre. London was a good place to be if you were a serviceman with time to enjoy yourself and I took full advantage of it. Once every three months I had to perform an all night duty which could be in any room in the War Office and that entailed general clerical work dealing with urgent things that cropped up. There was a couch provided if there was any opportunity to sleep but sometimes I had to work right through the night. On one occasion there was a huge document that had to be typed, one plus 3 copies on a cabinet typewriter with three spaces between each line of typing and no alterations were allowed so if I made a mistake I had to throw away the four pages, put new carbon paper in and start that page again. The classification was Top Secret so I had to take all my aborted efforts to the shredding room and shred them. The deadline was 7am and I just managed to finish at 6-30.

The comradeship in the digs at Kilburn was good, one chap played guitar and we joined in singing. His favourite was 'Poisoning Pigeons in the Park' and we got told off for singing it at midnight. I could go home from Friday until Sunday evening so used my James motor bike for the journey but on one occasion had mechanical problems and did not get to Kilburn until about 4am. I got to bed not knowing that the other two of my room mates had arranged to go straight into their offices that morning. I awoke with sunlight streaming through the window, it was 11 o'clock and I should have been in the office at 9am. I arrived after 11.30 and explained what had happened to the Colonel who was in charge of the office. He said, 'Have you just come in without any breakfast?' When I confirmed that I had he said 'Go up to the luncheon club and get yourself something to eat'. He was a descendent of the Russian Royal Family and was given the rank of Colonel because of the job he did and had no military background. We all just called him Colonel, he had constant meetings with a variety of shady but interesting looking characters.

After I had been at the War office for about eight months I was in the Nuffield Centre one evening and happened to meet a man who had been at Robert Mellors School whilst I was there. He was in the guards and could not believe what I was doing saying, 'You should sign on as a regular for three years, you would get more pay, and a married hiring flat, you've got it cushy mate'. I would not hear of it but discussed it with my wife the following day who was all for it. I requested a meeting with the Camp Commandant who said that if I signed on for three years I would stay in my job at MI3 provided I behaved myself. So on the 14 October 1959 I signed on for three years, I always had the worry at the back of my mind about being posted to some harsh military place but it never happened.

We were allocated a flat above a shop at North Cheam near Morden which is at the end of the Northern line, I was issued with a season ticket for the tube and given regular cash funding for the bus between North Cheam and Morden but after a while got a bicycle and season ticket to leave it at Morden Station so I saved a few bob a week. The flat was infested with mice and I spent ages getting rid of them and their nests, I filled every space with a mixture of Red Lead and Putty, I did eventually succeed. It was a nice place to live with interesting walks to Cheam village, Ewell or Worcester park and Nonsuch Park was not far away. After a while I obtained a part time job as a barman at the Queen Victoria, North Cheam, having got permission from the Camp Commandant.

With about two years still to serve the Colonel asked me to change jobs with one of the civil servants who worked in the office. It would not be prudent to explain why but he swopped to my job of filing, typing and tramping round with the green boxes and I did his job of extracting and collating necessary intelligence data from the various documents available. I found it very interesting and the longer I worked with the foreign team the more respect I had for them because I learned some of their background stories. My final day in the office was an emotional experience and my fellow workers presented me with a lovely gift.

National Service gave me a second chance in life, I learned new skills and though I hated the first six weeks I did 3 years and 9 months followed by 7 years on the Army Emergency Reserve.

34 Back Home

I HAD BEEN LOOKING FORWARD to returning to Nottingham after my Army service but it was an anti climax. I got a job as a cutter in a small cut, make and trim garment maker in the Lace Market area, they used to put impressive woven labels with a picture of the Eiffel Tower and 'Made In Paris' in some of the garments that went to well known London shops.

After about a year in this job I was walking in Nottingham one lunchtime when I happened to 'bump into' a man that I knew before going into the Army. He owned a couple of cafes plus, mobile hot dog sales units and had a franchise for selling hot dogs at Mallory Park, the motor racing circuit in Leicestershire. He and his father owned a baby clothes manufacturing unit and an embroidery business. I had worked part time in his catering outlets and we had worked together at Mallory Park so we knew each other well. He wanted to know what I had done in the Army and what I was doing now. When I told him he asked if I would consider working for him at his children's clothing factory, situated at a place called Clifton which is three miles south of Nottingham but I lived four miles to the north of Nottingham. We arranged that I would go for an interview at the factory the following Saturday morning. He offered me the job of, 'Cutting Room Manager' good wages and told me that, a car went with the job. The car was a Morris 1000 which was parked outside his office and he showed me around the factory where there were a few sewing machinists working. It appeared too good to be true and so it proved. The cutting room that I was to be the manager of was just a couple of tables in the machine room and the cutting staff were myself, an old lady and a young girl who had not been told that a manager was to be in charge of them. The car that went with the job, went, but not with the job because it was the one that the Owner's wife used and she resented the fact that her husband had said that I could use it. So, from those humble beginnings I grew with the business. After about six months the owner bought a green A35 van and I was allowed to use it for business, pleasure and transport from home to work.

The owner's objective was that the business would become a major supplier of children's school wear to British Home Stores and he achieved this aim after about three years. At this time a large extension was built, providing a cutting room, cloth and trimming storage and a design room. By that time I was working as cutting room manager, with a staff of ten people plus, calculating, ordering and stock controlling all the fabric and commodities used in the factory. The company got bigger, I became general manager with a proper car and assumed more responsibility. The company was bought out by a larger business that owned three other factories and they appointed me Production Director with a Managing Director appointed from the parent company.

For a number of years things went well, the business got bigger and computers were introduced. For many years I had been completing a Suppliers Report which had to be put in the post to reach BHS by Monday morning. It was a detailed document giving full details of work in progress and most importantly what garments of every style, size and colour could be despatched to all the stores if they 'called them off'. BHS eventually decreed that the report had to be completed and sent as an email attachment. This posed a problem because I was not computer literate so had to compile the report on a Friday afternoon as normal and give it to the only person in the company that could work a computer and she often had to work late to copy my figures and send it.

After some soul searching I went to my Managing Director, who could not use one himself, and suggested that I learned to use a computer so that I could generate the report myself. His reply was symptomatic of many people at that time. 'I pay you to manage the factory, not to mess about on a computer.' The company started to struggle financially and I often found myself in an awkward situation when chasing a supplier who had not delivered fabric on time, they would often tell me to speak to our accounts department because we had not paid for the last lot yet.

A proposition was put to me that I could help alleviate the financial problems facing the company by becoming a shareholding director which involved putting a large sum of money into the business by taking out a loan with the house, that Joan and I owned, as security. We discussed it and refused, no way would we risk losing our house for me to have the egoistic honour of being a part owner of the business. I suspected that the writing was on the wall and some months later, after a sleepless night, I said to Joan 'if I am made redundant I will do for elderly people what you and I have done for our own parents over the years.', we never mentioned it again but we were both prepared.

The Managing Director retired two years later and the business was bought by two computer expert men who were going to transform the business, one was an accountant, the other a production man. When they moved in they had a meeting with the company accountant and myself in which they said that they wanted us both because we were important parts of the business. After three months they discharged the company accountant and after six months they discharged me. My bombshell happened on a Friday afternoon in the middle of stocktaking. I was called into a meeting and given five minutes to clear my desk and one week to give up my company car. I was 49 years of age and had been with the company for 26 years and, although I had known that it was a possibility it was still a shock. The official reason was 'I was not computer literate'. Driving home and telling Joan what had happened was an ordeal I will never forget but she said 'We will have to do your plan'. I was helped by the government body, Advisory Conciliation and Arbitration Service (ACAS) of the ministry of labour who helped get a better severance deal and negotiated me keeping the company car for three months. I did not get a great financial deal but it was a start and I was lucky because a year later the company went into liquidation and if I had still been there I would have got very little.

By coincidence, I had an appointment with my doctor on the Saturday morning I told him about what had happened and that I planned to start a business with Joan where we would work for elderly people, doing the garden or anything they wanted doing and he said that we could get enough clients without even going out of the village, on the following Monday he phoned with a list of names and telephone numbers which was a great start.

The ACAS man told me about the Enterprise Allowance Scheme that would pay some money for a year and give various help like how to keep my own accounting records. I registered on the scheme and the help was invaluable.

35 Gardener and the Alzheimers Lady

WE DECIDED TO CALL OUR self employed business Care Club our mandate was to go to elderly people prepared to do anything from gardening, cleaning, taking them out in the car, shopping, decorating, advice on any subject that we were capable of helping or perhaps just to talk. We worked separately or sometimes together and it soon developed that Joan did mainly cleaning and I did mainly gardening. The local community soon learned about us and we quickly established ourselves. My plan was to organise myself so that I worked a regular session each week and a pattern emerged where I committed myself to four hours on Monday morning at one place and two, two hour, sessions in the afternoon and so on through the week. I tried to leave Fridays free for spasmodic work and although, I had to be flexible, it worked well. Monday mornings were at a large bungalow occupied by three ladies, one in a wheel chair, and I was immediately asked to pump up the tyres. Mary, one of the ladies used to work with me in the garden and I learned a lot from her because whilst I was good at general work, I did not have the skills that she had acquired over the years.

I used to venture about two miles from home for one morning a week working for a widow who lived in a huge bungalow, one of many expensive properties in a very posh area, and noticed that the garden three doors away was totally overgrown. The driveway to the garage was covered in shrubs and vegetation and it was not possible even to see the small path that had once led to the front door. The lady that I worked for told me that the owner was never seen out and that the neighbours thought she had Alzheimers. I scrambled diagonally through the large front garden and put one of my cards through the letter box and about a week later I received a telephone call from the residents sister who lived six miles away. Her name was Jane and she told me that her sister, Betty, suffered badly with Alzheimers and could not manage her own affairs so Jane had to do it for her. Jane also explained that Betty was very rude to anyone who came into contact with her. I suggested that I could gradually get the garden under control by working a regular four hours a week which suited Jane who told me that I was to send a weekly bill to her and I was to liaise with her if any problems occurred. There was big practical problem because I needed to use a large electrically operated hedge cutter and needed to plug into a socket in the bungalow so Jane told me to go round to the back door and speak to Betty to gain access and that Jane would give her sister a note about it.

The first time I spoke to Betty she was, as I had been warned, uncooperative and rude, I don't want you here, go away, the garden doesn't need doing, I'm not paying you, were just a printable form of what she said. I managed to open a window and get my electrical lead plugged in. My idea was to start at the front to uncover the little path to the front door but as soon as I started work I discovered why the vegetation was so thick, the ground was sodden and there was standing water not far in. There was obviously a water leak which must have been running for years, so I started on the drive side of the garden and phoned Jane that evening and she said she would report the leak, she apologised for her sister's rudeness and said she would never change. The following week Betty was just as rude and the leak had been fixed so I was able to start clearing the path on that side. During the morning a car stopped outside and the meals on wheels delivery man got out; he was delighted that I was starting to clear the path and told me that Betty was rude to him even though he went every day. It was nice to speak to a person who understood because it was lonely working in that garden although the job satisfaction was immense as I gradually made progress. I got the front garden under control and had done about half of the back over about ten weeks when I knocked at the back door as usual and got the usual response, I don't want you, go away, I'm not paying you, to which I responded, as usual, that her sister would look after that. Betty said something she had never said before: 'She is good at that, she used to work in an office'. That was the first coherent sentence that I had ever heard Betty say and I responded by saying 'What did you use to do?' She replied 'I was a piano teacher' to which I asked 'Have you still got your piano?' and Betty said she had. I asked 'Will you play for me?' and she said 'Yes'. Looking back, I was a bit silly then because I was aware of not exploiting her by getting her to play the piano whilst I should have been working so I said, 'I will come and see you when I have finished my work'. I completed my four hours for the morning, knocked at the door, but got the familiar response, 'Don't want you any more'. I explained, 'You said you would play the piano for me'. Betty said to come in, and ushered me along a corridor and into a beautifully decorated room dominated by a full size grand piano. She beckoned me to sit down and proceeded to perfectly play lovely classical music. Tears of emotion ran down my cheeks, how could a lady who was unable to do anything for herself play so beautifully? She must have played for half an hour when she suddenly stopped, looked at me and said 'What are you doing here? I don't want you'. I thanked her and told her that her playing was beautiful but I don't think she understood and with a parting statement, 'I'm not paying you', off I went. The next time I went she said the usual things to me. I got so much pleasure in getting that garden back in order and looking after it, my reward was of course, getting paid, but the lovely things that neighbours said to me were nice. I received a letter from Jane which arrived whilst I was on holiday a few weeks later, Betty had died and there was final payment with words of gratitude.

The Enterprise Allowance Organisation invited me to attend a course designed to show us how do our own accounting and it was fruitful because I did not have to employ an accountant. The man running the course started by telling us that no one knew as much about our business as we did so we could easily do our own books. He explained that the alternative was to throw all our receipts into a shoe box and pay someone extortionate money to sort it out.

People looked at me in a different light because I was a gardener, when I went to work wearing a suit and was a Production Director, friends used to respect me but not when I was a gardener, of course, I was still the same person. A friend asked me to look after his mother's garden and take her to the shops but she lived about a mile from the factory where I used to work and I was apprehensive about going back there. On the very first morning a lady walked into the garden next door, I recognised her as one of the sewing machinists that I had employed, she asked me what I was doing there and when I explained she commented 'a bit of a come down for you isn't it?'.

It was sometimes difficult working for a couple because they could have different ideas about how things should be done, one instance was a huge garden with a path winding down to a wooden building housing a sauna overlooking a stream. There were vertical conifers and shrubs growing over the winding path and the man told me to prune them to the side of the path so he could walk along the path without the vegetation catching his feet. He was pleased but the following week his wife said she didn't like it. She told me to tell her husband that she did not want it done like that if he asked me again. The next spring the man told me to do the same job again and I told him about his wife complaining to which he replied 'I pay your wages and I'm telling you to do it' so I did it. His wife saw me working and reprimanded me but I told her what her husband had said. Later that morning the lady came to me with the words, 'I know he pays your wages but I give you a cup of tea and I am not doing it any more.' I never did get a cup of tea there again. The same couple used to squabble about buckets. He asked me to clean the three cars one day and to ask his wife for a bucket, she was not playing ball, 'he can give you an outside bucket, you are not having my inside bucket.' He exclaimed 'women' and found me an old garden bucket which I had to clean out before using.

A lady who lived very close to us already had a gardener but she asked me to work for her as well, she was an ex school teacher and was a stickler for perfection; on one occasion she asked me to take the front off the gas boiler and clean any dust off it with a wet cloth and was instructed to tell her when I had finished, she inspected it and appeared almost satisfied before saying 'just give it another ten minutes' so I dabbed it a few more times until she approved. It was an example of my adage, I don't mind what I do provided I am being paid.

One of my daughters and her husband taught me how to use a computer and I bought an old one from them which I used for letters and accounts. One lady I worked for was a retired solicitor, she had her own car but was not able to drive so I used her car to do her shopping once a week, put all the provisions away on my return and she made me a cup of tea and we would chat. She became very unsteady on her feet and I fixed many handrails around the bungalow for her. She still had milk delivered but became unable to bring it in from the step so asked me if I could do anything about it. After some discussion I offered to fix a sort of shelf on the inward opening back door so she could open the door and remove the milk and other provisions that the milkman bought. I spoke to the milkman and he gave me a plastic milk crate which I reduced to half size by appropriate cutting and fixed it half way up the back door. It worked like a dream and the lady could always get her own milk inside without phoning people to go round and bring it in for her.

As I got well past retiring age I continued to work for my existing customers but did not take any new ones. Whilst I did not earn as much money in our Care Club venture as I did in the textile trade it was the most satisfying work that I ever did.

36 Tuneless Choir

AFTER I HAD ENTERED THE Trent Bridge cricket ground well before the start of the England v South Africa test match, in July 2017, I heard the sound of singing coming from outside the ground. I looked through some railings and saw a group of people who were obviously enjoying themselves so I got a 'pass out' and went to investigate. They called themselves the Tuneless Choir and the name needed no explanation, but the smiles of enjoyment from the singers and people going to cricket was a joy to see. Car and bus drivers were tooting their hooters and it was fun. They don't take themselves too seriously but just enjoy singing as a group and took it in good humour as I suggested that 'they are to singing what I am to being a young man'. This choir, set up by Nadine Cooper and Bernie Bracher on 14 January 2016 was the first one, they are not trained singers but just enjoy singing and the companionship of meeting other people for pure enjoyment. They were pleased that I videoed them and you can see it on YouTube title:- *Tuneless Choir, Trent Bridge Cricket Test Match, July 2017*

I know a lady that joined the West Bridgford choir and this is the message she sent to me about it:-

In January 2018, I joined the Tuneless Choir in West Bridgford, with my sister and a friend and we all really enjoy the sessions. They are everything I hoped they would be, everyone there enjoys singing, with energy, enthusiasm and enjoyment making up for any lack of expertise. The day after the first session my sides ached from laughing so much as it was so much fun. I look forward to the Choir night as I know its going to be a great time and I am so grateful to Nadine and Bernie for creating the choir.

From that first choir, others have been formed, and by March 2018 another nineteen have been set up. Bernie and Nadine, the founder members are proud of their achievement and have given me permission to load a presentation that Nadine created to my YouTube channel, this is the title *Tuneless Choir presentation by Nadine*

The new choirs are at:-

Sutton Coldfield
Maidenhead
Maidstone
Newcastle
Cardiff
Bourne
Oxford
Beeston
Edinburgh
Solent
Wallingford
Fylde Coast
Tunbridge Wells
South Lakeland
Lytham St Annes
London Vauxhall
Edgbaston
Chesterfield
Kendal

It will be interesting to see how the story develops, I am sure their website will let us know: **www.tunelesschoir.com**

Music has many faces

The next chapter is in total contrast to this one because it features a chamber choir who had travelled from Drake University in Iowa, America to perform a series of concerts in England, ranging from Coventry Cathedral to St Pauls Cathedral in London. Those students have been, and will continue, training for many years to develop their voices to produce the lovely sounds that I witnessed at Cambridge. But off stage they were just as fun loving and human as the people in the tuneless choir and to me, that is what music is about, a coming together of people for mutual enjoyment and pleasure.

Let us not forget the role of the audience because however much people enjoy singing, acting, or performing music of any kind the culmination of that enjoyment is to receive applause. As an audience member for many years I know what I like listening to and looking at and am lucky enough to be able to appreciate a wide range of entertainment.

What I find difficult to accept is the role of critics and the perception prevalent in modern society that one performer must be singled out as the best and the others dismissed and discarded. Surely every person is an individual with their own opinion of what they like or do not like. Anyway, that is enough of me prevaricating, it was just that the contrast between the tuneless choir and a chamber choir got me going.

37 Chamber Choir, Drake University, Iowa

In January 2018 Joan and I were invited to a wedding in Cambridgeshire so we booked into the Hilton Doubletree Hotel at Cambridge for a few days, on arrival I learned that a concert was to be performed that evening at the Cambridge University Pembroke College Chapel. The Drake Chamber Choir from Drake University, Des Moines, Iowa, USA were to be the performers. It was described as 'an inspiring and uplifting programme of classical music including works by Canadian, English and America composers'. I found that Pembroke Chapel was just around the corner and that the choir were staying in the hotel. On arrival at the chapel I asked permission to video with a view to loading to YouTube and my request was granted with enthusiasm. The conductor, Aimee Beckmann-Collier invited me to position myself in the choir stalls next to the choir. The lighting was almost non existent so I knew the visual quality would be poor. They performed and Aimee spoke some informative introductions.

After the concert, many of the singers spoke to me, they were all extremely friendly and were keen to know where they could see the videos that I had taken. I gave them details of my channel and we agreed it was a beneficial part of YouTube. I include some information about each piece followed by the YouTube titles:-

Missa Brevis, Kyrie & Gloria written by Ruth Watson Henderson, a Canadian composer, born in 1932, the whole mass lasts only 11 minutes and the choir sang just two movements.
Missa Brevis, Drake University Chamber Choir, Iowa USA

The Three Kings music by Canadian composer, Healey Willan (1880-1968) with text by Lawrence Housman
Three Kings, Healey Willan, Drake University Choir, Iowa USA

O verbum Patris (O word of the father), written by Frank Ferko, born in Chicago,1950, the text was written by an extraordinary abbess who lived in the 12th century, she was a physician, botanist, poet, visual artist, composer and furthermore was an advisor to Kings and Popes. She was taken by the idea of circularity, she saw the Trinity, Alpha and Omega of God and Love of God in this form which shows in her visual art. The singers moved around as they performed this piece.

O verbum Patris by Frank Ferko, Drake University Chamber Choir

The Dark Eyed Sailor arranged by Ralph Vaughan Williams (1872-1958), An English Folk Song

Dark Eyed Sailor, Vaughan Williams, Drake University Chamber Choir

Over Havat (Over the Sea) Written by American, Dan Forrest, born1978, based on a poem that commemorated the story of Peter Mandius Nerland, an 18 year old Norwegian who immigrated from Finnoy Island, Norway, to rural Iowa in 1899. On arrival he obtained work as a farmhand. The choir replicate the noise of the sea spray as he looks out and even the throbbing of the engines as the boat takes him to the USA. Drake University is based in Iowa where Peter Nerland achieved his ambition of settling in America.

Over Havet, Dan Forrest, Drake University Iowa USA, Pembroke College Chapel

Alleluia, was written in 1942 as a plea for peace by American, Randal Thomson (1899-1984) it contains only the title word.

Alleluia by Randall Thompson, Drake University Iowa USA Chamber Choir

The final piece was an arrangement by John Rutter of 'Sing a Song of Sixpence' and Aimee mentioned the connection of John Rutter and Cambridge in her introduction. John, born 1945 lives near Cambridge and attended Clare College.

Sing a Song of Sixpence, arr John Rutter, Drake Chamber Choir USA

The names of choir members are:-

Soprano

Rachael Demaree*
Megan Dworsky
Elizabeth Fisher*
Lauran Lundy
Audrey McGee
Emily Miller
Elizabeth Watson

ALTO

Kate Broderick
Caitlin Carr
Gabrielle Clutter
Macey Coppess
Megan Guest
Alyssa LaTragna
Mollie Lawler*

Tenor

Colin Glowienke
Sam Hagen*
Seth Hammond
Jack Hanrahan
Eli Jost
Trevor Ross
Alex Tillinghast
Trevor Wiley*

Bass

Reid Frederiksen
Paxton Gillespie
Isaac Lodwick
Daniel Minnie*
Samuel Nolte*
Charles Porter
Kellen Schrimper
Seth Tack

*denotes Section Leader

The Tour Itinerary

Thursday January 4	Central Presbyterian Church, Des Moines, Iowa
Sunday January 7	St Michael's Church, Bath
Monday January 8	Holy Trinity Church, Stratford upon Avon
Tuesday January 9	Coventry Cathedral
Wednesday January 10	Lady Chapel, Ely Cathedral
Thursday January 11	Cambridge University, Pembroke College Chapel
Friday January 12	St. Nicolas Church, Witham
Sunday January 14	Old Naval College Chapel, Greenwich
Monday January 15	Evensong, St Paul's Cathedral, London
Tuesday January 16	Saint Martin-in-the-Fields, London

The Drake University Chamber Choir is one of four choruses that provide singing opportunities for more than 250 students at Drake.

The choir tours throughout the United States annually and internationally every four years. The ensemble has sung in major venues in Austria, Germany, Italy, the Czech Republic, Ireland, Wales, Latvia, Estonia and Finland. The Chamber Choir has been selected to perform at several conferences of the American Choral Directors Association and its members have frequently collaborated with the Des Moines Symphony.

Aimee Beckmann-Collier is the Ellis and Nelle Levitt Distinguished Professor of Conducting and Director of Choral Studies at Drake University, where she has taught since 1989. She is a frequent clinician, adjudicator and guest conductor for high school and college choral festivals, contests, and All-States throughout the country, as well as in England and China. She has conducted in Carnegie Hall on several occasions and made her Avery Fisher Hall debut in 2014, conducting a professional orchestra, soloists, and the Drake Choir, the University's 75 voice touring ensemble, of which all Chamber Choir singers are members. Drake ensembles under her leadership have performed in prestigious venues throughout Europe, as well as for conferences of the American Choral Directors Association (ACDA).

Dr. Beckman-Collier has served as president of ACDA's North Central Division, chaired the 1992 and 2012 divisional conferences, and served as assistant chair of the 2015 ACDA national conference. She has served as president of the Iowa Choral Directors Association and editor of both state and divisional publications. Her articles on a variety of topics have appeared in *The Choral Journal and the Music Educators Journal.* Dr. Beckmann-Collier has also served as chair of the Iowa Comprehensive Musicianship Project, as a mastery teaching program for music educators, and is director of Drake's Summer Music Institute, which provides professional development opportunities for music educators.

A graduate of Saint Mary's College, Notre Dame, Indiana, which recently presented her with its Distinguished Alumna Award, Dr. Beckmann-Collier received master's and doctoral degrees in choral conducting from the University of Iowa where she studied with Don V Moses. She is the recipient of Drake University's Madelyn Levitt Award for Distinguished Community Service, as well as Drake's Stalnaker Lecturer Designation, the Iowa Music Educators Association Distinguished Services Award, the National Federation Interscholastic Music Association Outstanding Music Educator Award, the Robert McCowan Award, given by the Iowa Choral Directors Association, and the ACDA's Weston F. Noble Lifetime Achievement Award. In May 2017 she was named Drake University's Madelyn Levitt Teacher of the Year.

I am impressed that a lady with such a list of achievements treated me with immense respect and cooperation when I requested permission to video the Drake Chamber Choir at Cambridge University. Michael Parkinson

Drake University is a private, coeducational institution situated on a 120 acre campus in Des Moines, Iowa's capital. Drake offers more than 70 under-graduates majors and many graduate programs in its six colleges and schools - Arts and Sciences, including Fine Arts: Business and Public Administration; Journalism and Mass Communication Law; Education and Pharmacy and Health Sciences. The University blends a focus on the liberal arts and sciences with outstanding professional programs, providing students a rigorous educational experience balanced between the theoretical and the practical.

Drake faculty are experts and scholars whose top priority is teaching. Even introductory courses are taught by senior faculty, and no classes at Drake are taught by graduate assistants. Approximately 93 per cent of the University's faculty hold the highest degree in their fields. Drake students learn from each other too. The University's 4.900 undergraduate, graduate, and law students come from 46 states and 50 countries, and they're highly involved in Drake's more than 140 organisations and the Des Maines community.

A cultural asset to Des Moines and Iowa, Drake offers a wealth of fine arts activities, from theatre and music performances to art exhibits: speeches and appearances by internationally known experts on a variety of topics; and NCAA Division 1 athletic events, highlighted by men's and women's basket-ball. Every spring, Drake hosts the famous Drake Relays, which attract many of the world's finest track and field athletes. **www.drake.edu**

38 YouTube Subscriptions

WHEN I CREATED MY YOUTUBE channel in 2011 it was purely to load a specific video but since then I realised that I could load videos from previous shows that I had promoted. It is a fantastic opportunity for an ordinary person to present their work to the world and the people of the world will soon decide what they are interested in.

In the days of photography I only used automatic mode, I could never get my head round settings and aperture speeds so decided that was best left to the experts. When I bought an iPhone I found it was easy to take video and to erase what I didn't want. I do not profess to be clever but by trial and error I learned how to improve the quality of a video. One of the difficulties is lighting conditions particularly outdoor, where on an intermittently cloudy to sunny day conditions change dramatically and instantly. I started to video keyboard players either piano or organ and made an attachment so that I could attach my iPhone to a Manfrotto tripod that I had used to hold a super VHS camera. In my opinion watching and listening to a keyboard or string instrument player in particular is an art form and this can be captured on video very easily with the use of a tripod. After some time I treated my self to a small portable tripod which is not so heavy to lug about but does not smoothly pan and tilt like the Manfrotto.

As a cricket follower it is handy to have an iPhone handy to take opportunities that arise but I do not try to emulate the professional photographers who have expensive equipment with powerful telephoto lens. My equipment records sound combined with vision so it is ideal for capturing the crowd reaction and general atmosphere connected with cricket. I have developed methods of editing video clips and chaining them together before loading the finished video to YouTube.

Over first five years of putting videos on my channel I received many messages from YouTube encouraging me to monetise my videos so that I would receive payment so did this and ten months later, in October 2017 received a payment of £62. The figures were indicating that I was qualifying for about £9 every four weeks so was looking forward to another payment when the earnings reached the threshold of £60. However, on 17 January 2018 YouTube announced changes to the Partner Program where eligibility to receive payments was changed to 4,000 hours of total watch time per year AND 1,000 subscribers. I easily achieve the watch time criteria but only had 480 subscribers at that time so until my subscribers reach 1000 I will not earn a penny. At the time of writing (March 2018) my channel has 517 subscribers so I am pleading that 483 people subscribe to my channel so that I can earn the princely sum of £9 every four weeks.

My total channel views on 20 March 2018 are 662,616 over the 1054 videos that I have loaded. My most watched top three are:-

1 Billy Fury Graveside tribute by Michael Parkinson 45281 views

2 Saara Aalto X Factor Sings in Leicester Square for Michael Parkinson 28689 views

3 Cricket England skittle Australia 60, Broad 8 for15, Michael Parkinson 26828 views

I am proud of this, particularly as I was made redundant at the age of 49 because I was not computer literate.

The inspiration to write this book was triggered by the example of what Joanna Forest (Chapter 16) has achieved against all the odds and, words spoken by her husband Paul, when Joan and I met them at Brighton in September 2017.

Goodbye and thank you for reading *Michael Parkinson.*

39 Danilo Mascetti, piano

ON WEDNESDAY 28 MARCH 2018 I videoed a concert at Steinway Hall, London, performed by Italian pianist Danilo Mascetti who is a senior piano scholar of Professor Vanessa Latarche and Gordon Fergus Thomson at the Royal College of Music, London. Danilo impressed me because he gave permission to load the whole of his performance including two encores to YouTube, this is unusual because pianists usually say that they are not satisfied with certain things they have played in a live performance.

Danilo regularly performs as a soloist all over Europe, with orchestras including the Pomeriggi Musicali, Philharmonic Orchestra 'Miahil Jora' and the Symphonic State of Craiova, Romania. Since 2015 he has performed internationally in China, Japan, Hungary, Italy, Morocco and Greece. In 2015 he debuted in London for the Aspect Foundation, in Prague with the West Bohemian Symphony Orchestra and in Rome with the Nova Amadeus Orchestra. In 2016 he gave his American debut with the New York Concert Artists Symphony Orchestra. Upcoming concerts in 2018 will include Danilo performing Prokofiev's Piano Concerto No. 3 in Romania, Chopin's Piano Concerto No. 2 in Italy and Bach Concertos in the Czech Republic.

Here are the videos that I loaded to YouTube:-

Bach Toccata in D major BWV 912, **Danilo Mascetti piano, Steinway, London**

Ravel, Miroirs II Oiseaux tristes, **Danilo Mascetti piano, Steinway, London**

Ravel Miroirs III, Une barque sur l'ocean, **Danilo Mascetti, piano, Steinway, London**

Poissons d'Or Images II Debussy, Messiaen Etude, **Danilo Mascetti**

Stravinsky Firebird Dance Infernale Berceuse et Finale, **Danilo Mascetti**

Cimarosa, Sonata C minor, **Danilo Mascetti piano, Steinway, London**

Schubert Erlkönig arr Liszt, **Danilo Mascetti at Steinway, London**

Appendix

These are YouTube titles used in the book:

Chapter 1: Billy Fury Dance - Nottingham Arts Theatre
Mrs Jean Wycherley
Billy Fury Dance, Lady, Nottingham Arts Theatre
Billy Fury Dance, How Many Nights, Nottingham Arts Theatre
Billy Fury Dance, Gonna Type a Letter, Nottingham Arts Theatre

Chapter 3: Billy Fury Dance - Mansfield
Billy Fury by Vince Eager, Audition at Birkenhead Essoldo
Michael Parkinson's Billy Fury Show, Mansfield Palace

Chapter 4: Billy Fury Dance - Floral Pavilion New Brighton
Sweet Jessica, Hannah Bennet, Billy Fury Dance Show.
Jean Wycherley, Mother of Billy Fury, Speaks and sings, Tribute
Billy Fury In My Room, Wallasey School of Ballet
Billy Fury That's All Right Floral Pavilion New Brighton
Billy Fury Running Around, Floral Pavilion New Brighton
Billy Fury Maybe Tomorrow, Floral Pavilion New Brighton
Billy Fury Died 1983 Speaks & sings Forget Him

Chapter 5: Billy Fury Dance - Shaw Theatre, London
Billy Fury Dance Show, Cora Vanaman, Director
Billy Fury Dance Show, Craig Canning hit by David Essex
Billy Fury Dance 1 Heartbeat, Narration, Once upon a Dream
Billy Fury Dance 2 You're having the last dance with me
Billy Fury Dance 3 Give me your word, Narration
Billy Fury Dance 4 It's only make believe
Billy Fury Dance 5 Margo
Billy Fury Dance 6 Running around
Billy Fury Dance 7 I'll never fall in love again
Billy Fury Dance 8 Gonna type a letter
Billy Fury Dance 9 When will you say I love you
Billy Fury Dance10 Wondrous place
Billy Fury Dance 11 Maybe tomorrow

Billy Fury Dance 12 In thoughts of you

Billy Fury Dance 13 Don't knock upon my door (subject to video blocking)

Billy Fury Dance 14 Nothin' shakin' like the leaves on the trees

Billy Fury Dance 15 I'd never find another you

Billy Fury Dance 16 Like I've never been gone

Billy Fury Dance 17 Run to my loving arms, Dialogue

Billy Fury Dance 18 Colette

Billy Fury Dance 19 That's alright

Billy Fury Dance 20 Glad all over

Billy Fury Dance 21 Jealousy

Billy Fury Dance 22 My Christmas Prayer, Narration

Billy Fury Dance 23 Devil or Angel

Billy Fury Dance 24 Somebody else's girl

Billy Fury Dance 25 Hippy Hippy Shake

Billy Fury Dance 26 Because of love

Billy Fury Dance 27 Lady

Billy Fury Dance 28 Last night was made for love

Billy Fury Dance 29 In my room, Narration

Billy Fury Dance 30 In Summer

Billy Fury Dance 31 Psalm 23 Crimond, Sung by dancers

Billy Fury Dance 32 Billy speaks self written words, Forget him

Billy Fury I will, Michael Parkinson show

Billy Fury Dance 34 I'll never quite get over you, I'm lost without you

Billy Fury Dance 35 A thousand stars, Narration

Billy Fury Dance 36 Halfway to Paradise (Finale)

Chapter 7: Billy Fury Biography

Billy Fury Mother died age 96 Tribute, In Thoughts of You

Chapter 8: Billy Fury Graveside Tribute

Billy Fury Graveside Tribute by Michael Parkinson

Chapter 9: YouTube, How I started

Liszt Grand Galop Chromatique, Vanessa Benelli Mosell, Piano.

All That Jazz, Comedy version, Bear Left Theatre Company
Hamlet, Ophelia's Flower Speech, Lauren Nicole, Bear Left Theatre.

Chapter 10: Saara Aalto X Factor

Saara Aalto X Factor Sings in Leicester Square for Michael Parkinson
Half a Sixpence, Review by Michael Parkinson.

Chapter 11: Jessica May George, Jessie's Fund

Victoria Wood talking about Jessie's Fund.
Jessie's Fund, Jessica May George by Charlotte Griffin.

Chapter 12: Thames Path Walk, Barrier to Windsor

Thames Barrier to Greenwich Thames Path Michael Parkinson
Greenwich to Canary Wharf, Thames Path Michael Parkinson
Canary Wharf-Blackfriars Thames Path Michael Parkinson
Blackfriars to Chelsea, Thames Path Walk Michael Parkinson
Chelsea to Putney Thames Path Walk Michael Parkinson
Putney to Mortlake Thames Path Walk Michael Parkinson
Mortlake to Richmond Thames Path Walk Michael Parkinson
Richmond to Hampton Court Thames Path, Michael Parkinson
Hampton Bridge to Elmbridge Thames Path Michael Parkinson
Elmbridge to Shepperton Ferry, Thames Path, Michael Parkinson
Thames Ferry Weybridge/Shepperton, Nauticalia
Doyle Carte Island and House, River Thames
Pike caught in Thames at Shepperton, Michael Parkinson
Shepperton to Staines, Thames Path, Michael Parkinson
Staines to Windsor, Thames Path, Michael Parkinson

Chapter 13: Thames Path Walk, Windsor to Oxford

Windsor to Maidenhead Thames Path, Michael Parkinson
The Vicar of Bray-Stanley Holloway-1937
Gaiety Girls, Gaiety Row, Brunel Bridge, Maidenhead
Maidenhead to Bourne End Thames Path, Michael Parkinson
Bourne End to Henley Thames Path, Michael Parkinson
Henley to Reading Thames Path, Michael Parkinson
Reading to Goring Thames Path, Michael Parkinson
Goring to Wallingford Thames Path, Michael Parkinson
Wallingford to Shillingford Thames Path, Michael Parkinson
Stonemason Thames Bargeman talks to Michael Parkinson
Shillingford to Culham Bridge Thames Path, Michael Parkinson
Culham Bridge to Oxford Thames Path, Michael Parkinson

Chapter 14: Thames Path Walk, Oxford to Source
  Oxford to Bablock Hythe Thames Path, Michael Parkinson
  Bablock Hythe to Tadpole Bridge Thames Path, Michael Parkinson
  Tadpole Bridge to Lechlade Thames Path, Michael Parkinson
  Lechlade to Cricklade Thames Path Bull, Michael Parkinson
  Bull obstructs Thames Path, Cricklade by Michael Parkinson
  Cricklade to Water Eaton, Bull gone, Thames Path, Michael Parkinson
  Cricklade to Ashton Keynes Thames Path, Michael Parkinson
  Ashton Keynes to Ewen Thames Path, Michael Parkinson
  Ewen to Source Thames Path, Michael Parkinson
  Thames Source Flooded Jan 2013

Chapter 15: Blackpool Tower Ballroom - Phil Kelsall
  Rock n Roll Blackpool 79 years young
  Phil Kelsall Blackpool Wurlitzer Lilac Waltz Medley
  Jedward CBeebies, Katy, Waltz, Phil Kelsall, Blackpool Tower.
  Blackpool Tower Ballroom, Tea, Spectators, Dance, Phil Kelsall

Chapter 16: Joanna Forest, Feel your Boobs
  I dreamed a dream, Joanna Forest at Brighton
  Time to say goodbye, Joanna Forest at Brighton
  Oh Mio Babbino Caro, Joanna Forest at Brighton

Chapter 17: Cricket - Notts and England
  Hat Trick Bowler, Harry Gurney, Nottinghamshire
  Cricket, Australia You'll Never Get The Ashes Back, Nettleham School.
  Uptown Nettleham
  Jerusalem, Phil Hughes Tribute, England v Australia 2013 Trent Bridge
  Test Match
  You Raise Me Up, Rule Brittania, Eng v Aust, Trent Bridge 2013
  Cricket England skittle Australia 60, Broad 8 for15, Michael Parkinson.
  Hi Ho Silver Lining, Sung by Trent Bridge T20 Cricket crowd
  Freddie & Bumble, Sweet Caroline, Edgbaston T20 Final 2017
  Cricket Notts win T20 Cup at Edgbaston 2 Sep 2017

Chapter 18: The Seekers - Judith Durham
  The Seekers Georgy Girl, Golden Jubilee Tour, Nottingham Concert Hall
  2014

The Seekers, The Carnival is Over, Golden Jubilee Tour, Nottm 2014

Chapter 19: Scarborough Spa Music
Scarborough Spa Orchestra, Suncourt to Grand Hall, Rain
Bach to Beatles Howard Beaumont.
The Best Of Times, Howard Beaumont, Scarborough.
Goodbye, Howard Beaumont, Organ, Scarborough
Stingrays Rock n Roll, Matchbox, Scarborough Spa
Besame Mucho, Trombone, Scarborough

Chapter 20: Disneyland Paris
St Pancras Eurostar and TGV to Disneyland Paris via Lille
Disneyland Paris, Forest of Enchantment Part 1
Disneyland Paris, Forest of Enchantment Part 2
Walt Disney Studio Tram, Paris, Earthquake, Fire, Flood, Screams.
Disneyland Paris, It's a small world, Michael Parkinson's favourite
Disneyland Paris, Gota Lejon Band from Sweden, July 2017
Disneyland Paris Parade, July 2017

Chapter 21: Eric Coates - Viola to Composer
Tell Me Pretty Maiden (1930)
Wood-Nymphs, Valsette
Calling all workers - Eric Coates
Sleepy Lagoon Eric Coates Haruko Seki piano
Bird Songs at Eventide, Eric Coates Haruko Seki piano
Tit for Tat, Eric Coates Words, William Lyle
Dam Busters, Coates, Hucknall Torkard Ensemble
Bird Songs at Eventide, Hucknall Torkard Ensemble
Children's Hymn, Words & Music by Eric Coates

Chapter 22: Thursford Christmas Spectacular
Thursford Christmas Spectacular Entrance 2013
Thursford Christmas Fantasy Prince George visited 2014
Thursford Christmas Spectacular, wurlitzer, doves at end of show
Norfolk coast walk Cley-Blakeney Point-Seals-Cley
Thursford Christmas Spectacular, 28 Coaches

Chapter 23: Nottingham Organ Society

Dirkjan Ranzijn, Party Time, Paloma Blanca, Dog in Audience
Dirkjan Ranzijn, Sexy Camilla story, Nottingham Organ Society.
Robert Wolfe, Tiger Rag, Nottingham Organ Society
Mark Thompson, Theatreland, Jack Strachey, Nottingham Organ Society
Mark Thompson, Guess the Shows, Nottingham Organ Society
Theatre Organ Medley. Tim Flint, Nottm Organ Society
12th Street Rag medley, Nicholas Martin organ
Klaus Wunderlich Medley, Claire Greig, Wersi, Nottm Organ Soc
Minors of the ABC, Children's picture club Claire Greig
Brett Wales plays live at Wersi Summerfest 2009
Rock n roll Chris Stanbury, Nottingham Organ Society

Chapter 24: Royal Academy of Music

Bach/Busoni Chaconne, Mitra Alice Tham, Piano, Djanogly Recital
Piano String Duo Classics, Mitra Haru Jonathan Roger
Entertainer, Piano Quintet arranged by Mitra Alice Tham
Piano instant composition for Iris, Mitra Alice Tham

Chapter 25: Phab, Fanfare for Christmas

Christmas Day-Holst-London Orpheus Choir for Phab.
Shepherds Farewell-London Orpheus Choir For Phab.
Ding Dong Ding-London Orpheus Choir, St James Piccadilly, Phab
In the Bleak Mid Winter, Tribute to Ed Stewart, Phab 2016
Jingle Bells, London Orpheus Choir, St James Piccadilly
Anita Dobson, New President of Phab, intro, John Corless
Truth sent from above, 'The Shropshire Carol' London Orpheus Choir
The 12 Days of Christmas, London Orpheus Choir, Phab, Fanfare

Chapter 26: London Concerts

Fazil Say-Black Earth, Belle Chen Piano, extended technique
Nativity Wood Sculpture, St James, London.
Debussy, Berceuse héroique, Maria Marchant piano
Chopin Raindrop Prelude 28, Maria Marchant
Chopin Barcarolle Alvise Pascucci Piano.
Chopin Scherzo 3 Op 39 Giulia Rossini Piano.
Graham Fitkin, Fervent, Yoshio Hamano, piano.
Chopin Rondo E-Flat Major, Natalia Sokolovskaya piano

You Will Be Found, Melisa Camba, St Pancras Station London

Chapter 27: Scottish Army Invade Trafalgar Square
Scottish Army Invade Trafalgar Square, Bagpipes & Drum

Chapter 28: Victorian Ballads and Limericks
Hayley Griffin, Seen But Not Heard
Christmas Day in the Workhouse, Victorian Ballad, Hayley Griffin
Exam Nerves, Hayley Griffin, Nottingham Girls' High School
Old Soldiers Granddaughter, Hayley Griffin, Ted Wyke-Smith
Billy's Rose Victorian Ballad, Read by Hayley Griffin, G.R. Sims
Billy's Rose, Danced, Charlotte/Marcos Narrated, Hayley Griffin
Fish riding bicycle, Hayley Griffin reads Selwyn McGrigger

Chapter 29: Southwark Cathedral to Bonington Theatre
Vaughan Williams Piano Quintet C minor, 1st mvt Bonington Quintet
Schubert Piano Quintet in A major 'Trout' 1st mvt, Bonington Quintet
Schubert Piano Quintet in A major 'Trout' 2nd mvt Bonington Quintet

Chapter 30: Promotions, Concerts and Shows
Hershblume, Sagi Hartov cello David Smith piano
Le Jazz Hot, Dancers Trent Bridge Cricket
Liszt Liebestraum, Hannah Lewis cello Mitra Alice Tham piano
Chopin Fantaise Impromptu, I'm Always Chasing Rainbows
Prima Donna, Bonington Theatre, Arnold.

Chapter 32: Childhood Memories
Minors of the ABC, Children's picture club

Chapter 36: Tuneless Choir
Tuneless Choir, Trent Bridge Cricket Test Match, July 2017
Tuneless Choir presentation by Nadine

Chapter 37: Chamber Choir, Drake University, Iowa
Missa Brevis, Drake University Chamber Choir, Iowa USA
Three Kings, Healey Willan, Drake University Choir, Iowa USA
O verbum Patris by Frank Ferko, Drake University Chamber Choir
Dark Eyed Sailor, Vaughan Williams, Drake University Chamber Choir

Over Havet, Dan Forrest, Drake University Iowa USA, Pembroke College Chapel

Alleluia by Randall Thompson, Drake University Iowa USA Chamber Choir

Sing a Song of Sixpence, arr John Rutter, Drake Chamber Choir USA

Chapter 39: Danilo Mascetti piano

Bach Toccata in D major BWV 912, Danilo Mascetti piano, Steinway London

Ravel, Miroirs II Oiseaux tristes, Danilo Mascetti piano, Steinway, London

Ravel Miroirs III, Une barque sur l'ocean, Danilo Mascetti, piano, Steinway London

Poissons d'Or Images II Debussy, Messiaen Etude, Danilo Mascetti

Stravinsky Firebird Dance Infernale Berceuse et Finale Danilo Mascetti

Cimarosa, Sonata C minor, Danilo Mascetti piano Steinway London

Schubert Erikönig arr Liszt Danilo Mascetti at Steinway London

Acknowledgements

I HAVE BEEN HELPED BY many people and attempt to mention all of them but apologise if I have left anyone out.

Mags Cummings and Harry Whitehouse for information about Billy Fury. Chris Eley for his provision of CDs, continual support and permission to use Billy Fury pictures. To John Vanaman for the story about his parents. To Cora Vanaman for directing the Shaw Theatre show. Thank you to my friend and mentor John Gurnhill whose YouTube name is catman2007. Thank you to the parents of Jessica May George for giving permission to include Jessie's poems. A special thank you to Mr and Mrs Downes who allowed my dedication to their son Ellis. Thank you to Merlin Entertainments and Phil Kelsall of the Blackpool Tower Ballroom and to Joanna Forest for allowing me to include her story. To the Head Teacher, staff and pupils of Nettleham Junior School. Thank you to Harry Smith, curator of the Eric Coates Estate. To Charlie Cushing, to use extracts from the Thursford Christmas Spectacular programmes and for supplying pictures for the book cover. To the committee of Nottingham Organ Society for help and permission to video many of their concerts and to Organfax for their information. Thank you to the Phab team and London Orpheus Choir for Fanfare for Christmas. To Miss Hayley Griffin for permission to use her poems and recitations. To Nadine Cooper and Bernie Bracher for permission to use their tuneless choir presentation.

Most important of all, thank you to my wife Joan, who has read, made suggestions, and checked every word of each chapter, sometimes 3 or 4 versions, before I have been satisfied. Thank you to my grandson Craig Woods for his forward and synopsis but most of all for his words of encouragement.

Finally, thank you to Mark Webb of Into print at Paragon Publishing for help and advice along the way and for fitting in the extra chapter 39 at short notice.

Lightning Source UK Ltd.
Milton Keynes UK
UKHW02f1429290418
321828UK00002B/18/P